T0340338

Retail Security and Loss Prevention Solutions

Retail Security
and Loss
Prevention
Solutions

Retail Security and Loss Prevention Solutions

Alan Greggo, CPP, CFE
Millie Kresevich

CRC Press
Taylor & Francis Group
Boca Raton London New York

CRC Press is an imprint of the
Taylor & Francis Group, an **informa** business

AN AUERBACH BOOK

CRC Press
Taylor & Francis Group
6000 Broken Sound Parkway NW, Suite 300
Boca Raton, FL 33487-2742

First issued in paperback 2019

© 2011 by Taylor and Francis Group, LLC
CRC Press is an imprint of Taylor & Francis Group, an Informa business

No claim to original U.S. Government works

ISBN-13: 978-1-4200-9006-2 (hbk)
ISBN-13: 978-0-367-86568-9 (pbk)

Library of Congress Cataloging-in-Publication Data

Greggo, Alan.
 Retail security and loss prevention solutions / Alan Greggo and Millie Kresevich.
 p. cm.
 Includes bibliographical references and index.
 ISBN 978-1-4200-9006-2 (hardback : alk. paper)
 1. Retail trade--Security measures. 2. Shoplifting--Prevention. I. Kresevich, Millie. II. Title.

HF5429.27.G74 2011
658.4'73--dc22
 2010021128

Visit the Taylor & Francis Web site at
http://www.taylorandfrancis.com

and the CRC Press Web site at
http://www.crcpress.com

CONTENTS

FOREWORD

The authors of this book set out to write an introduction to retail loss prevention mainly directed at college students in the criminal justice field of study. Many fine universities offer criminology, police science, and corrections and prepare students for a career in the public service sector. We recognized the shortage of private-sector preparation available to the student in criminal justice who may want to specialize in asset protection, loss prevention, or security management. Preparation for those careers is usually not found in a university's business management school. A few universities are starting to recognize that preparation for private-sector criminal justice careers is a new niche to be filled. Our intent was to make this study of problems and solutions available as an introduction to the field so students could decide if they were going down the right path and if retail loss prevention interested them.

As the book progressed, we also recognized the recurring theme of a culture of integrity being central to a successful loss prevention program. This book is very appropriate for recent criminal justice degree graduates who find themselves on the private-sector side of law enforcement and in the retail industry. There is a lot to learn in those initial few years to be successful and to feel comfortable functioning in loss prevention in a retail establishment. Much of what graduates take from the criminal justice school does not prepare them to be loss prevention managers handling problems in retail business. Understanding how a loss prevention department works and what a culture of integrity is will make the transition so much easier. We hope this book will help raise questions and inspire readers' thought processes to make them curious in the right directions so they might find the answers they need.

We have assembled our very best theories and experiences from a combined 45 years of experience in retail loss prevention from a number of businesses. We have brought thought-provoking discussions from a group of professionals and experts in their fields to the pages of this book to enhance the learning experience. We hope anyone who reads this book will come away with an understanding of retail loss prevention, the most prominent problems, and some of the available solutions. We hope readers will understand what a culture of integrity is and how important it is to the retail business as a whole and to the loss prevention department, which must be the catalyst for integrity in the organization.

This book does not represent legal advice. For example, in discussions on shoplifting, internal investigations, and addressing organized retail crime, readers and practitioners are urged to involve their own corporate legal department for legal advice. No book can give the rigorous examination of problems and recommended solutions that are necessary for specific instances within your business.

All statements, recommendations, and ideas are the opinions of the authors or contributors involved in these chapters and do not in any way represent the statements, recommendations, ideas, or opinions of any companies for which authors are currently or may have been employed in the past.

Now with all the formalities out of the way, let us get started discussing some problems and solutions in retail loss prevention.

ABOUT THE AUTHORS

ALAN F. GREGGO CPP, CFE
Principal

Alan Greggo is the principal and founder of PROFIT Rx, an asset protection and fraud investigation firm. He has a BS in law enforcement administration from Youngstown State University, is a Certified Protection Professional (CPP), a Certified Fraud Examiner (CFE), and a member of the American Society for Industrial Security (ASIS) and the Association of Certified Fraud Examiners. He serves on the Retail Loss Prevention Council of ASIS as the chairman of the Organized Retail Crime Committee. He has over 28 years of loss prevention experience in specialty retail and discount mass merchandise retail.

Alan has authored magazine articles for *Security Management*, *Loss Prevention Magazine*, *Retail Construction Magazine*, and *Optometric Management Magazine*. He is on the editorial review committee for *Fraud Magazine* published by the Association of Certified Fraud Examiners.

Alan is the primary author of Chapters 5, 6, 7, 8, 9, 11, and the Conclusion.

MILLIE KRESEVICH
Senior Manager–Asset Protection

Millie Kresevich is a Senior Manager–level executive in the field of retail loss prevention, and has over sixteen years of experience in big box, corporate, and specialty loss prevention. Millie holds an AAS in criminal justice and a BS, *summa cum laude,* in social psychology. She has several published articles on the topic of workplace dishonesty and has been interviewed for many magazines and papers including *Loss Prevention Magazine* and *Security Director News.*

Millie serves on the Legislative Committee for the National Retail Federation (NRF), is the legislative chair for the Coalition of Law Enforcement and Retail (CLEAR), and has contributed to the development of certification programs for the Loss Prevention Foundation. Millie is a member of a nationwide Organized Retail Crime Task Force.

In 2008, Millie was a recipient of the 20 Under 40 Security Executive Award given by *Security Director News.* Most recently, Millie is involved with a project with the National Institute of Standards and Technology, involving developing behavior indicators for groups of organized criminals involved in retail theft. She frequently speaks nationally and internationally on loss prevention topics.

Millie is the primary author of Chapters 1, 2, 3, 4, 10, and 12.

CONTRIBUTORS

Richard C. Hollinger, Ph.D.
Professor, Department of
 Criminology, Law, and Society
University of Florida

Paul Jones
Global Director, Asset Protection
eBay

W. Michael Kotyk, CFE
Loss Prevention Practitioner

Daniel Mania
Director of Corporate Security and
 Aviation
Delaware North Companies, Inc.

Judge James McKenzie
Tennessee General Sessions Judge
Rhea County General Sessions
 Court

Frank Muscato
ORC Investigations Supervisor
Walgreens

Gene Smith
President
The Loss Prevention Foundation

David E. Zulawski, CFI, CFE
Chair CFI, Senior Partner, Speaker
Wicklander-Zulawski &
 Associates, Inc.

1

An Introduction to Retail Loss Prevention

Those outside of the business rarely understand the complexity of retail loss prevention. When members of the general public are provided with a brief synopsis of what goes into being a loss prevention professional, they often correlate the position with a security guard. As we know, the job of a security guard usually entails safeguarding people and property, as does the job of a loss prevention professional. But it is at this point where the similarities end and how each profession achieves the goal varies drastically.

To articulate the profession of loss prevention by associating it with known professions, it is necessary to take components such as accounting practices, forensics, fraud detection, human behavior analysis, and interview and interrogation skills into account. Many retail loss prevention professionals do not initially set their sights on entering the business of loss prevention. Rather, many are pursuing degrees in criminal justice, business administration, or related fields while in college and happen to fall into the career. Often they start off as store detectives and move up through the ranks.

The position of store detective teaches that no one is exempt from the potential of thievery. From business executives to nuns and drug addicts, the different classes of society that engage in deviant behavior seem to be endless. As store detectives begin to gain tenure with their organization, they also gain experience in understanding the motives behind the actions of the individual. Some people shoplift because they don't have

the means to provide for their family or themselves, whereas others steal to support addictions. In today's society shoplifting has advanced drastically to organized retail crime (ORC) in which participants are no longer individuals; rather, a criminal enterprise exists with multiple players who have individual roles. The topic of organized retail crime will be explored in great depth later in the book.

From shoplifting in department stores to shoplifting in the grocery business, the pattern of human behavior remains the same: only the type of product being stolen differs. Recognizing who is going to steal eventually becomes instinctual. Store detectives can watch a front door of a store or a camera system and pinpoint individuals who are entering for one purpose: theft. The recognition process is not based on clothing, race, and gender; rather, it is based on the physical behavior of the individual. The way a person walks or the way his or her eyes are moving plays an important role in the recognition process. Knowing who is going to steal before it happens is the first step in protecting the company assets. From there, concealment, consistent surveillance, and the apprehension will soon follow. Loss prevention managers usually teach store detectives all of the components of the business.

As store detectives gradually move to higher positions, they begin to get more involved with the other ways losses can occur besides externally—internally and operationally. Employee theft is the biggest contributor to shrinkage in retail, accounting for approximately 42.7% of all losses, according to the 2008 National Retail Security Survey conducted by Dr. Richard Hollinger from the University of Florida. It is also the most difficult to control. It can be summed up as, "If there is a will, there is a way."

In 2008, The National Retail Security Survey Final Report says retailers experienced shrinkage of 1.51% to sales, and that translates to roughly $36.6 billion in retail lost annually. This is the national average. Each year organizations spend millions of dollars on theft detection and prevention devices such as exception reporting, cameras, and article surveillance, yet they still incur losses at the hands of their own employees. The most important and pressing question isn't how theft occurs because investigations easily answer that question. The important question is why employees bite the hand that feeds them and their families. This is the area where loss prevention professionals truly learn the different types of motivators between those outside and those inside the organization who cause losses to an organization.

A later chapter disucsses the theft triangle, which entails the components necessary for theft to occur. The triangle includes low deterrents,

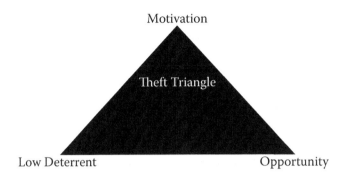

Motivation

Theft Triangle

Low Deterrent Opportunity

Figure 1.1 The theft triangle, developed by Read Hayes, PhD.

opportunity, and motivation. The first two—low deterrents and opportunity—are closely shared by people and employees who cause losses to an organization. But the motivation behind the actions of employees is much more complicated than that of people from the outside (Figure 1.1).

This book will delve heavily into the motivational factors that contribute to organizational shrinkage. It is important for retailers to understand that an employee who is on a mission can defeat even the best, most expensive deterrent systems. While tackling the topic of motivation, readers will learn how a philosophy can change the entire spectrum of employee dishonesty. It is not much different from the one adopted several decades ago by the New York City transit authority. The subway system had a terrible problem with crime, including vandalism, and nothing seemed to deter it. Two individuals, David Gunn and William Bratton, with a totally different philosophy on how to handle crime and reorganization stepped in to curb the problem. These individuals didn't add cameras or high-tech devices on the subway, nor did they have undercover agents to increase payroll on the trains. To be completely honest, they didn't deal with the most significant crimes at all. That may seem ludicrous, but it worked. They dealt with the graffiti on the trains and with turnstile jumpers. Each believed that the overall presentation of the subway system as a whole was the driving force behind the crimes being committed. It is true, there were small issues that eventually led to bigger issues. They contended that if everything preceding the crimes could be changed, perhaps the crime itself would not occur. Getting people to think this same way about retail loss prevention can put organizations on a path to eradicating losses due to employee theft.

The title *Loss Prevention* implies that losses are being stopped before they occur. In most cases by the time the event reaches loss prevention the damage has already been done. At this stage of the situation it is time to recoup the losses and get rid of the problem. If organizations learn more about the behavior that precedes an event, more losses can be prevented. Loss prevention is a discipline of learning and applying deterrent principles in light of what was learned to stop further occurrences of loss. Later chapters will discuss theoretical perspectives so readers can understand research being conducted on the topic of employee deviance. Chapters to follow will also explore ways to control employee dishonesty through impediments and will provide ways to build an ethical infrastructure within the organization.

Prior to 2002, organizations could make their own choice as to whether to prevent fraud. Employers controlled their own financial statements as they wished. The Sarbanes–Oxley Act of 2002 now holds organizations that are publicly traded in the United States accountable for preventing fraud and being able to prove to the government that they are doing so. The law also mandates that all financial disclosures have been reviewed and certified as accurate by the top executives of the company. Specifically, Section 404 of the act includes retailers in its scope. Noncompliance by organizations can lead to hefty fines and can include imprisonment for executives. Now more than ever the need for well-trained loss prevention professionals is in demand. Later chapters will discuss selecting the right individuals for the job and how to build a loss prevention department, should you ever have a chance to do so. Some parts of the book will provide the fundamentals for individuals entering the business of loss prevention, whereas other parts will cover the more integral components for those who have many years of experience. The book will educate on the topic of retail loss prevention through real-life case studies and interviews with people involved in the business and will discuss the problems as well as the solutions for businesses as a whole.

2

The Root of the Problem in Retail Business Cultures
Promises, Promises

From the first interaction with a new hire, agreements are starting to be made. The employer tells the new hire what the job entails, and the new hire absorbs all the information as it is being said. The new hire is also walking into the job with certain expectations. Neither the employer nor employee declares that a contract is being made, but essentially that is what happens during the conversations (Figure 2.1).

The creating of the contract doesn't end at the hiring stage; rather, it continues throughout employment. Agreements such as initial wage may be very concrete, but other promises may not be so clear. Some made between employee and employer do not include words. The silent promises are based on one's own expectations about how the other should behave. For instance, the employee is thinking, "My boss should treat me with dignity and respect; in turn, I will treat my boss and others with dignity and respect." The employer is thinking, "The new employee should show up to work on time everyday, and that is how I will know that the new employee is reliable and can be considered for advancement."

Another type of agreement is the implied promise. The employer implies that something can happen but does not clarify the conditions that need to occur for it to happen. The employer may know that he or she does not have what the would-be employee wants at this time and may

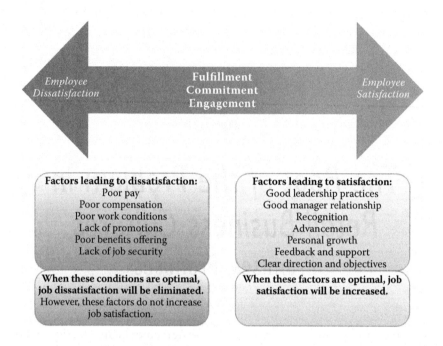

Figure 2.1 Job satisfaction model. (© 2008 Justin Field.)

never have it but alludes to the potential that it can occur. Consider the following example:

> An employer must fill the open position. The person applying for the job is looking to be in management, but the open position is nonmanagement. The employer has no evidence that a management position will open in the near future. The interviewee tells the employer that he really would like to be in management to consider taking the job. The employer tells him that if he takes the entry-level position a management spot could open, and he will be the first to be considered. The employee goes into the position thinking he will soon be in management. The employer recruited the candidate she liked, but at what cost?

Yet another type of promise is made for the current condition. The employee tells the employer during the interview that it is impossible for her to work certain days of the week because of personal reasons. At the time of the interview, that promise can be kept because the employer has enough resources to allow the employee not to work those days. The

employer cannot be certain that things will never change but does not tell the employee that if staffing should change she might have to work the days. Instead, they agree that the employee will not have to work the days, and she takes the job with the perception that she will never have to work those days.

So what happens when there is a broken promise or what would otherwise be considered a breech in contract? We will share the story of Bob and his broken promise.

Bob worked for an organization for over 10 years; He was a great employee and was already in a lower-level management position. One day Bob's boss left the company, and Bob became indirectly in charge of managing the location. He eagerly picked up where his boss left off and assumed the duties without being asked. The organization knew that Bob really wanted to be a higher-level manager because he spoke of it frequently.

Bob came in early and stayed late to get his current job plus his new job done. He put in many hours and regularly communicated with his supervisor, who was previously his supervisor's supervisor. During the conversations Bob was told what a great job he was doing filling the roll of the manager and that the organization really appreciated all of his hard work. When Bob asked for an increase in salary, his supervisor told him that she was working on it. Months went by with Bob working an excessive number of hours and still no pay increase. One day Bob's boss walked into the location and introduced him to his new supervisor.

The look on Bob's face said a million words. Bob could not believe that he worked two jobs for one salary all of those months under the pretense that he would become the manager of the location and now was being introduced to the person who just took his job. Bob did not receive so much as a call letting him know that he would not be getting the job; rather, just a few days before the introduction he was again told what a great job he was doing. An organization he trusted and loved had just let him down in the worst way. He thought if someone had the nerve to call him and let him know before they slapped him in the face it might have been a little easier. Bob began to think of all the time he lost at home working the excessive hours in the hopes that he would soon receive a bigger salary and new position. The supervisor told the new manager what a great job Bob did in holding the store together and that he will be a great resource in the location. Bob was of the opinion that the supervisor could take all of her lip service and give it to the new person.

Bob was no longer the Bob everyone knew over the last 10 years. He was disgruntled, angry, and disappointed. Bob knew he wanted to get back at the organization and his supervisors for what they did to him, so he figured out a way to do it. He decided that he would compensate himself for all the extra hours he put in by doing fraudulent returns. At random, when a customer paid for product, Bob would go into the register and refund the amount in cash. Bob would pocket the cash and continue working throughout the day. Bob felt better that he was getting something back for all of his hard work and rationalized that he was doing to the organization only what had been done to him. He was eventually

7

caught and terminated and shared his story during the loss prevention interview with the individuals investigating the case.

Bob's story isn't much different from many others who had similar treatment in the workplace. Bob believed he would be getting more money and the management position because his supervisor allowed him to believe that. If the supervisor had told Bob up front that he wasn't going to be the manager but had asked for his help during the interim, the outcome would have been much different. But the supervisor knew that she needed Bob to work the extra hours to ensure that all the work would be done, so she allowed Bob to believe things she knew were not going to happen. A tenured employee who gave so much to the organization became another statistic in the loss prevention department because of broken promises.

Loss prevention professionals who don't take the time to learn about cause and effect in the workplace are missing out on understanding the bigger picture. An inexperienced person could have discounted the causes behind Bob's story by not delving deeper into the situation. Conversations about dishonesty should not end at the point where an admission is reached. They should continue until the interviewer has an absolutely clear understanding of what led this individual down a path that would ultimately cost him his job.

Societies as well as the employees within the workplace are very quick to position themselves for the company and against the individual who committed the act of dishonesty. It is true that everyone has a choice to steal or not to steal, but there are always contributing factors to the result. Loss prevention people need to be consistently assessing the contributing factors to make change for the good.

Often overlooked are actual or implied promises by employers to employees. This may happen mainly because it may not be an immediate issue. For example, say someone needs money for rent on Friday, so he steals the bank deposit on Thursday. When the interviewer asks that ever so daunting question of why he did it, the answer seems clear and simple: He needed money, so he took it from the first place an opportunity presented itself. The answer provided by the interviewee is one that is believable and understandable because it relates to basic needs. This reason is also easily accepted by the organization because according to what is conveyed, the organization did not play a role in the person's decision-making process.

The beginning of the chapter discussed an employee being promised she would not have to work certain days of the week. These particular conversations usually take place before employeees actually begin working at an organization. If the broken promise is what actually caused the dishonesty and the event did not occur until later, it can be considered a delayed issue. It is difficult for some organizations and interviewers to believe that one simple conversation about something such as a work schedule can lead someone to steal. Even when told, organizations tend to shrug at something like this and can cause someone to take such action. Again, it is easier to blame the individual alone than to deal with the bigger picture.

When sales get sluggish, the first item to be addressed is accountability. Training department members will begin to focus on programs that hold management and employees accountable for the condition of the organization. They will develop new or modify existing coaching and counseling methods to produce results. If the company was not extremely results-oriented before the sales slowed, it will certainly adopt the methodology after the fact. Thousands—if not millions—of dollars will be spent on consultant research, program development, and implementation. The goal of the organization is to increase sales and to regain investor confidence in the reliability of the organization. Employees are put under extreme pressure to deliver results. Their productivity levels are closely monitored, and their superiors scrutinize individuals responsible for the districts or regions. At this point in the organization's life cycle, it is either swim or sink. To those who fly at 10,000 feet above store level, the answer seems to start at middle management and below. During this phase, some jobs will be eliminated, and individuals will begin to crack under the pressure, in turn resigning from their positions. Many wonder how the organization's leaders allowed things to get to this point and why it was not disclosed prior to everything getting so bad. No one comes forward to truthfully declare all the circumstances that led to the organization's current condition; rather, it is assumed that starting at store level will fix it. Some organizations will recover from their predicament, whereas others will perish.

Accountability or ownership for results is nothing new in the business world. In fact, it is easy for an organization to implement an atmosphere where accountability is paramount to gaining necessary results. One would think that organizations are eager to hold individuals accountable for all their actions, but that is not the case. Managers who make silent promises, implied promises, or promises made for the current conditions

are often not held accountable at all. Most organizations pay little or no attention to this topic and do not realize how much impact these promises have on employees. If organizations were able to remove the blinders, they might realize that perhaps executive-level promises led to the current condition of the organization, not front-line employees' inability to sell product.

Organizations need to take the time to train supervisors on not making promises and having truthful discussions. "Desperate times call for desperate measures" should not apply to hiring individuals. When loss prevention finds out during the course of an investigation that any of the three promises were involved with the situation, action should be taken based on that information. Loss prevention members who are not currently probing for how it all began need to start assessing the topic. Training employees who supervise others on proper conversations—the do's and don'ts during the hiring process—is important. It must be understood that when something is implied to an employee, it is taken to heart and expected to happen. Proper education regarding promising conversations can lessen the number of employees who engage in deviant behavior as a result of what they believe should have happened.

MONKEY SEE, MONKEY DO

Supervisory-level employees are always on display. Every move they make is being observed and monitored by store-level employees. Without even uttering a word, their actions or inactions are being taken in by subordinates and used as a lesson learned. Once an employee sees how a supervisor reacts to something, the employee learns the level of tolerance that will be accepted for that particular situation.

An example of this is attendance. If an employee comes in late, other employees are waiting to see how the supervisor reacts. If the supervisor does nothing, the supervisor ultimately declares that coming in late is acceptable. Employees believe management condones this type of behavior and that they too can do it. In turn, this teaches employees that a slight deviation from the rules will be tolerated. Employees will monitor what happens to each of their co-workers for similar infractions. They will gauge if preferential treatment is occurring by what happens to each individual and if they are all held accountable the same way.

There are implications both for inaction and for treating employees differently. Employees begin to think that if supervisors accept a deviation

from policy for attendance they will also accept a deviation in other categories. Employees will also monitor who is getting away with what and how often. In all retail environments there are great, good, and not so good producers. It is often found that the great producers are held less accountable for infractions than are the not so good producers. The reasoning for this inequality of accountability is simple: managers do not want to lose their top-performing people for any reason because it impacts sales and them directly. It is also known that managers will challenge terminations for their top producers by finding reasons for counseling rather than a termination. If an employee is not producing, a loss prevention investigation is kindly welcomed. But if the person is a high producer, a loss prevention investigation is often frowned upon.

Although employees do not know what happens behind closed doors between a manager and employee, they can guess fairly well as to the dialogue taking placed based on many different factors. For instance, an employee shows up to work 10 minutes late, and the manager immediately asks the employee to come into the office and closes the door. Others on the sales floor know what is going on, but no one has said a word. This type of immediate action makes a statement to employees that the manager will address violations in policy and will not let them go. In turn, employees who thought about being late know the outcome before they do it. As long as everyone receives the same consequences, the manager is building a foundation that does not accept bad behavior. Even worse than not holding other employees accountable for rule breaking is managers themselves breaking the rules. They can hold every individual accountable in the store for violating policy, but if they engage in the same action without consequence, the morale in the store will begin to deteriorate and disgruntlement will set in.

A case study involving region X demonstrates the "Do as I say, not as I do" methodology.

Region X is situated in the southern half of the Midwest territory of Company A. Sales were stable; the region was not the worst or the best. Many working in region X were long-term employees. Some had been with the organization for more than 20 years. The region also did not have much manager turnover. For the most part this region ran under the radar. For someone from the outside looking in, the perception initially was that the leadership was consistent and doing a good job. Times became tough within the organization, and there was a demand to increase the key performance objectives within the stores for the entire company. Region X had not reported many issues related to loss prevention, and not many investigations took place in this market.

11

All of that changed one day. The usual loss prevention investigation took place for a case of money loss; it did not seem out of the ordinary compared with any other case where employees committed acts of dishonesty for various reasons. What was different about this one is that it opened the floodgates for others to happen, or so it was believed. After the resolution of one case, many followed. The unique correlation between the cases was that almost all directly involved were management-level employees. Another unique component was that the cases were not related in any way other than that the managers belonged to the same region and that there were small time gaps between the incidents. Because the actual crimes being committed varied drastically from stealing money to falsifying statistics to theft of services, it was not easy to pinpoint the exact problem. There were some common denominators but it was unclear why. During one of the investigations, a manager who was helping gather the necessary documentation was asked, "What is going on in this region to cause all of this dishonesty?" It was like a weight had been lifted off this manager's back. She responded by providing the underlying cause as she and her peers saw it.

It was questionable why it took so long for everything to come to the forefront in this region because the lack of ethics by leadership was so apparent. Violations in ethical judgment, such as passing employees up for promotions based on likes and dislikes to expecting managers to cover multiple locations on one salary in excess of six months, were frequent occurrences. The regional supervisor left threatening voicemails, which explained why no one was willing to come forward. The manager also discussed content of routine conference calls held by the supervisor. An example of the calls were managers asking questions directed the content of conference calls with this supervisor. Someone in the region would ask a question directed to the supervisor on how to increase the store performance objectives that he or she knew was against company policy. The supervisor would not indicate that no one should cheat to reach a goal; rather, he would say every store needs to reach its goal and however it gets done is how it gets done.

The information received over the next several months during the investigation was not only shocking but disappointing as well. During some of the dishonesty interviews, the managers indicated that their supervisor had driven them to take action against the organization. People felt violated and alone in their battle against one person and reacted in a way that was adverse to the organization. After an extremely lengthy investigation and documentation gathering, the supervisor was eventually terminated for his actions.

It was believed that all the managers who lasted throughout this ordeal would be thrilled and would immediately be able reach their full potential because the weight had been lifted. However, the morale was still low, and people just seemed depressed.

The manager who provided the information that led to the termination of the supervisor was asked why things were not improving as quickly as they should. She stated that it was not that easy to recover from what they all went through. She said the situation was analogous to a woman or child who is being abused by a loved one. Statistics show that many women will go back to their abuser even after the abuser has been punished for the crime. She said that the managers who remain seem to be lost without the supervisor and scared as to what will happen without him. They all knew what he was doing was wrong, but for whatever reason they had learned to accept it. This was strange, but it was reality

for those who lived it. To make matters even worse, years after the situation concluded in the region and the supervisor was gone, the manager who was so insightful and had provided all this information ended up stealing back deposits and was terminated. Although the investigator who handled the original case did not handle this one, a fellow investigator stated that the manager who took the deposits mentioned the whole ordeal and could not understand why she herself engaged in dishonesty.

Region X illustrates the downward spiral that can take place if some-one who leads others does not have integrity. At no point during any of the conference call conversations did the supervisor tell anyone it was okay to steal or tell anyone to violate the rules, but his own actions as well as the questions he did not address gave everyone who was listening the answer. The Region X case study demonstrates the extreme end of what can happen when employees observe their supervisors being unethical. Most of the time, so many people will not lose their jobs and an entire region will end up in turmoil.

Region X represents a situation where employees observe behavior and adjust their behavior to accommodate the conditions. Therefore, it can be assumed that managers who always hold their employees accountable for their actions will have an area that thrives and that ethical standards will be followed by all. This is both true and false. It is true that managers who do not tolerate rule breaking and address it immediately will have fewer employees engaging in deviant behavior. However, this is false if how managers handle the rule breaking is a violation.

We will go back to the example of tardiness because it is one of the most prevalent forms of policy violation in a retail environment. The employee walks into the store late, and the manager decides to immedi-ately address the situation. But this time the employee is not taken into an office. This time the manager yells at the employee in front of all her peers and whoever else can hear. Yes, the situation is being addressed, but this scenario can be worse than not addressing it at all. The employee on the receiving end of the hostility is embarrassed and feels violated and angry. The employee has a couple of choices: either yell back or accept the behavior and walk away, depending on her personality type. Both have their own set of ramifications. Others who witness this act are very clear that tardiness will not be accepted, but they have also lost respect for the person who leads them. Employees want to be respected, and in turn they will respect others. If they are treated like children being disciplined by their parent, all the respect for their supervisor goes away. A lack of respect for superiors leads to different forms of deviance that are more

difficult to catch quickly. Employees who respect and have loyalty for a person or organization are much more likely to remain honest than those who lack respect and do not have a vested interest in their workplace. If the manager believes he was right in his actions and does nothing further, resentment sets in for the employee receiving the incorrect form of discipline.

So far we have covered employee observation and behavior adjustment and incorrect disciplinary action that leads employees down a path that will negatively impact the organization. The last part of this section is probably the most frequent improper performance and least to be recognized. The next few paragraphs will discuss managers who are not following operational controls but are not necessarily violating the policy as already covered herein. Among the three departments, loss prevention, human resources, and operations, many controls and best practices are set forth that will help prevent, deter, and eliminate dishonesty. When operational audits are conducted, the decencies within a location become extremely apparent. It is logical to believe that if managers are not following the controls put in place to combat dishonesty, the likelihood of them being able to identify it lessens. But that is not the only implication of not following the controls.

Many employees are aware of what is expected to be followed and enforced by the management staff. Through conversations, audits, visits, or reading policy manuals employees can figure out what controls are in place and what management should be doing to comply with the controls. When management is intentionally not following what needs to be done due to pure laziness, staffing shortages, or a variety of other reasons, this makes a statement to employees: It is acceptable not to follow procedures all the time. These managers may be as honest as they come, but intentionally not following procedures will overshadow that in the eyes of their employees. An example of this is package checks. If policy states that it is necessary to conduct daily package checks of employee belongings upon departure, the management staff should be conducting daily package checks. If the management staff decides that they will ignore the policy and not check employee contents upon departure, the employees may think it is acceptable not to follow the controls that are put in place. Some managers may feel that by not checking employees' packages they are nonverbally announcing to employees their level of trust in them. This is not the case. Employees want and expect management to follow the rules; in turn, most will also follow all the rules. As a result of managers not following known controls, some employees will

take advantage of the situation, and some will lose trust in their supervisors. The ones who take advantage are opportunistic and wait for a situation to present itself so they can go for it. If they know the manager is not ever going to check a package, they will risk concealing product in a personal belonging and remove it from the store. Others who lose trust may begin to take extended breaks or call in sick when they really are not sick because their supervisor is willing to bend the rules a little bit. Neither of the two groups—those who are opportunistic or experience a loss of trust—is productive for the organization, and both can be caused by observations in the workplace.

Employee observation and behavior adjustment, incorrect disciplinary action, and management not following known controls are all areas of retail that can contribute to losses occurring in one form or another. Some are intentional, and others are more subtle. Loss prevention professionals who interact directly with store personnel or present at district and regional meetings should be covering these three areas so that employees can understand how their behavior directly impacts others. When covering employee observation and behavior adjustment, the main point of the conversation needs to focus on communicating and following through. Store supervisors, as well as other leaders up to and including executive leaders of the organization, need to realize that saying one thing but doing another will be detrimental. In addition, if managers do not clarify that something is absolutely wrong when they know it is a violation of policy, they are essentially condoning the behavior. Managers must publicly state when asked if something is against policy. If they are not sure of the answer, they need to find it and convey it to everyone who reports to them. Some personality types are more direct than others. Directness that turns into outright verbal abuse toward employees who do wrong is not acceptable. Managers need to be taught how to properly address situations with their subordinates. All employees do not need to know every word said to their peers during a disciplinary action. The employee being disciplined should be removed from the sales floor and out of earshot. Just because someone did not meet an expectation does not mean he or she should be treated without dignity and respect. The disciplinary action should be conducted in private, and the manager should not discuss what happened behind closed doors with anyone who does not need to know. Last, the importance of following procedures and best practices needs to be communicated not only by loss prevention but also by regional and district managers. If during an audit or store visit it was determined that the store was not following all procedures, an action plan should be developed to

identify specifically what needs to be corrected and how to correct the problem. During the recap of the findings, the manager should understand what happens when controls are not being followed. It is important to discuss how employees see the bigger picture and the implications of their perceptions.

THE RELATIONSHIP

According to an article by Barbara Wold, seven strategies allow businesses to strengthen their relationships that will in turn provide a competitive edge:

1. Communicate frequently.
2. Offer customer rewards.
3. Hold special events.
4. Build two-way communication.
5. Enhance your customer service.
6. Launch multicultural programs.
7. Visit the trenches.

Building relationships in business can be considered one of the key components in determining the success of an individual. If we take each of the seven strategies and apply them to the relationship between loss prevention professionals and their customers, not all will be easy to achieve. In most organizations loss prevention is not directly responsible for individuals outside of their own department. In addition, the geographic areas covered by loss prevention people, excluding single store level, are usually relatively large, which makes it difficult to consistently communicate with everyone. Beyond single store level loss prevention much of the conversation being held is between loss prevention individuals and individuals responsible for regions or districts. This is where the frequency in conversations will take place. Celebrating what employees are doing right is something that probably needs a little work in most organizations when it comes to loss prevention. During audits and investigations, issues such as dishonesty, operational deficiencies, and lack of proper training are identified. These are all considered negative items and rightfully so. A key motivator in human behavior, especially in business, is that individuals are recognized for a job well done. Because loss prevention is rarely called to action for good, individuals working in the department must learn to

create their own "good." Some examples of loss prevention recognition are as follows:

- Yearly award for lowest store shrinkage and region and district shrinkage. The award can be a framed certificate mailed to the store along with a gift card.
- Small trinkets brought with the auditor during audit to be given to managers who score above a certain percentage.
- Allowing managers who excel in operational controls to be loss prevention captains. These individuals will be the go-to people for others who have questions about proper procedures.
- Having managers interested in loss prevention in conjunction with their own abilities that are above and beyond when it comes to shrinkage control travel with loss prevention.
- Sharing stories about employees who assisted loss prevention or uncovered issues that were costing the company money. The stories can be relayed through newsletters or other means available.
- Recognizing employees during a meeting being held by loss prevention.

These suggestions are just a sample of what can be done to develop meaningful relationships between loss prevention and others in the organization.

The ability to build two-way communication will be determined by how much effort each party is willing to put forth and also by how the loss prevention department is viewed by the entire organization. If loss prevention is viewed as a department that is a necessary business entity and provides value outside of its main functions such as auditing and investigation, the two-way communication building will be easier. But if the loss prevention department is viewed as the necessary evil that needs to be called upon for terminations and when employees are being bad, the two-way communication building will be difficult. The perception of the loss prevention department as a whole does not start at the the bottom and move to the top; rather, it begins directly at the top. If the individuals leading the loss prevention department do not build a foundation with executives in the organization, everyone in the department will be affected. Starting the two-way conversation or relationship may be one-sided for a while before it becomes fully evolved. Even if loss prevention is viewed as a business partner, others in the organization are still going to be a little leery of people within the department because they are involved with so many negative situations. The field personal in the organization or stores will want to watch what they are saying in front of loss prevention team members for fear that what

they are saying will somehow get them in trouble, therefore limiting their exposure to the department. The calls will come from those who need loss prevention interaction until the relationship between loss prevention and its partners reaches a new level, which will not be accomplished until trust is built. Once this occurs and the partners understand that loss prevention has the same goal as they do—which is to keep the company profitable—the partners will realize they go about achieving goals differently. Making managers and employees feel at ease during any loss prevention encounter is a key to developing the relationship.

To enhance the level of customer service, some simple steps need to be followed:

Step 1: Follow through on the commitments.
Step 2: Treat everyone with dignity and respect, regardless of the situation.
Step 3: Do not violate the trust of others.
Step 4: Provide clear and understandable answers to questions or concerns.
Step 5: Recognize individuals for a job well done.
Step 6: When unintentional deficiencies are found, treat the situation as a learning session for the individuals and help them improve those deficiencies.

Because loss prevention is a support department in most organizations, enhancing customer service allows others to communicate to upper management that loss prevention is more than just a necessary department. Often, once a trusting relationship has been built, individuals in the organization will latch on to loss prevention people for support they cannot get anywhere else. The latching that takes place can be very beneficial to loss prevention because the employees are willing to have open communication without fear of repercussions. The conversations can lead loss prevention to direct or underlying causes of losses within the organization. But the latching can also cause loss prevention people to become overwhelmed by the amount of time each employee occupies for the conversations depending on how much territory they cover. There needs to be a balance between becoming the go-to person for everything and being there for employees who need to convey information about issues that can adversely affect the organization.

Organizations that are doing very well today are also embracing diversity. Diversity should not be mistaken for a quota system that looks

to hire individuals because of a specific race or gender. According to Cornell University,

> Workplace diversity is a people issue, focused on the differences and similarities that people bring to an organization. It is usually defined broadly to include dimensions beyond those specified legally in equal opportunity and affirmative action non-discrimination statutes. Diversity is often interpreted to include dimensions which influence the identities and perspectives that people bring, such as profession, education, parental status and geographic location.

Differences of opinion as well as different approaches to the same issue can be considered diverse. Loss prevention professionals should be encouraged to be creative in their thinking and to broaden their horizons. Because loss prevention deals with such a diverse group of employees, it is important that members of the department also be diverse. For example, in Florida, Texas, and California, loss prevention people need to be able to speak Spanish to interview employees. In Quebec, loss prevention employees have a need to speak French. Knowing the needs of the geographic area is important before hiring. If someone is hired to conduct interviews in an area where there is a large population of foreign language speakers and the person does not possess the skill set, it will impede his or her ability to be successful in the position.

Having conversations over the phone with store employees is effective, but it cannot replace in-person visits. The current century has allowed for the reduction of human contact through e-mail, online shopping and banking, and delivery services so people never have to leave their house. People learn and develop through socialization, which is achieved through human interaction. Technology has made people's lives easier but has removed a very important part of human development. Only so much can be achieved through a virtual setting. Again, the quantity of stores' loss prevention people are responsible for will determine how often they can interact with people. Stores with significant shrinkage problems or integrity problems warrant visits from loss prevention. Putting a face with a name is also important in building a trusting relationship with people. Employees will feel more comfortable calling someone they have met before for information regarding dishonesty than they will calling someone based on a business card posted on a wall. During in-store visits it is important that employees gain much knowledge. The learning will occur not only through audits; in addition, sitting down with employees

to discuss loss prevention and all the components that go with it can be a very powerful learning tool. Employees will walk away understanding shrinkage, how their actions affect others, and what they can do to create an environment where honesty prevails. Following is an outline of what topics can be covered during the conversations in the form of a checklist as well as examples of the answers.

AREAS FOR DISCUSSION
Shrinkage

- Give the definition of *shrink*.
- Explain how shrink occurs.
- Talk about what causes shrink.
- Discuss ways to reduce shrink.

Internal Theft

- Talk about employees' temptations and opportunities and their implications.
- Discuss the top reasons for employee theft at the organization.
- Explain the controls in place at store level to combat theft.
- Provide information on what loss prevention does to prevent dishonesty.

Shoplifting

- Conduct a role-playing session on how to address shoplifters.
- Discuss organized retail crime and the impact on the organization.
- Give tips on how to decrease shoplifting.
- Go over the shoplifting policy for the organization if there is one.

Operational Controls

- Discuss refund and void control procedures.
- Talk about daily paperwork review.
- Discuss package checks and how to avoid complacency.
- Provide statistics, and talk about how to combat missing deposits and chargebacks.

Hiring Employees

- Provide information on how to test for integrity during the hiring process.
- Go over the hot points of the employment application related to loss prevention.
- Talk about getting the right fit and not hiring out of desperation.
- Ensure there is an understanding of what happens with broken promises.

Reporting Information

- Discuss the use of the incident report form.
- Talk about the reporting hotline and where the number should be posted.
- Provide information about Sarbanes–Oxley and what the organization is doing to comply. (The Sarbanes–Oxley Act, passed in 2002, holds publically tended companies accountable for reporting accurate financial numbers.)
- Discuss reasons people do not report information and how to overcome this.

Create a Culture of Honesty

- Discuss ways to create an environment of open communication.
- Talk about giving clear and consistent messages about dishonesty.
- Discuss proper treatment of employees.
- Provide tips on how to immediately handle policy violations.

ANSWER SHEET

Shrinkage

- Shrinkage is the difference between the book inventory (what you should have) and the physical inventory (what you actually do have).
- Shrink can come in three forms: internal, external, and operational errors:

- Internal: Shrink is caused internally when employees choose to steal from the company or intentionally cause losses to the company.
- External: Shrink is caused externally when customers or delivery drivers steal merchandise.
- Operational errors: Shrink is caused through errors when employees are not following the proper operational protocol that allows us to protect the company profits.

- The ways to reduce all forms of shrink are as follows:
 - Internal: Good hiring practices, open communication, and good store controls.
 - External: Excellent customer service, keeping shelves full, alarms systems, and key control.
 - Operational: Education, communication, and follow-up.

Internal Theft

- Employees cause losses to the company by engaging in theft of bank deposits, credit card fraud, refund or void fraud, and dropped sales. Employees take from the company if they feel mistreated, need money, are mad at their supervisor, or see other employees doing it and not getting in trouble. The implications of employee theft include reduced sales, lower store morale, counterproductive behavior, and turnovers.
- If possible, provide a recap of what employees said during dishonesty interviews with regard to why they stole from the organization.
- Manager should be reviewing daily paperwork. Everyone should be following all policy and procedures as listed in the employee handbook, and this information should continue to be discussed. Inventory should be taken accurately.
- Provide examples of the tools loss prevention uses to detect and deter dishonesty, such as software for exception reporting, software used to find stolen product on the Internet, and camera systems.

Shoplifting

- Role playing should include different scenarios depicting events that could occur in the store as they pertain to shoplifting. Loss prevention should provide guidance on how to handle multiple customers and situations involving theft.
- Organized retail crime can range from a single theft or removal of understock to the use of fraudulent credit cards and checks in stores. All involve taking illegally, reselling, or returning for the benefit of the group. These people are professionals, also known as boosters, and are well structured, entering stores to remove property to be resold at fences. Fences then resell the product at flea markets, pawn shops, and on the Internet, to wholesalers, merchandise distributors, and even neighborhood stores.
- To decrease shoplifting use excellent customer service, keep displays neat and full, and be observant of people who wear loose clothing or don't buy anything and continue to come into the store and groups of people who try to distract employees by taking them away from other persons in the store.
- Provide the actual policy—if there is one—on how to handle shoplifting. This should include a "who to call" list and "what to do" procedures.

Operational Controls

- Refunds and voids are an easy way to steal cash from the company. To combat these problems, managers should be reviewing all returns and voids on a daily basis. Both returns and voids should have an original purchase that can be substantiated. Managers should complete a customer service call to a customer if they feel there is a suspicious transaction.
- All managers should be reviewing daily the prior day's business. Managers should be looking for any inconsistencies or irregularities in the prior day's business.
- Package checks should be completed daily. All bags, lunchboxes, backpacks, and other carrier items should be checked prior to employees' departure. If this is done daily, employees expect to

have it done and are less likely to conceal stolen merchandise in their bag.
- Provide current data on areas of vulnerability. Provide specifics on how to protect those areas.

Hiring Employees

- Provide examples of what questions employees can ask during the interview process that would allow them to understand where a person stands with regard to integrity. For example, "If you see a manager borrow $10 for lunch and place an IOU in the drawer, what would you do?" If they say, "Well, it's the manager, and they know what they can and can't do," that's a bad answer. If they say that they would report it immediately, that's a good answer.
- Employment applications should be examined carefully in the following areas:
 - Information that talks about convictions.
 - Information that talks about discharges from previous employment.
 - Reason for leaving other employers.
 - Fair Credit Reporting Act (FCRA).
 - Large gaps in employment history.
- Organizations are looking for the best employees. Ensuring that managers are hiring employees that fit the scope of what is desired, such as good salespeople with integrity is an integral part of the hiring process. If a red flag is found on the application or during the interview process, do not hire the person because you need a body in the store. Hiring a person who is not the right fit because of a need only will cause the organization problems down the road.
- During the first interactions with a new employee, a contract between the manager and employee is being built. The employee listens and believes everything the manager says. If a manager misleads or implies things that cannot or will not happen, this is a breech of contract. As a result the person feels betrayed or lied to, and this will cause problems for the manager.

Reporting Information

- The incident report form is used to document incidents of theft, burglary, and robbery. All stores should have these documents on hand and use them for the aforementioned incidents.
- Provide the number for the anonymous reporting hotline and uses.
- The Sarbanes–Oxley Act of 2002 was passed by Congress as a means to restore investor confidence in corporate executives, corporations, and public and financial disclosures. It was a result of the crisis in business ethics that included Enron, WorldCom, and Tyco fraud scandals. As a result of this act, publically traded companies must ensure that they are complying with the review of their paperwork and must take responsibility for their business.
- There are several reasons employees do not report information pertaining to dishonesty. The next section titled "Conversations" will provide a flow chart that can be used during the discussion.

Create a Culture Of Honesty

- Always tell the truth. Deal with issues as they come; don't allow them to sit. Allow employees to disagree, but commit to a plan. Create an environment that allows people to come forward with information. Reward people who are honest and provide information. Declare your beliefs and talk about a foundation built on the truth.
- Managers must often tell employees that any form of dishonesty will not be tolerated. When the company is offering a contest or special incentive, managers must tell the employees that they should not cheat to win the contest. If store internals are low and there is pressure to increase sales, cheating gets the person terminated.
- Employees need to feel like they are part of the team. They need to know they are valued and contribute to the bigger picture. They should be kept informed of company information, and their concerns should be taken seriously and addressed.
- Provide information on who to call if someone suspects that others are stealing from the store. Also discuss the don'ts of knowing such information:

- Don't inform people that you are aware of what they are doing or ask them why they are stealing.
- Don't make it known to any other employees in the store that someone is suspected of theft.

Some of the aforementioned areas may or may not apply to the reader's current employer. This is an example of what can be used to open a conversation around the topic of loss prevention. The checklist can be modified to fit the current organizational methods, or components of the checklist can be used to implement areas that are nonexistent.

Organizational relationships are the building blocks to successful partnerships that allow organizations to flourish. More so than other departments, loss prevention depends on trusting relationships to get the job done. The stronger the foundation of the relationship between loss prevention and its customers, the easier the job becomes. Loss prevention is a team effort, not a lone ranger business. Once the auditor, investigator, or trainer from loss prevention walks out of the location he or she is visiting, it becomes the choice of the location to continue what has been started or pretend like it never happened in the first place. Loss prevention individuals who understand the importance of relationship building will spend time doing so before they venture further into other duties. Those who are under the misconception that everyone has to comply because loss prevention said so will have a very difficult time being successful.

THE CONVERSATION

As we covered in the previous section, relationships are the building blocks to successful partnerships. This section will cover how the relationship develops through conversations. Loss prevention people spend a significant portion of their time engaging in conversation. Some of the conversation takes place during the audit or training session, whereas other portions take place during an interview. Loss prevention must look at every conversation as a fact-gathering session. Many clues must be detected to probe for further information, such as the following:

- The tone in employees' voices when being asked a general question.
- The hesitation to answer questions regarding their supervisor.
- Avoiding the actual subject by deflecting the question.

- Remarks such as "If you only knew" or "Do you really want to know."
- Sensing frustration in interviewees when they did not know or understand something.
- Employees want to tell more, but something is stopping them.

If loss prevention investigators are able to pick up on subtle clues, they will be able to generate a conversation that is beneficial to persons holding the information as well as the organization. Many employees holding on to information are willing to share it if they feel safe. Employees do not want to convey information that is affecting the organization for many reasons.

Figure 2.2 represents the steps necessary to report information. It also depicts human behavior that gets in the way of reporting the information. The employee response process is similar to that of the Bystander Effect. Researchers have concluded that certain conditions need to be present before society is willing to help those in an emergency situation. Much of the research was prompted by the Kitty Genovese case. In 1964 Kitty Genovese was stabbed to death in a public area while dozens of people witnessed the gruesome attack. No one rushed to Kitty's aid. As with employees who witness occurrences of dishonesty within the workplace, society also has a duty to act but often does not for various reasons. There must be a situation occurring to prompt employees to react or not react:

Step 1: Notice That Something is Occurring. Employees may not understand that something is right or wrong, but in this step they are realizing something is going on. Between the situation beginning and the realization of occurrence by an employee, self-concerns begin to erupt. Employees begin to think that it is not really their problem and that they do not want to be part of it. To move to Step 2 they must overcome their self-concerns and be willing to make it their problem.

Step 2: Interpret the Situation as Out of the Norm. Employees are used to seeing specific things take place daily. In Step 2 employees must be able to decipher what is normal and what is not. Once they have determined that something just is not right, they can move on to the next step. But again there are self-inflicted barriers in the way of moving to the next step. This time ambiguity, relationships, and pluralistic ignorance impede information reporting. With ambiguity employees try to place gray into a black-and-white situation. This allows them to free their conscience of

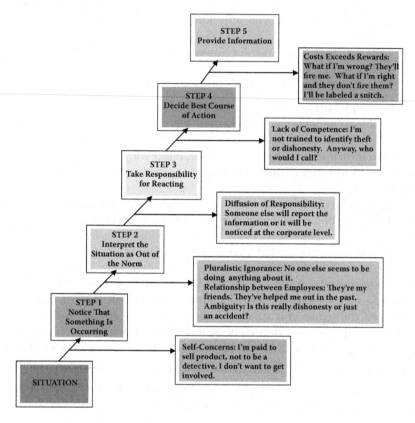

Figure 2.2 The steps af reporting information, and behaviors that may interfere.

not reporting by convincing themselves that maybe what they see is not what they think it is. They also dwell on relationships with coworkers and supervisors. They realize that what they are seeing cannot be good for the organization, but they do not want to get their "pals" in trouble. The last barrier between Steps 1 and 2 is pluralistic ignorance. Employees think there is no way they are the only person who noticed the situation. Because others are not reacting, or they do not believe are reacting, why should they get involved if no one else is coming forward?

Step 3: Take Responsibility for Reacting. During Step 3 employees acknowledge that they have a duty to act. They also begin to feel

offended that another employee is willing to take advantage of the organization they work for. But again a barrier gets in the way of taking responsibility—diffusion of responsibility. Diffusion of responsibility is similar to pluralistic ignorance in that it relies on others for decision making but is different because it does not place blame on others. Rather, it assumes that others will handle the issue without their direct involvement or it will somehow be noticed. This barrier does not allow for a conscience-free approach. The employee is not sure that the situation will be resolved without their intervention but hopes that it will.

Step 4: Decide Best Course of Action. If employees reach Step 4, they have made the decision that without them the situation cannot be resolved. Employees are deliberating how best to convey the information. If they are aware of all the tools available, such as an anonymous hotline, open door policy, direct contact with field management, or a call to loss prevention, the decision is made easier. If they are not sure how to proceed, they will need to research how to provide confidential information. The barrier between Steps 3 and 4 is lack of competence. Employees know what they are seeing is wrong, but they do not feel like they are competent to diagnose the problem completely. As mentioned in Step 4, not knowing who to call can get in the way of making any call at all. Employees can take the attitude that no one trained them on how to handle this type of situation so there is nothing more they can do.

Step 5: Provide Information. If all barriers are overcome, the end result is Step 5. Employees will provide the organization with the necessary information. Some employees never reach Step 5 because of the barriers stopping the flow of information. Some of the barriers have validity, but others are just figments of their imagination. On the other hand, if employees have actually witnessed one of the barriers come true with someone else who has tried to report information, this will only confirm their suspicions. The barrier between Steps 4 and 5 is along the same lines as the barrier between Step 2 and self-concern. Employeees begin to think of what can happen once the information is provided: if for some reason what they saw was not a violation, they will be fired. On the flip side, if they are right that can be bad as well. If their boss likes the person and somehow they are saved from termination they will have to deal with them knowing they are the one who tried to get them fired.

An extreme psychological process takes place for employees when they need to have a conversation. Some of the barriers are so intense that it does not allow for the movement to the next step that will eventually lead to releasing information. Having conversations with employees about what to do if they notice dishonesty and how to report information can lessen the barriers. If there is a hotline for reporting business irregularities it should be posted in visible area. Knowledge is power in this type of situation because if employees know the protocol prior to being involved it allows the entire process to move more freely.

The reporting of dishonesty that is discussed in the flow chart describes a situation noticed by employees and reported by employees. Information also can be delivered in different ways, but with similar results. Tying in the goals of loss prevention with operations can be a hurdle worth jumping. In other chapters the struggle between loss prevention and other departments will be discussed more fully, but for purposes of this section it will be only briefly mentioned. Loss prevention must understand what the immediate needs of the organization are. Most loss prevention people will find that reducing shrinkage is not at the top of the executive "to do" list. But that does not mean that loss prevention cannot find another angle to attack shrinkage or potential ethical issues occurring in a location.

CATEGORIES AFFECTING EMPLOYEE PERFORMANCE

There is usually a correlation between poor store performance and high inventory loss. The problem is usually with the leadership at the store or regional level. With that being said, a different angle is to approach the situation with trying to correct the poor performance, which is usually at the top of the executive to do list. Addressing the topic of poor performance will also be accomplished through conversation. The unique outcome of this type of conversation is that it will serve two purposes: understanding why there is a performance issue and uncovering underlying causes that can be contributing to loss prevention situations. Categories that affect performance in the workplace are as follows:

1. Training, skills, and knowledge.
2. Motivation.
3. External factors or factors beyond employees' control.

Especially important to loss prevention is the motivation category. Motivation drives much employee behavior and can work either for good

or bad. The following section provides examples of questions that can address employee performance. Each question can be given a yes–no answer. Interviewers can assess which of the three categories is the biggest contributor to the problem by the number of yes and no answers. Providing a recap of the assessment to field partners and executives of the findings will also be beneficial.

TRAINING, SKILLS, AND KNOWLEDGE

1. Did the organization provide adequate training?
2. Do you believe you received the same training as everyone else?
3. Did the organization provide adequate coaching and opportunities to work with others who could help?
4. Does the coaching you receive help better you in the current role?
5. Do you feel as though you understand what is expected of you on a daily basis?
6. Do you believe you possess the skills necessary to perform your job at the level the organization expects?
7. Are you armed with the knowledge necessary to fulfill your role?
8. Do you receive feedback on your performance?
9. Do you know how to fix areas of opportunity when you receive feedback?

MOTIVATION

1. Do you like working for the organization?
2. Do you believe that everyone in the store is treated the same?
3. Do you feel the incentives are fair?
4. Are you recognized for a job well done?
5. Do you believe you have a good level of autonomy?
6. Do you feel like you can advance within the organization?
7. Do you believe promises the organization makes are kept?
8. Are all employees in the store accountable for their actions?
9. Do you believe your needs are addressed?

EXTERNAL FACTORS OR FACTORS
BEYOND EMPLOYEES' CONTROL

1. Have you noticed a decrease in store traffic?
2. When walking near or through the mall do you notice customers carrying bags from other retailers?
3. Have any new retailers of a similar nature opened in the area that would be impacting your business?
4. Is the economic growth strong in the city where the store is located?
5. Would you say your personal quality of life is good?
6. Are you happy outside of work?
7. Have you experienced any life events over the past year?
8. If you feel pressure from work, is it revealed when you are at home?
9. Are there enough employees in the store to do the job?

One of the most profound statements made regarding conversations came from Susan Scott, the author of *Fierce Conversation,* during one of her presentations for an organization. She spoke about a marital relationship that was not going so well. For years, conversations had been occurring between the husband and wife, but no resolution ever came of the conversation. She said, "The conversation is the relationship." In other words, the relationship could not exist without the conversations. This is true for most relationships. Conversations need to continue to occur for the relationship to move forward. Problems are resolved through discussions with others. Without conversations it would be difficult for people to exist.

3

Exploring the Psychology Supporting the Theft Triangle
How and Why Does Criminal Behavior Begin?

As loss prevention professionals ponder the reasons for dishonesty, understanding human behavior will help put everything into perspective. Significant research has been completed on why people commit crimes in general, but an insignificant portion is geared toward theft specifically. It is obvious that individuals who cause external or internal theft do not just wake up one day and decide this is the way to go. Research on adolescent behavior shows that early life influences will impact decision-making ability throughout adulthood.

Adolescence is a time of physical and emotional growth. The adolescent life stage is a period of increased risk for the onset of several problems, including delinquency. Being able to identify the early warning signs of deviance and early intervention can play a key role in adolescents' future development. Parental involvement and discipline consistency will determine how adolescents perceive the act of deviance, the level of awareness toward consequences, and effects on their conscience concluding an event. Peer and sibling pressures will leave an emotional wake concluding a conversation or request for engagement in acts that would otherwise not be thought of. Environmental situations and socioeconomic issues

are contributing factors when adolescents are contemplating making the right or wrong decision. Knowing right from wrong or moral development begins early in life. When children need nurturing or feeding and their parents fulfill that need without excessive indulgence, they develop character that accepts rules and tolerates frustration later in life.

We now turn to a discussion of different theories associated with crime and deviance. Understanding the theories will allow the readers to tie the concepts into retail loss prevention.

SELF-CONTROL THEORY

Gottfredson and Hirschi's self-control theory assumes that individuals are rational in their decision to commit a crime. Individuals will weigh the costs against the rewards in any decision to commit a crime. Therefore, individuals pursue crime because it promises rewards with little threat of pain. This particular portion of the self-control theory ties in well with what retailers face on a daily basis when it comes to employee theft. Because employees go through an interview process, the ability to determine whether they are rational or not happens before the hiring process. If they are hired, it is assumed that they are not only rational but also competent enough to satisfy the requirements of the job. However, being rational is not the only factor that goes into individuals' decision to engage in behavior that will negatively impact an organization. If we take the second part, which is weighing the costs against the rewards, it is easier to understand how the decision is made. Costs and rewards make up one of the most important perspectives in retail loss prevention and can be combated easier than others. The theft triangle involves opportunity and how eliminating opportunity can reduce the amount of theft that takes place. Costs and rewards focus on one's perception of getting away with something and how much it is worth. If employees realize that there is little chance of getting caught when committing the act of dishonesty, their willingness to take the risk increases. Please see Figure 3.1 showing how infrequently retail crimes, especially shoplifting, employee theft, and employee fraud, are reported to the police.

Gottfredson and Hirschi equated individuals' desire to commit crime against their level of self-control. Gottfredson and Hirschi argued that individuals with low self-control are unable to restrain themselves from the temptations of immediate satisfaction and that low self-control develops early in life. According to Higgins and Rickets's recap of the

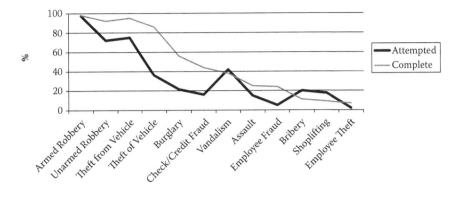

Figure 3.1 Percentage of attempted and completed crimes reported to police. (Source: AIC Small Business Crime Survey, 1999.)

self-control theory, low self-control could be the result of ineffective or inadequate socialization. Ineffective socialization includes weak or poor attachment, supervision, and discipline from parents before the age of 8. After that age, individuals' level of self-control will remain stable into and throughout adulthood.

Empirical literature supporting the self-control theory includes a meta-analysis by Pratt and Cullen, who provided 20 studies showing that self-control is at least a moderate predictor of crime and deviance. Other studies also show support for the hypothesis that parental management is an antecedent to self-control. Higgins and Ricketts, in their evaluation of the self-control theory, found that self-control has a direct effect on the intent to commit academic dishonesty. Their study also indicated that self-control does not have an indirect effect on intent to commit academic dishonesty through opportunity, but it does through freedom.

DIFFERENTIAL ASSOCIATION THEORY

Edwin H. Sutherland developed the term *differential association*. According to Giddens, Duneier, and Appelbaum, differential association states that some cultures encourage illegal behavior whereas others encourage legal behavior. I interpret this to mean that in some parts of the world it is acceptable to break the rules, but in other parts it's not a condoned practice. If we

relate this concept to retail, it is the culture within a store, region, brand, that will determine which behavior is acceptable...one that is good for the organization or one that is adverse to the organization. Individuals on both sides of the fence (illegal–legal) view their behavior as the norm. Therefore, in a culture that accepts illegal behavior, it would be considered the same as law-abiding citizens' behavior. These cultures would just consider the approach to be different. This is true in a retail store environment as well. The culture created within the store will dictate the behavior of employees. If the manager accepts or participates in deviant behavior, others are likely to follow. The manager's behavior dictates to employees that it is okay to bend or break the rules and that there are not consequences. Even if the employees had no intention of bending or breaking the rules, watching a superior do it and get away with it opens the door. On the other hand, if a manager clarifies his or her level of tolerance (what is and what is not accepted), then the employees are being told that bad behavior will not be condoned. Consequences must accompany both good and bad behavior. Those who consistently follow the rules should be rewarded, and those who do not need a reprimand; otherwise, as the book *Absolute Honesty* warns, "When the culture authorizes aberrant behavior, aberrant behavior becomes the norm and a culture of honesty ceases to exist." If the behavior is accepted, it will be repeated.

Erickson et al. evaluated Sutherland's differential association theory and Hirschi's social control theory. The study found that deviant friendships and susceptibility linked social bonds to substance use and delinquency. Bonds were more consistently related to friends' substance use than to friends' delinquency, and deviance of males was more strongly affected by the actions of friends than was deviance of females. Although there is not extensive research on the topic of male versus female dishonesty in the workplace, some evidence supports that males are a bigger contributor to dishonesty than are females.

MERTON'S STRAIN THEORY

According to Agnew, Merton's strain theory assumes aspirations of fairly uniform economic success across social classes and attempts to explain why crime is concentrated among the lower classes, which have the least legitimate opportunity for achievement. Merton states that the theory is the combination of cultural emphasis and the social structure, which produces intense pressure for deviation. Members of lower classes are the

most vulnerable to this pressure, or strain, and will maintain their unful-filled economic aspirations in spite of frustration or failure. Merton's the-ory can be tied into shoplifting from retail stores. A significant percentage of individuals caught shoplifting are from lower classes. These individu-als have found a means of supporting themselves or their habits through illegal actions. Individuals stealing for personal reasons often have not learned how to make it through life legitimately. Shoplifting is an easy way to get what they need with little consequence.

COHEN'S STRAIN THEORY

According to Agnew, Cohen argues that working class boys are not equipped, because of socialization, to compete with middle-class boys in societal states. Because of this strain or inability to compete with classes above their own, the attitudes develop into exaggerated hostility towards societal and middle-class values.

AGNEW'S STRAIN THEORY

Agnew wrote that strain is neither structural nor interpersonal but is instead emotional, involving a breakdown of beliefs in the role others play for expectations about normally occurring events. Perceptions of an adverse environment will lead to strongly negative emotions that motivate people to engage in crime. Agnew stated that crime is sporadic and that people would "desist" if not for persistent negative events and effects. He identified three types of deviance-producing strain:

- Failure to achieve positively valued goals, which is the gap between expectations and actual achievements and the difference between the view of what a person believes the outcome should be and what actually results.
- Removal of positively valued stimuli, which occurs primarily during adolescence when a dramatic change or loss happens.
- Confrontation with negative stimuli, which is applied most to adolescents. Usually the individual is forced to remain among negative actions that through an anger-induced response create deviant behavior.

MORAL DEVELOPMENT

Loss prevention professionals often wonder where employees' morals have gone when being interviewed for dishonesty. Often, dishonest people who want others to believe they are honest and not guilty will bring up their childhood. Comments such as, "I was raised better than that," are not uncommon when dishonest employees are probed about the event that got them into trouble. They feel that if someone believes their moral development was adequate, they are more likely to believe they did not commit the act of dishonesty. These comments are deflectors of the situation and should be recognized as such.

Kohlberg presented adolescents with stories of moral dilemma and was able to identify three levels of moral development:

1. Preconventional level (up to age 9):
 a. Moral law is developed by children seeing rules set, mostly by parents.
 b. Satisfaction of children's needs is seen as good and moral.
2. Conventional level (age 9 to adolescence):
 a. An understanding of expectations as laid out by role models such as parents and teachers is beginning. Morality is seen as achieving these expectations.
 b. A fulfillment of obligations and following expectations are seen as moral law for children.
3. Postconventional level (adulthood):
 a. Adults learn that there are varying opinions about morality and that people or groups evaluate it differently. Morality is seen as upholding the values of your group or culture.
 b. Those who understand their own beliefs allow others and themselves to judge and be judged upon higher levels of morality. Right and wrong are based on the circumstances surrounding an action.

PARENTING AND CULTURAL INFLUENCES

According to Santrock, parents are neglectful when they are very uninvolved in their adolescents' life. It is believed that neglectful parenting is associated with adolescents' socially incompetent behavior, especially lack of self-control, and they do not handle independence well. Adolescents

who have experienced neglectful parenting develop the sense that other aspects of their parents' lives are more important than they are.

In Baer, a study conducted on family cohesion found that cohesion is important to family functioning and that levels of cohesion have been implicated in both positive and negative outcomes. It was predicted that cohesion would be negatively correlated with deviance; results indicated that deviance was predicted by the changing trends in family. Cohesion may not be static, and levels may shift across the family life cycle.

Lerner, Noh, and Wilson examined one study indicating that among 14- to 19-year-old African American youth social support from kin was related to self-reliance and good grades; however, when kinship support was low the youths experienced feelings of distress. Students with intact families were least likely to drop out of school and were less likely to experiment with drugs. In another study of more than 1,800 Latino, African American, and European American parents of adolescents, conflicts were said to occur mainly over everyday matters like chores and styles of dress rather than related to substantive issues like sex and drugs. Depression in both European American and Asian American adolescents is correlated with family relations marked by low warmth and acceptance and high levels of conflict with mothers and fathers. Anger, hostility, coercion, and conflict shown by both parents and siblings have a detrimental effect on the adolescent adjustment.

The International Study of Adolescent Development (ISAD) found evidence suggesting that differences in family processes (parental monitoring, the affective mother–child and father–child relationships) and levels of self-control largely accounted for the differences in self-reported delinquency between males in Switzerland and the United States. The select variables explained more than 70% of the total variability in self-reported delinquency between the two nations. The results indicate that finding such differences in individual socialization and differences in contextual experiences may inform the understanding of the etiology of various developmental outcomes and processes in adolescents and may provide information for intervention and prevention efforts.

Organizations are full of people who grew up in environments where good morals were taught and in environments where no morals were taught. Even those who grew up in morally stable environments—where right and wrong were clearly different—can make decisions as adults that can adversely impact their place of work.

To further understand why adolescents make bad decisions and to provide useful information for retail loss prevention, research was

conducted at a juvenile detention center. The purpose of the research was to determine what has the greatest influence on the decision-making process of adolescents and how the decisions affect their mental health. The study focused on adolescents who committed acts of thefts.

Method

Procedure and Sample
A total of 12 adolescents were interviewed in person and were also observed in their natural setting. All participants were males ranging in age from 10 to 18 years of age. Of the total population interviewed, 33% were white, and 66% were African American. Of those interviewed, 10 of 12 were incarcerated at a juvenile detention center. Of the participant population at the detention center, 80% were African American, and 20% were white. The other two males were perceived to be law-abiding citizens. The counselor assigned to the facility selected the sample from the detention center. Only males who had been convicted of theft-related crimes were able to participate in the research. Prior to the interviews, all participants agreed to join in the discussion. A list of 20 questions was given to each participant (Table 3.1). The participants at the detention center were asked one extra question: to discuss the crimes they had committed. The questions pertained to relationships (with family, peers, and teachers), self-perception, honesty, and future plans. The answers to the questions and notes were documented and were included as an appendix to the paper provided to the detention center at the end of the study.

Results
The research shows that there is a great deal of support for Agnew's strain theory, specifically confrontation with negative stimuli response. The 10 incarcerated males indicated that they grew up in negative surroundings. They explained observing significant violence, theft, and drug activity. A total of 9 out of the 10 incarcerated males were raised in the inner city. The one raised in the suburbs had negative influences in the household. The two males who were not incarcerated did not mention any observations of negative stimuli. All 12 boys did not live with their biological mother and father. Three lived with their father, four lived with their mother and a stepfather, and the rest lived with other family members or a girlfriend. Several did not know who their father was, and several others had fathers presently or previously in prison. All 10 incarcerated boys mentioned being involved with drugs—mostly selling. All were repeat

Table 3.1 Interview Questions

What is the difference between the truth and a lie?

How did you learn the difference?

What happens when you tell your parents a lie? What about when you tell the truth?

If you did something wrong and you are not sure if your parents will find out, what would you do?

What are some of the decisions you are allowed to make by yourself?

What happens when you do something good and your parents know about it?

What happens when you do something bad and your parents know about it?

If you have something special going on at school or outside of school, who comes to see you?

If you are having trouble with your homework, who do you ask for help and how do they react?

How do you feel about your parents?

If you could change one thing about your life, what would it be?

If you told your parents you would be home at a certain time and you did not make it home at that time, what would happen?

How often do you talk to your parents about friends and school?

What are some of the things you think your parents do not know about you?

If you feel your parents did not treat you fairly or you are angry with a decision they made, what do you do?

What do you think is your biggest accomplishment?

What do you think is your biggest failure?

How do you get along with friends, teachers, and parents?

What do you want to be when you grow up? How do your parents feel about that?

If you could change one think about yourself, what would it be?

offenders. Only one mentioned using drugs. Among the 10 boys, their first theft offense occurred between the ages of 7 and 17. The items they first stole ranged from candy to cars. Of those incarcerated, 3 of 10 first stole a bike from the neighborhood. Only 1 of 10 first stole a car. A total of 8 of 10 admitted to being shown by a peer or family member how to steal. This provides support for the differential association theory. Only 1 male showed remorse for what he had done to others, and 1 of 10 admitted to receiving significant punishment due to their acts of deviance. The other 9 had little or no consequences for bad behavior. The lack of consequences

or accountability was one of the significant contributors to deviance. This also provides much support for the self-control theory. Several males mentioned that if the consequences had been worse they could foresee choosing a different outcome. Only the two boys not incarcerated seemed to have the ability or desire to discuss their parental relationship.

The research showed correlation between environmental factors, cultural factors, and family and peer relationships and adolescents' decision-making process. One question posed to the interviewees returned surprising results. All interviewees were asked whether they would tell their parents about something bad they had done even if they knew their parents would not find out. Both males who were not incarcerated would not tell the parents, and 2 of 10 incarcerated males would tell their parents. The reason this was surprising is that the boys who were not incarcerated did not declare any fear of their parents. It could be argued that the thought process of boys in that age group, regardless if they've been in trouble or not, will withhold information if the risk of getting called out on it is low. This question goes back to consequences and accountability. Those who were not incarcerated had a greater consequence for being caught doing something wrong than those who were incarcerated. The two incarcerated males would be willing to tell their parents because there would be no repercussions. The incarcerated males have less than desirable living conditions when they are free; most live in areas where children are exposed to violence on a daily basis. Often, people who grow up in this environment believe that they do not have a choice in committing crimes because of the conditions around them. They exhibit very little self-control and easily give in to temptation.

The 10 incarcerated boys interviewed for the study wondered how they were going to be able to change their lives once they returned home because they were going back to the same environment that created the problems to begin with. They were alarmingly affected by their peers' perception of them. If their peers teased them or dared them to commit a crime, they went along so they were not singled out. Their parents, through neglectful parenting, gave too much freedom, which contributed to their current predicament. For these incarcerated boys to have any chance at a normal adult life, something in their home environment would have to change. Their lack of remorse for the crimes they committed is an indicator that they were likely to be repeat offenders.

The incarcerated young males were angry. Some declared that they were even angrier when they were younger but that as they grew older they learned to accept what their lives were. Bottling up emotions and not

having an outlet to discuss problems festered within; as they continued to see more violence and crime, it continued to build. They saw crime and deviance as an escape.

Further research is needed on this topic. One question to explore is what role gender plays in the decision-making process when adolescents are contemplating acts of deviance. Cross-sectional research can be conducted to further explore the topic of deviance and adolescents. The advantage of cross sectional research is that it is relatively inexpensive and demands less time.

Adolescents are society's future. Eventually the incarcerated males will have served their time and will be released into society. If they are not provided with a way to stop the vicious circle of deviance and criminal behavior, they will continue to be a hazard to those around them. Some will eventually obtain employment and will be predisposed to theft and deviance, causing a financial impact on organizations. Early intervention is the key but cannot be considered without caregivers' proper involvement. The justice system is not the answer to fixing these problems; it is simply a temporary solution to a foreseeable problem. Using shaming as an alternative to incarceration is a very effective tool in Japan. The crime rate of both adolescents and adults is significantly lower in Japan than in the United States because in Japan when a crime is committed it brings shame and embarrassment to the offender's family and friends. Parental involvement and intervention as well as community involvement are the keys to resolving crime-related problems in the United States.

Ideally, anyone applying for a job would also provide a truthful account of the first 18 years of life. However, we know this is an unrealistic expectation. Tools such as preemployment screening can weed out potentially bad employees, although some who pass the preemployment screening eventually end up stealing from the organization. There is no guarantee that anyone will or will not steal from the workplace.

CONTRIBUTING FACTORS OF DEVIANCE IN THE WORKPLACE

Adverse employee behavior impacts the employee, organization, and coworkers. As organizations try to keep profits high and losses low, they must first uncover the root cause of why employees choose to engage in acts that do not have the company's best interest in mind. Some employees'

willingness to jeopardize their personal integrity should not be taken lightly. They must have the motivation to commit the act and be able to rationalize their behavior before they ever make the first step toward counterproductive behavior.

It is more important than ever for corporations to ensure they are keeping honest employees honest. Organizations have an obligation to treat employees properly; in turn, employees will have an increased loyalty to the organization. Each year corporations invest millions of dollars in recruiting, hiring, and training quality employees. Businesses pride themselves on achieving high profits and maintaining a highly motivated workforce. What they sometimes overlook is that when things such as employee dissatisfaction, personality traits, negative attitudes, and changing perceptions heavily impact work places, counterproductive and sometimes even deviant employee behavior may follow.

The following sections address the different factors that affect employee behavior and the key role they play in employees' decision-making processes. The objective of this review is to inform the business community about how counterproductive behavior originates in the mind of the employee and how organizational behaviors contribute to the entire spectrum of employees who choose either to remain positive or to become negative, thus adversely impacting the organization.

Expectations

According to the 2008 National Retail Security Survey, employee theft accounts for nearly 43% of all retail losses in the United States. The financial loss caused by a dishonest employee is an average of $1,023 (Figure 3.2). An employee typically works for his or her employer an average of nine months.

Social scientists have concluded that a variety of factors contribute to theft occurrence; logically, three must be present, making up what is called the theft triangle (refer to Figure 1.1 in Chapter 1):

1. Motivation
2. Opportunity
3. Low deterrent

The transition for employees from honest to dishonest takes much rationalization. They must feel like what they are doing is justified in some way. The motivation that leads to dishonesty can begin either in the workplace or at home.

Figure 3.2 Causes of inventory shrinkage according to the 2008 National Security Survey.

According to Hollinger, most incidents of employee pilferage are unrelated to employees' particular financial situation. In addition, average employee thieves are not embezzlers of large amounts of cash; rather, they steal small amounts of company merchandise or cash on a regular basis.

Job dissatisfaction plays an important role in employees' minds when they are contemplating theft. If they feel as though they have been treated unfairly or that the company owes them something, the decision to steal is made much more easily. They rationalize that they are getting back at the employer for unresolved feelings of perceived inequity in the way they have been treated.

Paul, Niehoff, and Turnley conducted a literature review involving employees' and employers' evaluation of empowerment. The authors suggested that empowering employees results in employers' creating beliefs about entitlements that will go unfulfilled eventually. The unfulfilled beliefs about entitlement may constitute a breach of the psychological contract between employer and employee, which may result in employee behavior that is counterproductive in terms of organizational goals.

Average employees want to do a good job but also expect things in return for their good job. If employees are presented with more and more duties, they believe that something good is going to happen in their near future and may perceive this even though a conversation has not taken place about how they might be rewarded. If what they expect and believe they are entitled to does not arrive, negative emotions will begin to build. If the manager does not recognize a problem with the employee, it can lead to counterproductive behavior based on false perceptions.

Dissatisfaction

Hollinger and Clark examined the job satisfaction hypothesis with a larger data set and discovered a more consistent pattern of support. As covered in an earlier chapter, employees' very first meeting with their employer builds a psychological contract—an agreement between them and their employer. The employer could have implied something but not actually meant what he or she said. In this meeting, however, employees take what their employer implied or said and put it as part of this contract. Once there is a breech in the contract, employees feel as though they have been lied to or misled. As a result of this breech, they become dissatisfied.

Researchers concluded that the most common reason employees committed fraud had little to do with opportunity but more with motivation: the more dissatisfied the employee, the more likely he or she is to engage in criminal behavior. Employees and executives who feel unfairly treated sometimes believe they can right the scales by committing occupational fraud and abuse. Getting even with the company for unfair treatment is more common than many would like to believe. When people hear about highly paid executives who steal from their company, they wonder why. Most turn their thoughts to greed but do not consider that these executives may have been trying to even the score. Organizations do not have to get inside the mind of every employee; rather, they should observe employees' behavior and intervene when necessary.

Attitudes

Bolin and Heatherly evaluated four different employee attitudes—theft approval, company contempt, intent to quit, and dissatisfaction—in predicting deviant employee behavior. One purpose of this study was to assess the utility of classifying deviant workplace behavior based on the offense. The samples used were entry-level employees, and the method was the Employee Perceptions Survey. Overall, the results indicated that theft approval is the most important predictor of workplace deviance across the current criteria and group. (Please see Figure 3.3.)

Gauging employees' attitudes to determine if they will become dishonest is not an easy task. Research in this area can help business owners reduce the losses because they can know what to look for. Employers aware of what to look for in employees' attitudes can begin the intervention process. This can be a conversation with employees regarding their attitude or asking general questions to test their loyalty to the company.

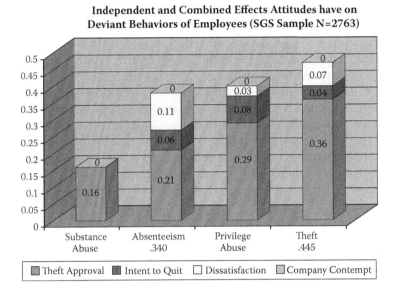

Figure 3.3 Bolin & Heatherly evaluation of four different employee attitudes.

If their attitude is based on what they have witnessed by others or what they have found to be acceptable, a redirection by their supervisor may put them back on the right track.

Personality and Perceptions

Colbert focused on the joint relationship between personality and perception of the work situation and deviant behavior. Seven hypotheses were developed to evaluate the relationship between employee perception and personality to the withholding effort and interpersonal deviance. The model used in the study indicated that a negative perception of the workplace may lead employees to deviant behavior, but this may be suppressed or facilitated depending on personality traits.

Stamper and Masterson theoretically and empirically explored the concept of perceived inside status (PIS), or the perception employees have about the relationship between them and the company. Balu's social exchange framework best represents perceived organizational support. There was evidence to support that perceived organizational support influenced PIS. There is no support for actual inclusion in the

organization leading to PIS. The findings indicated that PIS is positively and significantly related to a positive discretionary behavior (altruism) and negatively and significantly related to production of deviance. Actual and perceived inclusion in the organization matter. Production deviance was not as prevalent as altruism.

One instant motivation crusher is when employees think another employee is getting preferential treatment. This could be projected in a variety of ways, such as better work hours or days, more money, or job scope. If employees believe that their supervisor likes people in the work group more than they are liked, problems can occur. Employees want to believe that everyone is treated equal, and if a manager proves otherwise, employees can lose their interest in working for their manager.

Personal Integrity

Mikulay, Neuman, and Finkelstein examined the relationship among personal integrity, situational factors, and counterproductive workplace behaviors. Three broad predictions were offered:

1. Is it possible that integrity does not interact with desirability, group norms, or risk?
2. Is it possible that individuals low in integrity react to situational factors by adjusting their likelihood of committing counterproductive behavior?
3. Is it possible that individuals high in integrity respond to the situation and individuals low in integrity do not?

As the level of integrity decreased, the likelihood of counterproductive behavior increased. Low-integrity individuals indicated a higher likelihood of absence, tardiness, committing theft, and vandalism. The likelihood of theft by high-integrity employees did not increase as risk of exposure decreased, whereas the opposite occurred for low-integrity individuals. The only significant interaction was integrity and the risk of theft.

Many preemployment tests screen for integrity, which many individuals caught engaging in counterproductive behavior took and passed. This can mean one of two things: either the test is not valid, or something caused the employee to go from having personal integrity to not having any. Because employers use a variety of tests, the chances are slim that every test is invalid or unreliable, so the latter scenario is more likely.

Personal integrity is something everyone should be proud to have. When Thorsborne asked people to describe integrity, they answered in a variety of ways, including the following:

- Strength of character
- Walking the talk, doing what was promised
- Open, honest, and direct dealing with others
- Authentic, straightforward, what's on the inside is displayed on the outside

According to Thorsborne, trust is an incredibly precious commodity and is always the first casualty when relationships in the workplace are damaged. Integrity is something people own and can be taken away only if it is given. So why do so many people in the workplace give it away—make a conscious choice to simply throw away their self-worth for a few dollars? That is the issue almost all corporations deal with at some level.

One could argue that the "me" generation has made a priority of self-interest. The pursuit of profit at all costs has seduced people away from responsibilities to relationships with others. Self-interest is certainly an issue in the workplace, but is it a contributing factor for counterproductive behavior? Employees who are concerned with getting promoted, doing a good job, and being productive enough to move ahead are less likely to engage in behavior that would lead to termination. They do not want to jeopardize in any way their employment with the company because they wish to remain employed. Employees with no self-interest or without a vested interest in the company should be of utmost concern to the organizations in which they work.

Summary

All of the studies in the preceding sections indicate that even if employees start off with integrity, something may happen to change them during their time with a company. This change may be a result of their dissatisfaction, expectations, perceptions, or personality. Once employees have made a conscious decision to move from honesty to dishonesty, there is no turning back for them. Corporations should have as a goal to make sure their employees never make this transition for any reason. It could be stated that people with a good attitude and positive perception of the organization are less likely to engage in counterproductive behavior. Managers must make efforts to ensure they understand where their subordinates stand. Open lines of communication between employee and

employer are essential for productive workforces. If employees fear retribution for discussing matters, animosity will build.

Managers cannot engage in deceptive methods to lure potential applicants to the job just to hire a warm body. They must understand that once applicants are hired under false pretenses, the organization will pay through revenge from that employee. Most employees do not intend to be dishonest on their own without any contributing factors. To fully understand and attempt to eliminate counterproductive behavior, we must first understand how the thought process behind the behavior is developed.

MORE DETERRENTS OR BETTER LEADERSHIP?

The first part of this chapter focused on adolescent behavior and factors that contribute to workplace dishonesty. As discussed, there is evidence to support that children who grow up in morally challenged households are more likely to engage in theft-related offense. In addition, research has shown that happy employees are less likely to steal. Does this mean that employees who were raised right and seem to be happy will definitely not steal? The answer is no. As mentioned in this chapter, the theft triangle focuses on motivation, low deterrents, and opportunity. The motivation part of the triangle was discussed in the first part of this chapter. Low deterrents and opportunity will now be discussed and evaluated against motivation.

Crime Prevention through Environmental Design

Crime prevention through environmental design (CPTED) is a concept that has not been explored in great detail related to retail loss prevention but that should be. This chapter focuses on internal issues, or employees, not external issues such as shoplifters. The concept of CPTED was originally formulated by criminologist C. Ray Jeffery. The goal of CPTED is to create an environment that is risky for crime. Four elements surround CPTED.

Natural Surveillance
With natural surveillance there is an increased perception of being seen or apprehended. The environmental design is conducive for rule followers but impedes rule breakers' ability to get away. Store design is an extremely important consideration for employees contemplating whether

to be dishonest. Blind spots without camera systems are frequently used by employees who want to get away with something. Register placement is also important. If the register is in an open area where the public and other employees are consistently walking by, it makes it more difficult to take money.

Natural Access Control

Natural access control limits the opportunity for crime by taking steps to clearly differentiate between public space and private space. This can include the placement of entrances and exits, fencing, lighting, and land-scape. Many retailers already employ several different methods of access control such as one employee entry and exit. Making it mandatory to enter and exit through the same door makes it difficult for employees to walk out of the door with concealed product because their fear of being caught is higher: they will not know who will be standing at the door and poten-tially conducting package checks. Dumpsters or garbage areas are often used for the concealment of stolen merchandise that will be picked up at a later time. Limiting the number of employees who can take out garbage and placing the dumpster in a well-lit area will help decrease merchan-dise leaving through this method.

Natural Territorial Reinforcement

Territorial reinforcement encourages individuals to have a vested interest in their surroundings, which motivates them to keep out individuals who do not belong or who will negatively impact their environment. It boils down to a sense of ownership of the area. Employees who feel like their place of employment is also part of who they are will be more likely to want to remove anything that negatively affects their daily lives. They will not tolerate others who blatantly jeopardize their livelihood by engaging in behavior that will adversely impact their organization. This is a form of employee self-policing one another that drastically reduces the amount of losses that can occur because dishonesty is clearly unacceptable to others.

Maintenance

The broken windows theory, developed by criminologists James Q. Wilson and George Kelling, is a valuable tool in understanding the impor-tance of maintenance in deterring crime. Wilson and Kelling believed that evidence of neighborhood deterioration, such as broken windows, could bring about social disorder because there is a perception that no one cares. Maintaining a store environment is crucial in motivating or demotivating

employees. Employees who walk into a clean, organized store daily are more likely to be productive than those who walk into a store that is dirty and disorganized. You can often tell the quality of a manager by going into the restroom of the store. If the manager allows the restroom to be dirty and does not have a program in place to ensure cleanliness, it is safe to conclude that the other controls are probably not in place either. Outside of employees' expectations regarding how they should be treated, they also want to have adequate physical working conditions. For instance, different smells can help spark different behaviors, and realtors frequently tell home sellers to bake cookies right before an open house because this will be more inviting and encouraging to potential buyers. Something as simple as cookies can be the difference between selling a house or not. Employees who enter a store that is well maintained, smells nice, and looks nice will have a sense of pride in their workplace. On the flip side, employees who walk into a store that is not maintained, stinks, and is messy will wonder why they should care if the organization and management do not seem to care. If employees have reported to upper management that the store is in need of maintenance, the belief that no one is going to do anything about it especially increases.

Employing the techniques discussed in CPTED will help foster a climate that is conducive to employee productivity and will decrease occurrences of dishonesty.

Other Deterrents

In today's world, advances in technology provide for myriad devices that will detect and deter employee dishonesty. A very useful software program used by retailers is exception reporting. The great thing about exception reporting is that employees do not know when it is in use, therefore making it unobtrusive. This allows employee point-of-sale (POS) activity to be monitored for fraud but does not affect honest employees. Exception reporting captures transactions for which desired queries are created. It allows stipulations and criteria to be built within the queries. The queries make it much easier to isolate the problem and illuminate the suspected fraudulent situation. For example, an investigator runs a report for a region and notices that the percent to sales for returns is high. This is good preliminary information, but the scope is not narrow enough. The next query selected should be individual store refund percentages. This allows the investigator to narrow down the stores that are contributing most to the percentage. Once the stores are narrowed down, individual

employee transactions should be reviewed. The query will identify the particular employees who have the most (most can mean quantity or value) refunds. The report should be able to identify the employee, date of refund, dollar amount, and possibly what specific SKU was returned. Many exception reports will also identify the original transaction if there was one. The reporting will make it easier to identify potential fraud, but it is not conclusive. The next step in the process is to retrieve the actual paperwork involved with the transaction to confirm what the reports are indicating.

Discussing the topic of exception reporting and providing copies of the reporting to managers and employees during store visits are excellent deterrents. After a conversation regarding exception reporting, employees will understand that everything they enter into the POS system is always being monitored. To further the deterrent potential of exception reporting, add a function in the POS system that clearly flags high-risk transactions. A suggestion is to have a pop-up screen follow a high-risk transaction on the POS system. An example would be a refund transaction in excess of $100. As soon as the transaction is entered, the pop-up can say something like, "This transaction is being monitored by exception reporting." If the employee did not know about the capabilities, the visual pop-up would make them think twice about pocketing the money.

Another effective tool is closed-circuit television (CCTV). In years past, loss prevention relied on employees to change videotapes. Today, new technology has allowed for camera systems to be continuously backed up to an internal hard drive within the unit. Aside from physically destroying the unit, this type of system is difficult to defeat. Even tampering with the buttons on the recording unit usually does not affect the camera footage being backed up. Camera placement is important and should be evaluated by someone in loss prevention before installation occurs. Cameras over sensitive areas such as registers, safes, hallways, high-dollar products, and exits are good places to start the installation. Loss prevention monitoring of employees' activity within a store is much easier today than it has ever been. Technology allows for remote computers to watch live footage as it is occurring. To make it even easier, many CCTV companies provide a Web site that loss prevention team members can log onto to watch a specific store. If employees know their behavior is being monitored, they are less likely to chance stealing because the risk of getting caught is great.

Again, technology has made the inconspicuous monitoring of different systems easy. Internet auction sites provide a venue for both internal and external thieves to dispose of stolen product. Software is available to track

particular product on the auction sites. If the software picks up on large quantities of a particular product being sold by someone, it can flag the seller. The average person would have no way of knowing who the seller is without purchasing something and the seller providing an address for payment. But today, auction sites such as e-Bay can be solicited for a personal information request (PIR), which will provide the seller's registered name along with an address. This is effective if a store has high shrinkage and no suspects. Once the PIR information is received, it can be cross-referenced against an employee roster. If the seller is also an employee, you may have just figured out where your product has been going.

Telling managers and employees about this software and monitoring process is a deterrent for anyone who was going to put stolen product for sale on an auction site. One noteworthy case occurred in Chicago, Illinois. A manager for a specialty retailer was apprehended after stealing in excess of $200,000 in product from three different locations. The process took place with the software flagging the product, and a PIR identified the manager. During the investigative process, it was discovered that the product was being removed from the store in a soft-sided lunch box. However, the most interesting thing about this case is that the manager got away with it for 3 years before it was discovered.

A method that is not used much by retail loss prevention but can be very effective is scientific content analysis. When loss prevention people first hear about this, they often think it has something to do with handwriting analysis. In fact, there is no analysis involved; it is necessary only for employees to write their statement on paper and not type it so errors (or slips) can be easily seen. Content analysis evaluates such things as sentence structure, pronouns, verbs, nouns, and length of paragraphs. It is a very effective method when there are losses, but anyone in the store could be responsible. The analysis can usually weed out people who definitely did not do a crime and others who are suspect. Following is a statement written by an employee who later admitted to stealing a bank deposit. Following the statement, information is provided on where the deception occurred and how the investigator knew this person was guilty before any conversation took place. The name of the individual and some facts have been changed to preserve privacy.

To Whom It May Concern:
This is regarding the deposit I, Jane Doe, was to make on July 20. I understand that the deposit bag was unsealed, short $145.01 and was a day late. I was told to write a statement recounting the events of that day.

I remember that day only because it had rained a great deal and on my way to work my windshield wipers stopped working. I stopped and changed the fuse, but the wiper blades fell/broke off rendering them useless and instead of looking for a place that sold them I decided to drive without them. I arrived at work frustrated and angry at the circumstances. I worked and finished the day as usual but I was in a hurry, anxious to get home as soon as possible in case it rained again that night. I was closing starting with the deposit first. I left it unsealed in case I had another customer that night. When it came time to leave I threw the deposit in my bag and left. On my way to my car I tripped in/on a hole along the path leading to the parking lot outside the mall. I dropped everything I was carrying. I didn't notice anything amiss. I got into my truck and went home. I didn't realize I failed to make the deposit until I was at the end of my driveway and instead making a 48-mile round-trip drive back to the store, I decided I would drop it off the following day. I honestly cannot recall any events that may have lead to the loss of the money. But seeing as how my name is on that bag I accept full responsibility.

On July 29, Jane Doe was phone interviewed. Jane admitted to stealing the $145.01 out of the deposit. Jane said that she needed to repay the remainder of a debt she had from two years ago. Jane was asked why she thought she could steal the money. She replied that due to the change in management the validated slips were not being picked up from the bank daily. Because the slips were not picked up daily, she said she figured she could get the money back into the bank before anyone noticed.

The content analysis made the interviewer very confident that Jane was lying about the missing money before an interview took place. This confidence allowed for a quick and easy admission and repayment of the loss. Looking at the statement, the interviewer noticed several red flags immediately. People who write statements such as Jane's do not notice that they are inserting these flags because they are all subconscious attempts to deceive the reader. The first flag was the length of the paragraph discussing the rain. This is an attempt to stay away from the actual topic (missing money) and to focus on something that has no relevance to the issue at hand. The rain becomes the focal point of Jane's entire statement, which in her mind makes it easier to deflect the actual events. People trying to deceive also use the word *left*. If you notice, Jane uses the word *left* twice before she allegedly trips and drops everything. Jane wants the reader to think that her tripping may have accidentally led to the loss of the money, but the word *left* is inserted twice because she knows what she is going to write next is a lie. The most crucial piece of evidence leading to confirmed suspicions that Jane is dishonest is how the bank deposit is referenced throughout the statement. She calls it "the deposit" throughout most of the statement but eventually changes "the deposit" to other terms. After

she has decided to steal the money, the statement ends with, "I decided I would drop *it* off the following day. I honestly cannot recall any events that may have lead to the loss of *the money*. But seeing as how my name is on *that bag* I accept full responsibility." The deposit becomes "it," "the money," and "that bag," all within three sentences. The "it" allows Jane to disassociate herself with the events so she is able to rationalize her own behavior. It becomes "the money" and no longer a deposit because Jane has ownership of the stolen funds and intends to use it. She finishes it off with "that bag" because she knows she is guilty of not only breaking company policy but also violating the law and wants to remove the situation away from herself. Finally, Jane never states that she did not steal the deposit. She dances around the topic by using different verbiage but never comes out and says, "I did not steal the deposit." She uses the words "cannot recall any events" at the end of the statement to softly tell the reader that she is not saying she did not do it but rather that she cannot remember doing it. The final statement where she accepts responsibility for the loss of "that bag" is a ploy to take responsibility of the lesser offense, which is just for missing money, not stolen money. It is much easier to say that you are responsible for a loss that occurred simply because it was in your possession than to admit to stealing it all together. If employees are aware that loss prevention people have the ability to analyze statements, they will be afraid to write the statement entirely if they are guilty of something. Therefore, when employees are asked to write statements recounting the events of a day and refuse to do so, this may be an indicator of guilt. Most employees are very willing to write a statement if it will clear their name quickly and will help find the person who violated the rules.

One method most retailers stay far away from due to liability issues is polygraph testing. Many retailers are also under the misconception that they cannot ask employees to take a polygraph examination because of the Employee Polygraph Protection Act (EPPA) established December 27, 1988. This federal law established guidelines for polygraph testing and imposed restrictions on most private employers but did not take away all the rights for employers to ask employees to take the examination if certain criteria are met.

The American Polygraph Association suggests that the following elements be met before an employer can ask an employee to take an examination:

1. The incident must be an ongoing, specific investigation.
2. It must be an identifiable economic loss to the employer.

3. Obtain a copy of the Employer Polygraph Protection Act of 1988.
4. Provide the employee with a written statement that includes:
 a. Identification of the company and location of employee
 b. Description of the loss or activity under investigation
 c. Location of the loss
 d. Specific amount of the loss
 e. Type of economic loss
 f. How the employee had access to the loss (Note: Access alone is not sufficient grounds for polygraph testing)
 g. What kind of reasonable suspicion there is to suspect the employee of being involved in the loss
5. The statement provided to employee must be signed by someone other than the polygraph examiner, who is authorized to legally bind the employee, and must be retained by the employer for at least 3 years.
6. Read the Notice to Examinee to the employee, which should be signed, timed, dated, and witnessed.
7. Provide the employee with notice 48 hours in advance (not counting weekends or holidays) of the date and time of the scheduled polygraph test.
8. Provide employee with written notice of the date, time, and location of the polygraph test, including written directions if the test is to be conducted at a location other than at the place of employment.
9. Maintain a statement of adverse actions taken against the employee following a polygraph test.
10. Conduct an additional interview of employee prior to any adverse action following a polygraph test.
11. Maintain records of all of the above for a minimum of 3 years.
12. Employees may not waive their rights.
13. Police and investigators are not exempt and must comply if they are conducting an employment related polygraph test, that is, when conducting a polygraph test on an internal theft for a missing deposit. Information about a polygraph provided to the employer by a police officer or investigator is prohibited under the act, since employers are not allowed to use, accept, or inquire about the results.
14. There is a $10,000 penalty for each violation of the law.
15. Check out the credentials of the polygraph examiner that you use and verify that the examiner meets EPPA requirements. Never

hesitate to ask for written proof of licensing, liability insurance, and so forth.

16. Use your company letterhead on all forms you provide to the employee. Have your corporate attorney review your actions to assure your compliance with EPPA.

These are the recommendations of the American Polygraph Association, but the organization's internal legal department should also be in the loop about polygraph examinations. Letting potential employee suspects know that there is a chance that they could be given a polygraph regarding a situation where money or merchandise is missing will serve as a good deterrent.

In every business, including retail, there is usually a system for checks and balances. The checks and balances keep order within the establishment and allow checkers to understand what is going on in their business. Most retailers have a protocol in place that has a manager of the store completing some type of daily reconciliation. The reconciliation allows the manager to know if the store is meeting its goal and if the store internals are in line with what is expected. In many cases there is also a protocol in place for the manager to check the operational controls. This can focus on reviewing items such as returns, voids, discounts, and other transactions that can lead to the loss of money in the store. If there is no such program in place for managers to check high-risk transactions daily, there should be. If the checks and balances are completed daily and to the level that is expected, the opportunity to engage in risky behavior will definitely decline. Most managers are provided tools that allow them to be excellent deterrents for dishonesty, such as double checking paperwork. There are many reasons for this. Retailers' first priority is ensuring that the sales goals are being met. Sales should be the number one concern, but not at the expense of operational controls. Another reason is the time allotted for the review process. If managers do not set specific time aside to review the paperwork, it probably will not get done. Finally, leading by example is another reason for the lack of emphasis on the review process. If the district or regional manager visits the stores within his or her region and never checks anything regarding the controls and focuses only on sales, this demonstrates to the management team where the priorities are and where they are not. Regional or district managers should encourage their management staff to set time aside each day to focus on maintaining operational controls. After completion of the review process, managers should select transactions that they feel are suspicious or they cannot

easily explain. They should bring those transactions to the attention of the employees who completed them and ask for an explanation. This process does two things:

1. It answers the question of what happened
2. It tells the employee that someone is reviewing the paperwork every day.

Sales are important, but profit leaving through various venues through the hands of employees defeats the whole purpose of selling.

Regional or district managers should make it a point to inspect controls on every visit. After they are finished discussing the store internals, they should ask to see a few controls they expect to be completed, such as a daily bank deposit log of all deposits. This tells the management team members that their supervisor sees operations as an important part of the process. It also creates the same effect as employees knowing their managers are looking. Loss prevention people should be communicating to the store managers that they should never discover fraud in paperwork before their managers do. This communicates to management staff members that they are responsible for their business but that the business goes beyond ensuring a sales goal is met.

WHAT WORKS BEST

This chapter focused on the contributing factors to workplace deviance—specifically motivation, low deterrents, and opportunity. The first part of the chapter covered employees' motivation as a contributor to dishonesty, and the second half of the chapter demonstrated that the most effective way to control dishonesty in the workplace is to institute the proper controls to eliminate opportunity and to evaluate the deterrents. The truth is that all three must work in sync with one another to keep honest people honest. Keeping associates happy and having dilapidated controls will not work. On the flip side, having all the controls in place and treating employees poorly will also not work. Two real-life case studies involving members of field management for a retail business illustrate in this section what works best and what does not. The first study is about a regional manager who had the tightest controls on operations she could have.

Susan inspected what she expected, which is very important in eliminating opportunity and keeping the deterrent level high. She did not treat employees poorly, and she did

59

recognize outstanding performers in the region. If a dollar were missing from a location, she would absolutely know about it, sometimes even before the store knew. If an exception report were sent to her, there would be an answer as to what happened by the end of the day. She could have been considered loss prevention's best friend. There was not an operational task she would not do or an audit she would not attend. When inventory results were posted, she went through them with a fine-toothed comb and called all locations to understand what happened if they had losses. She invited loss prevention to attend meetings and gave them more time to speak than most regional managers. She was so operationally insistent that she would even go into the stores when managers went home for the day so she could go through their paperwork. On occasion, she would send in her friends to secretly shop the store so she could understand the level of customer service being delivered. Of course, she would review those results with her managers after they were completed.

Does it sound like the controls were tight enough that employees would not dream of attempting to do anything bad? The answer is no. This particular region had more turnover—specifically manager turnover—than other regions. This region also had several cases of dishonesty. I would assume that readers are wondering what the problem was if opportunity was low, deterrents were high, and people were not being treated poorly. The problem was that everything was done to the extreme, and employees felt like they had their mother watching every move they made. Remember how Susan went into the stores when managers left for the day to see what they were doing? She also confronted them after a bad shop that she deceptively set up without their knowledge or the company's knowledge. Managers felt like one eye was always on them and that their supervisor did not trust anything they did. The lack of trust turned good managers into poor performers who ended up quitting or dishonest.

There has to be a balance, and supervisors need to show their managers that they have trust in them. As with any relationship, trust is usually the factor that either makes or breaks the relationship. When couples are in a committed relationship, they usually begin with trusting the other person until the other person breaks that trust with his or her own actions. The same should be true with supervisor–subordinate relationships. The supervisor should instill trust in her people until something happens to take the trust away. Susan never gave her people a chance to be trusted; rather, she expected that if she did not find anything suspicious with all of her sneaking around, it would eventually lead her to trust them. This behavior manifested itself in an environment of "her against them." The relationships that formed were unhealthy, but no one said or did anything about it. Susan believed that she was inspecting what she expected, and

her people believed that an eye was constantly watching to see if they did anything wrong. The scenario relayed in Susan's story can be correlated to many different relationships where one person's behavior will eventually lead the other person to do what is believed about him or her. Accusations from an insecure wife to her husband about infidelity, even though he has done nothing, will ultimately lead to an undesired result. Either the husband will grow tired of the futile accusations and leave, or he will comply with it and do what he is accused of. The wife wants neither of the outcomes, but it is inevitable if it is not curbed in a timely manner. Such is the case with Susan's story. Her folks either left the organization or gave her what she was always looking for. Again, Susan wanted neither of the outcomes, but it was inevitable because of the behavior.

The next scenario deals with a supervisor who gets the desired results with little effort. This is a story about a field manager named Paul.

Paul ran a region in the South that had low shrinkage, great sales results, and very little turnover. Those three factors—low shrinkage, good sales, and low turnover—are indicators of a region that is running well. Paul chose to tackle motivation first and developed strong relationships with each of his managers before anything else took place. The relationships went beyond supervisor–subordinate relationships and ventured into nonwork-related relationships where both parties believe the other is looking out for the other's best interest. Paul believed that his people produced such good results because they cared about themselves, their boss, and the organization. His people believed that Paul's interest in them went far beyond the confines of the organization and into their families and who they were as people. These beliefs between Paul and his people allowed everything to function as a well-oiled machine. Paul satisfied the requirements for eliminating motivation by building strong genuine bonds between him and everyone who worked for him. The next thing he did was to clarify expectations and consequences for not complying with the expectations. This is where Paul dealt with the opportunity aspect. Paul did not leave any opportunity for misunderstanding or anything to be unknown. People who violated the expectations were absolutely held accountable for their actions. However, Paul's approach to holding them accountable was diplomatic and respectful. Next, managers were very clear on what each visit would hold and what Paul would be looking at. Paul thoroughly checked the paperwork that loss prevention would look at as part of a routine visit. This was not done when managers were not in the store or for the purposes of catching anyone; rather, it was part of every store visit. Making it routine helped everyone feel comfortable and allowed managers to know exactly what would be done. The action of checking increased the level of deterrents, which made it difficult for someone to get away with something because it would eventually be revealed during the visit. Paul's management techniques produced individuals who were willing to give extra effort and did not want to risk their own personal integrity for anything.

61

Throughout this chapter we have evaluated and reevaluated the components of the theft triangle and hopefully have conveyed the message that all three areas—motivation, deterrents, and opportunity—will either negatively or positively affect everything and anything within a retail sales environment. We also tried to determine which of the three is the most important. Realistically the answer is all three are equally important. But individuals who tackle the motivation aspect first will come out ahead of those who do not. So, to answer the question of what works best, refer to Paul's management style and how he was able to tackle all the integral components of the theft triangle and make them work in his favor.

4

How It All Ties Together

One of loss prevention's most difficult components to achieve within any organization is consistency among all practices. Much of the information delivered is subject to the audience's interpretation, and not everyone delivers the message the same way. In addition, loss prevention people usually cover a vast territory, and information will flow through others until it reaches the store-level personnel. When store-level employees are uncertain about how to tackle a particular operation or task, they will often call someone at another store in their same position. This is where much of the consistency breakdown occurs, because these employees are not getting the information directly; rather, they are taking information from someone who may or may not be doing things correctly. The vicious cycle of inconsistency continues as more and more store employees call one another to gain information instead of going to a source that is foolproof.

BUILDING AN EFFECTIVE TRAINING
AND AWARENESS CAMPAIGN

Achieving consistency through the loss prevention message is difficult but not impossible. Launching an effective training and awareness campaign is one of the first steps in getting all employees on the same page. Documenting who participated in a specific training can also be useful for investigations. If associates are being interviewed for some type of policy violation and say they did not know they were not supposed to do

something, documentation that says otherwise could be invaluable. Over the many years the authors have conducted loss prevention interviews, countless employees who have stolen or violated policy stated they were never told they could not. A rebuttal that works fairly well is, "It doesn't state in the policy manual that you can't burn down the store, but common sense tells you otherwise." Letting everyone know the major dos and don'ts is the best course of action, and ensuring that managers have all the correct tools at their fingertips for the daily operations is a best practice.

Rolling out the loss prevention "good word," propaganda, or message is best done by first initiating some sort of an awareness campaign. The campaign can serve different functions such as integrity adherence, operational controls, and general loss prevention training or can be specific to something that is being introduced at the time. One key factor is to keep the campaign alive for as long as the organization wishes to disseminate the information. If the information is not kept fresh with different techniques, people either will forget about it or will believe that the organization does not feel like it is a priority any longer. Think of it as an organization letting its guard down. To put this statement into perspective, think back to what happened immediately after 9/11 with airport security. Security became so tight that it was nearly impossible to get on a plane without a hassle. Yes, the wait was longer and more aggravating, but the awareness of what happened was very clear each time you stepped foot into an airport. It also made people feel secure that once they entered the plane, the likelihood of a terrorist being able to take over the aircraft was minimal. I remember shortly after 9/11 being pulled out of line by Transportation Security Administration (TSA) and taken to a "special area." The x-ray device found a metal fork in my bag, and the security department wanted to know my intentions for the fork. I chuckled a bit when they asked my intentions; they did not find it funny at all. I explained that I ate breakfast on the run and must have just placed the fork in my bag because I did not have anywhere else to put it. The look on their faces told me that I better check next time. I was asked to remove the fork and place it into the "weapon holder." Now, years later, the thought of terrorists taking over a plane probably is not the first thought when people sit down in their seats. Taking off your shoes and eliminating all liquids more than 3 ounces did not happen until someone decided to smuggle explosives onto an aircraft. The airlines began to let their guard down, and someone took advantage of the situation. As with most events, good or bad, the time immediately following is the most action oriented. Society is pumped and ready to take action. However, as time goes by, fewer and fewer people are involved, and the event is not as

significant because it is no longer part of everyday life. The reason for this lack of significance is that society members are not reminded of it consistently. If they were, the message would be kept alive.

The same is true with keeping honest people honest in an organization. Employees must be consistently reminded what is right and wrong. Employees must also be empowered to run the business with the proper tools provided. The next section will discuss how to build an effective training and awareness campaign by targeting the different areas necessary for introduction, compliance, buy-in, and how to promote it.

HOW AWARENESS OF A PROBLEM IS ACHIEVED

There is no need to raise awareness if there is not an issue. In addition, not everything needs to be so significant and made part of employees' daily business. Addressing only the most critical matters will serve as a best practice and will prove to be more efficient. Because specialty retail loss prevention people are not in daily communication with every employee and in most cases not every store consistently, they must rely on others to disseminate information. The following three items will help determine which issues are pertinent to the business.

Talking to Field Partners and Store Associates

Talking to employees about the topic of loss prevention will provide the department with information regarding what people are thinking. Many people might not understand what is expected or believe that their supervisor does not value loss prevention as an important topic for discussion. The goal is to inspire a shared vision of how loss prevention is a necessary part of doing business and protecting company assets.

Asking Questions and Listening to What Associates Are Telling You on Store Visits

Asking specific questions about dishonesty or the understanding of auditing procedures will allow the loss prevention department to know just how much everyone else knows: don't leave any stones unturned. If an employee makes a comment such as, "Everyone is doing [violating a certain policy]", explore that topic further. The incorrect information may stem from much higher up in management ranks than at the store level.

Clarifying the Reasons Associates Provide
for Stealing or Resigning

People who leave the organization either willingly or unwillingly are a wealth of information for loss prevention. Never leave an investigative interview with a lack of understanding of underlying causes. Do not hesitate to participate or conduct exit interview calls after managers resign from the organization. Past employees give such good interviews because they really have nothing to lose. Current employees are often reluctant to provide useful information because of fear it might implicate them or others in wrongdoing, which may lead to job loss.

UNDERSTANDING THE NEEDS OF YOUR BUSINESS

Not every organization needs the same awareness message at the same time. Understanding where the deficiencies are and targeting them for maximum exposure to attentive awareness training are the most effective. One specific campaign will not work for all retailers, but the general foundation will be the same. For instance, a grocery store may want to target employees eating candy that has been damaged out of stock. They believe that employees will intentionally damage bags of candy so they have something to munch on later in the day. The practice within the grocery store has been to allow employees to have out-of-stock candy, but an increase in "ripped bags" has occurred over the years, which has cost the company unnecessarily. The campaign or training could focus on destroying candy immediately after a bag has been found to be compromised. This type of campaign or training is specific to grocery and would not be useful for an apparel chain. However, the concept can be applied to apparel, because if employees are allowed to purchase damaged clothing at a discounted rate, they are more likely to damage the clothing themselves. There are three questions to ask when attempting to understand the needs of your business.

What Types of Tools Are Most Effective
for Training and Awareness?

Again, this depends on the business. For distribution or delivery centers, posters are a good reminder for loss prevention messages. It is necessary to update the posters with different messages to keep interest. For a retail

store with limited space, pamphlets and wallet cards given to associates are good reminders. Having a loss prevention manual available is also a good choice.

How Do You Intend to Get the Message Out?

As discussed already, there are different ways to get the awareness message out, but not all are through a physical or written means. You will find that stories with a message stick in employees' minds. Provide them with a story that has a message embedded, especially if people have lost their job because of an investigation. Talking about the merits of the investigation's most interesting characteristics, without using names or identifiers, is a good way to get the awareness story across to employees.

What and How Will the Information Be Absorbed and What Information Will Be Retained?

Not everything that someone hears or reads will be retained. Make sure to reiterate the most important parts if providing training in the form of facilitation. Begin with what is most important, and end with what is most important. If a phone number on a poster is what should be remembered, make it bigger than the rest of the information. Repetition of the important communication points helps employees to remember them.

INCORPORATING INTEGRITY AWARENESS INTO YOUR CULTURE

Is every organization ready for a culture that flourishes with integrity? You would hope the answer is yes, but that is not always the case. Some organizations are used to cutting corners or just bending the rules and not having to answer to anyone. For anything to work properly, it must begin at the top. An organization cannot expect store-level employees to comply with directives if higher-level management is not complying. There are three areas to consider when incorporating something new into existing organizational culture.

Have a Clear Understanding of Where Your Culture Currently Is and Where You Want It to Go

How an organization carries out terminations gives many loss prevention people a very clear understanding of its culture. Some organizations do not have a culture of equality and terminate with a "depending on who it is" attitude. Associates can often be "saved" from termination if they have the right advocate looking out for them. Wwhat was once completely black and white is contaminated with a clouded shade of gray. If these organizations are not ready for a complete overhaul, help them to start off small and work their way back up.

Prepare for Resistance and Commit to Overcome It

It may seem like everyone would embrace developing a culture conducive to integrity, but in reality many who do not play by the rules find absolute integrity to be a burden. Positioning your proposal to highlight the benefits and how the organization will benefit is the most effective way to achieve buy-in.

Ensure That You Are Modeling the Way

One important rule in the world of loss prevention is to never let any employee from the organization see you bending or breaking the rules inside or outside of work. Loss prevention people—also considered to be the protectors of the organization—are held to a different standard. They are expected to play by the rules at all times. One individual in the department who does not play by the rules could ruin it for everyone else.

BUILD RELATIONSHIPS AND GET CONNECTED

In an earlier chapter we discussed the importance of relationships; this theme will be evident throughout the book. Launching an awareness campaign requires good relationships. Loss prevention team members may have devised the best program on the planet, but if they have not taken the time to get to know their audience, it may have been time ill spent because employees will not understand the whys behind the program.

Spend Time Traveling with Partners and Getting to Know Them and Their Needs

There is something to be said for the human relationships that develop between loss prevention people and others within the organization. Loss prevention people who are doing things right are often the most trusted in the organization. This level of trust is developed from consistent, non-threatening interactions between individuals. Spending time with field management people and really getting to know who they are will open the door for them and for you.

Build Trust

Trust does not happen overnight with any relationship; therefore, it should not be expected to happen automatically simply because someone is in a position of authority. Loss prevention people will realize they have achieved trustworthiness when they are overwhelmed with unsolicited phone calls from employees who want to provide information on integrity issues.

Follow through on Commitments and Provide Feedback

If commitments were made to someone in the organization, those commitments should be kept. If commitments cannot be kept for whatever reason, peers and leaders within loss prevention should be asked to give a hand in getting that audit done or investigation started. Letting employees know where they stand is important for auditing and investigations. It is also important if the campaign focuses on providing information or getting information.

GET COMMITMENT FROM FIELD PARTNERS

Regardless of what type of campaign is initiated, the only way for it to survive is to have the targeted audience comply with what is advertised. A solid relationship in the beginning with the people toward whom the campaign is geared will allow them to accept and embrace the message.

Get a Commitment that They Will Support Your Efforts

Support is even more necessary if the campaign is not something that the entire company is asking for. If something is specific to a region or particular area based on specific factors, discuss why you believe it is necessary for this particular area to have extended or new rules when no one else does. Employees are more likely to comply with change if they understand why the change is necessary and how it will benefit them.

Ensure that All Field Managers Are Promoting Awareness on Their Individual Store Visits

If the awareness campaign has some type of handout for employees to view, provide them to the field people responsible for the stores. This will not only get the message across but will also show that the direct supervision of the store is supporting what is in the message. If the campaign is geared toward new procedures of some sort, ensure that field people are checking compliance during their visit and are reporting the findings.

REWARDS AND RECOGNITION

In the world of loss prevention it is very easy to address everything that is being done wrong because that is what we look for. Things done right, though, often go unnoticed because they are expected. Employers have certain expectations of the people they hire, and one of those is that the rules of the organization will be followed. If that were always the case, loss prevention within organizations would not be necessary. Recognizing and rewarding employees for adhering to rules and regulations will ensure that correct behavior will continue.

Find Ways to Reward Associates for Doing the Right Thing

There is a great video by National Geographic photographer Dewitt Jones titled *Celebrate What's Right with the World*. It is a powerful documentary that teaches people not to ignore the little things in life but to celebrate them. Loss prevention departments can learn a lot from this video because it puts aside the everyday negativity in the world and illuminates the wonder of human simplicity—people doing what they love to do for no given reason, and appreciation of one another just for being human

beings. Catch employees doing the right thing, even if it is expected, and reward them. Positive reinforcement for employees, as with children, is a key factor is sustaining the desired behavior.

Single Associates Out and Recognize Them for Making an Impact in the Field of Loss Prevention

Meetings are a great place to celebrate employees, and to thank them for making a difference in the organization. Creating a certificate or some kind of physical reward and presenting it to employees in front of all their peers can be instrumental in reinforcing positive employee behavior. Many employees desire to be part of the loss prevention department, but not everyone will have that chance. Those making a difference and desiring to contribute more can play a small role in training their peers on the topic of loss prevention.

Publicize What Associates Are Doing to Contribute to Training and Awareness.

If your organization has an internal Web site or newsletter, find a way to incorporate employees who are contributing in a good way to loss prevention. Most organizations will have something that celebrates good internal results such as sales; therefore, it should not be too difficult to find a place for advertisement.

IMPLEMENTING AN INTEGRITY AWARENESS CAMPAIGN

The first step after developing a program is to get your department's buy-in. If you want to roll out a new program to the organization, complete the necessary research for the topic first. After the research is complete, put together a prototype of what the program will look like and give it first to people in the loss prevention department for their suggestions. This will provide many points of view as well as potentially missed items.

Have Peers and Supervisors Provide Feedback on Changes

Not everyone will always agree with the approach or perspective taken on various topics. Even people within loss prevention believe differently about

the topic of dishonesty and how to best control losses. When people do not agree with your views, it does not always mean they do not have anything valuable to contribute. It is better to get the disagreements dealt with in the department as opposed to having field- or store-level employees disagree with something that could have been fixed had you taken the suggestion.

Target Influential People

This is the time when it pays to know people. If your loss prevention department does not have a group that can build a campaign or program from start to finish (as most do not), you will have to rely on others to help the cause. Be patient with the people you need. Loss prevention initiatives are usually not a first priority and will almost always take a second seat to those such as sales programs. Because you probably can't do it alone, figure out who will be necessary to help you. But, understand that you will be on their "list," so remain patient until they can meet with you.

Know Who Has the Power to Promote the Program

The people who help you develop the physical program are not the same as those necessary to promote it. In most organizations it is imperative to have the support of the operations department for any program to survive. The people in this department will drive the field- and store-level employees to do what you need them to do. If you can get them to send out a communication supporting what you are trying to do, you have won the first battle.

Understand Who the Key Players Are in the Rollout

As with the development and promotion, yet another group will need to be involved with the rollout. If the intent is to saturate the entire organization, usually training and development team members will be the key players. They are responsible for most rollouts and know how to make it work. They will also understand the challenges and how to overcome them, one of which is often making sure the information is saturated throughout the organization. Having the program on CD or DVD will be easier than disseminating the information firsthand because of the time involved. But if each store does not have access to a computer terminal to watch the CD or DVD, that will also be a challenge. If the program requires every associate to complete it, such as ethics training, how will

it be known that every associate has indeed completed it? The training and development team will also help standardize the program from a formatting standpoint. Organizations usually have a logo or coloring that is standard for their advertising; therefore, if something is going to be introduced company-wide, standardization is often required.

Make Sure Information Is Moving up the Ladder

The success of the campaign or program is also dependent on how many people at the top believe in it. If there is not any executive support, it will likely not stick. The higher-level executives within the loss prevention department will play a key role in moving the information up the ladder.

Write a Business Proposal

If there are costs involved—either actual monetary cost or employee productivity costs—it is usually necessary to create a business proposal outlining the following three items:

- Proposal description
- Justification
- Cost benefit

Proposal Description

Define what the program is and what it entails. Use terms easily understood by the general population about how the program will work. Be very specific about what you want. For instance, if the intent is to roll out the program company-wide, make sure to include that information in the description.

Justification

Define why it is necessary to have a program such as you are describing. If the program is focused on dishonesty, broadly describe how employee dishonesty adversely affects organizations. Also make specific reference to your own organization and why this type of specific program is necessary. If there is a way to quantify information and to place statistical data, do so in this section. If the person reviewing the proposal cannot understand why it is necessary to make change, the program will likely die at this stage.

Cost Benefit

Everything is about return on investment (ROI). Explain how the program will save the organization money in the short- or long-term. It may be impossible to accurately forecast exactly just how much money can be saved, but an educated guess based on facts will be sufficient. Something such as employee dishonesty costs the company directly by actual inventory loss and productivity loss because of the people, and indirectly by those who must investigate and resolve the claims.

The following sections cover some topics that can be addressed in an awareness campaign to capture management attention and collaboration.

METHODS TO CONTROL AND UNDERSTAND TURNOVER

One statistical figure often consistent among organizations is that if turnover is high in the organization, or one brand of the organization, high shrinkage will often follow. Low turnover usually equates to lower shrinkage. Turnover costs companies large amounts of money each year because for every one person who leaves there must be a new untrained person to replace the person who left. Hiring and training costs are staggering for business in America today. Any awareness campaign or program with results proven to lower turnover either directly or indirectly will be welcomed.

Research How the Organization Evaluates Turnover

A breakdown of turnover statistical figures usually can be reviewed, such as the breakdown of hourly versus salary, part time versus full time, and geographical information. Then move on to research the causes of turnover.

Understand What the Causes of Turnover Are

Figure out how many employees are leaving willingly and unwillingly. Also contact the human resource department to receive the findings of exit interviews, if they are completed. If a particular region is having more turnover than other similar regions, place emphasis in that area.

See How Loss Prevention Awareness
Can Help Decrease Turnover

Develop an awareness campaign that focuses on decreases in turnover, but with a loss prevention spin on it. Since a correlation is known to exist between turnover and shrinkage, a campaign geared toward turnover will conquer two never-ending retail battles. It will be much easier to promote a campaign that focuses on something everyone in the company is concerned about as opposed to something that is very specific to one department.

NEW MANAGER ASSIMILATION

Getting to managers before they have a chance to make poor decisions or learn poor habits is one of the most important components to controlling shrinkage. After interviewing a new manager for posting thousands of dollars of stolen product for sale on eBay, it was learned that if she had known the company could monitor eBay she would not have done it. Something as simple as information can be the difference between someone stealing and not stealing. Developing a protocol for new managers that focuses on loss prevention training and awareness will decrease the number of managers who are willing to risk being dishonest. It will also teach managers on what they should be looking for to identify dishonesty in their own environment.

Loss Prevention and Associate Relations or Human
Resources to Target New Managers for Awareness

As new managers are hired, one of their first training sessions should revolve around the role of associate relations (AR) and human resources (HR) and loss prevention. Making the training part of the orientation process will ensure that every manager receives it. It is not a bad idea to have new managers sign an integrity statement and place it in their file. During the training managers should have a good understanding of exactly what AR/HR and loss prevention do for the company. This information should be very specific in explaining that loss prevention conducts investigations to figure out who is stealing from the company and that AR facilitates decisions on what the company reaction would be to someone who stole. If your company prosecutes internal theft, make sure to explain that as

well. This approach hopefully will "scare" new employees into doing the right thing.

New Managers Should Go into Their Role with Clear Understanding and Expectations

Getting to new managers before they have a chance to do anything wrong both intentionally and unintentionally will greatly benefit the organization. Laying down clear expectations will undoubtedly create a platform for success. Many companies have something like a "Duty Act," which requires managers to speak up. If managers do not know they could lose their job for ignoring loss prevention problems, they may be tempted to do just that.

Building a training and awareness campaign will frequently pose a challenge for anyone who desires to make change. A compilation of many different methods may be the best way of providing the full effect. Remembering that tying in the goals of the campaign with company initiatives will strengthen the likelihood that the entire company will embrace the cause. Knowing who to go to for different parts of the campaign will also be instrumental in speeding up the rollout.

HOW TO GET EXECUTIVE BUY-IN AND DEALING WITH RESISTANCE

Many loss prevention people feel like they are in a never-ending battle with people outside of their department. This is true for both store- and field-level loss prevention personnel. The "us against them" mentality is very hard to overcome. This seems absurd because the loss prevention department is usually the group to enforce policies and procedures. Why would anyone resist such a valiant effort put forth by a group with the utmost interest in protecting the company profits? Many executives in organizations have the perception that "if it isn't broken, don't fix it." If often seems like the only time many executives are willing to tighten the controls quickly is if the government mandates such an action. This should not be the case since the loss prevention goals within the organization are aligned with company goals but are just achieved differently. The next section discusses creative ways to get buy-in and how to overcome resistance.

Get to Know the Decision Makers

The perception that loss prevention team members are the organizational police cannot be changed unless the people in charge have a chance to interact with the departmental activities. Executives should be invited to participate in an audit or at least to see the results of the audit findings. Executives should also understand what type of infractions are plaguing the organization and being eradicated by loss prevention. So many people in loss prevention are stretching themselves far beyond the confines of their demographic organization and are helping other organizations or individuals with their expertise and wisdom assisting other companies as well as their own. When people in loss prevention are recognized outside the organization for their achievements, this should be brought to the attention of the company executives.

Ensure that Executives Understand the Different Roles of Loss Prevention

When I started in business over a decade ago, my job was to remove customers and employees who stole from the company. There was not much training going on or anything outside of getting rid of the bad guy. Loss prevention departments nationally and internationally have come a long way since then and have advanced to a multifaceted brigade of individuals with diversified expertise. Loss prevention team members today wear many hats, such as auditor, investigator, trainer, speaker, consultant, and someone to be relied upon by their constituents. Executives should understand that the role of loss prevention within an organization is more than just a necessary evil.

Talk Their Talk

If you want to positively influence and win admiration quickly with executives, leave loss prevention alone in the beginning and discuss the organization's current events. All loss prevention people should know where the company stands financially, how sales are for the current period, and stock prices. Knowing information that executives are drivers of and cannot live without will give you insider access. It will also probably catch executives off guard because most believe that the only item up for discussion with a loss prevention person is theft. One additional key point is that all company acronyms and any current terms or jargon should be

known by loss prevention. Many organizations have different promotions that they have unique terminology for such as "BOGO" (i.e., buy one, get one free or half off). Loss prevention should be up to speed with current promotions circulating in the organization.

Provide Statistics on Savings

Loss prevention should provide some type of biannual or annual report to the organization that reflects what the department is recovering or removing. It is always good to include information such as admitted dollars by employees. If there was a large case resolved during the year, it might be wise to project how much loss there would have been if loss prevention had not dealt with it. For instance, assume that an employee admits to stealing $5,000 in fraudulent returns over the last four months. This equates to $1,250 per month, which in turn amounts to $15,000 for the year that would have been lost had the employee not been caught. If audits are being completed and the store's shrinkage lowers after the employee is caught, provide that type of statistical information.

A Place for Information

Most retail stores will have some evidence of loss prevention within the confines of the establishment. Physical reminders like posters and pamphlets are reminders to line-level employees that loss prevention exists in the organization. A sample of an awareness pamphlet is shown in Figure 4.1. It can be folded in three to make a nice handout during store visits. Because corporate executives are not often in store locations, employees should receive information about the existence of a loss prevention department in their organization in a readily accessible place, such as an Intranet site if there is one. Loss prevention should have its own portal page displaying the department matrix, forms (e.g., incident reports), noteworthy cases, and current events. This provides executives with an avenue should they want to learn more about what it is the department is doing.

Attend Meetings

Most executives do not routinely travel to stores, but many will venture out for a meeting in which something new is being rolled out or in which they wish to have input. Meetings such as this are always good grounds

Integrity Expectations	Preventing Loss, what the Company does for you:	Preventing Loss, what is expected of you:
• Commit to Being Honest • Report Dishonesty • Help Create a Culture of Integrity • Foster a Climate of Open Communication • Say what you're going to do and do what you say • Comply with Sarbanes Oxley financial and inventory requirements	• **Audits:** Help strengthen store's procedural adherence. • **Investigations:** Resolve situations involving integrity issues. • **XBR Analytics® Exception Based Reporting:** Monitored by full-time CSC LP staff. Detects dishonesty in all brands without affecting honest, hard working associates. • **Internet:** VigilActive software is utilized by LP staff to find stolen product on the Internet. • **Training:** Conduct individual or group presentations. • **Sales Audit:** Tracks all financial variances, including bank deposit loss. • **Professional Relationships:** Partnering with authorities on issues that can't be resolved at company level. • **Incentive Monitoring:** Regular review of contests and incentive programs. • **Pre-employment screening**	• **Create a culture of integrity:** Set and maintain high standards. Treat each other and customers with respect and follow all policies and procedures. • **Provide exceptional customer service:** Deter shoplifting and report all incidents of loss. • **Internal controls:** Follow company guidelines on returns, voids, package checks, bank deposits. • **Inventory control:** Utilize perpetual inventory system (shipment tracking and preparation and execution and proper damage control). • **Compliance with high-shrink programs:** Follow all guides associated with shrink program. • **Incident reporting:** Report associate dishonesty or business abuse to appropriate parties (Loss Prevention, Netclaims, and Associate Relations).

Figure 4.1 Sample loss-prevention awareness pamphlet.

to interact with executives. Loss prevention team members' attendance will demonstrate to executives that they are team players. If a presentation by the department is requested, always start with the celebratory parts first. Recognize employees for a job well done and how they contributed to the good of the organization.

Gaining Key Support

Departments such as inventory control, operations, and sales audit are absolutely necessary to the loss prevention department. If loss prevention members discover some type of systematic issue affecting the inventory, it is always advantageous to have someone available to call. Often the lower-level employees are not willing to put in the time to resolve problems found by loss prevention for fear it might cause them more work, so having someone higher in the department's structure may help. Operations is usually the group that puts roadblocks in the way of loss prevention initiatives. Before trying to roll out something that might be viewed as controversial, it is a good idea to review it with someone in operations to gain the department's support and input. Sales audit is the group that deals with missing

bank deposits and credit card charge backs. Both deposits and charge backs are heavy hitters of profit and a big interest to loss prevention. To make matters worse, this is also the area in which loss prevention usually has the most trouble gathering information because of account numbers and confidential information that the bank and credit card company are hesitant to provide, especially with privacy concerns and credit card industry controls. Knowing someone in the sales audit department who has the ability to gain confidential information will be critical in gathering evidence for a case.

All of these areas will help a loss prevention department build a good foundation to support its initiatives. Resistance is encountered because many loss prevention people approach the topic through their own eyes rather than through the eyes of the executive. When loss prevention people want to get something done in this field, they must walk in others' shoes. Many loss prevention people see everything as black and white, whereas everyone else in the organization either intentionally or unintentionally inserts gray into situations. If any unclear issues are dealt with prior to the proposal by the introducer, the resistance may not even be an issue. Timing is also an important component for not encountering resistance. If loss prevention team members wish to roll out a new program, they must learn to time it effectively, especially if it costs money. If sales are weak and the program or initiative costs money, waiting to propose it to the executive committee is a grand idea. If what the loss prevention department wants to implement can be tied in with something the organization is bringing out, this is another step in the right direction. This way it is not something costly or extra for stores to do; rather, it is just an additional tool of a familiar program. Most executives want to run an organization they can be proud of and that exhibits integrity. With the right approach, even the most reluctant executive will agree to what is best for the organization.

BUILDING A CULTURE OF INTEGRITY

Every organization is looking for the foolproof method of dealing with losses. As many loss prevention people already know (and this book discusses), there are countless ways to deal with losses. Some methods are more effective than others for sustaining the desired results. We have all probably been to a restaurant at some point in our life where children were completely out of control, disrupting everyone and everything in their path. I will also guess that many of us have looked at the parents and

perhaps have even commented about their parenting skills. Much of the blame is put on the parents for children behaving poorly because society believes that the children are a reflection of the parents and their ability to properly raise them. In the same way, children who are respectable and behave properly in public are viewed as descendents of their good child-rearing parents. The same is true for employees of an organization: they are a reflection of their employer. If the employer accepts a culture that tolerates losses, then losses are what they get. It is very easy to put up a camera or run exception reporting excessively to uncover dishonesty, but it is much more difficult to create an environment where employees do not tolerate losses and help to reduce them. That is why organizations spend millions of dollars in their attempt to deter losses: it is the easiest way out.

Creating a culture of integrity within an organization is one of the more difficult tasks to undertake, especially if the current culture is not conducive to doing the right thing. Harvey Helms made one of the most profound statements I have ever heard during a seminar: "Culture eats policy and procedure for lunch." Regardless of what parameters are in place, the culture within the store or organization will overtake any initiatives loss prevention attempts to implement. A store culture in which a blind eye is turned to theft and then installs cameras will not eradicate the problem. The employees will figure out what is going on and simply find a safe alternative to steal product or money from the organization. The goal of building a culture of integrity is to have employees do the following:

- Respect the rules because they want to.
- Be shameful of any wrongdoing.
- Not accept anything that is adverse to the organization.
- Police one another.
- Report abnormalities immediately so they can be dealt with.

Another reason employers are reluctant in even attempting such a concept is because results cannot be seen quickly. To successfully implement a program that focuses on employee integrity, employers will reap the rewards in the future, not in the immediate present. It takes time to recondition employees to a new way of thinking and behaving. Consider it a way of desensitizing employees from what they are accustomed to. If done correctly, employers will have created an environment where employees flourish not only in integrity but also in productivity.

When deciding to implement a program that focuses on reconditioning employees to be pro integrity, one must understand why it is not

already in existence. To some degree, most organizations will have a culture of integrity in place, but when employees are not flourishing in their positions, most employers will not look in the direction of integrity playing a part in lack of productivity. It is very apparent when integrity is one of the most important aspects of an organization and not just words posted in an organizational mission statement attached to a back wall. The difference between having a true culture of integrity and a fake one is the will of the employees. Organizations that have developed the true concept do not have to force their employees to do the right thing because employees do it on their own. Understanding the areas that restrict organizations from having a true culture of integrity is an important determinant to whether the blinders can be removed to make the organization open to such a concept. If the top-level leadership is causing the lack of integrity, it will be a long row to hoe. If it is simply inconsistency among employees, however, this will be an easy path. Each organization must first evaluate its roadblocks before deciding that a culture of integrity is the way to go. In addition, if the foundation is not solid, the rest of the parts will crumble. The process is built from the bottom up to ensure that the ethical foundation is the strongest part to the program.

Japan is a good example of where culture works as an effective deterrent for crime. Its justice system is not significantly different from other countries, but its results are. Countries such as Jamaica and Russia have an enormous issue with murder and other violent crimes. Japan's economic success over these two countries contributes somewhat to the lower crime rate. However, Japan's crime rate is even lower than it is in the United States, and that is because the culture within the country does not tolerate bad behavior. It is unacceptable to be deviant. Individuals in Japan who decide to engage in deviant behavior are treated like outcasts in society. These individuals lose the respect of their families, friends, and society in general. After their period of incarceration they are allowed back into society but are forced to live a life of isolation. There is no greater pain than having persons you love and know wanting nothing to do with you. Japan's culture allows for safer streets and less burden on police and creates well-rounded human beings.

On the other hand, countries such as the United States tolerate crime and accept criminals back into society. Family members often welcome home, upon release, husbands and wives who have gone to prison. Serial killers receive fan mail and wedding proposals from those who know how heinous their crimes were. How mentally damaged does someone have to be to propose marriage to an individual incarcerated for dismembering

another human being? It is absolutely ridiculous that people in the United States will tolerate such behavior.

I have had the distinct pleasure of getting to know Judge James McKensie (*Taboo* on the National Geographic Channel), who became the judge of Dayton, Tennessee, which is part of Rhea County, in 1998. When he became judge, he evaluated the types of crimes and sentences associated with them and found that most shoplifters were put on probation without doing any real jail time. Giving shoplifters probation is fairly standard practice throughout the nation. Prior to 1998, Dayton, Tennessee, was no different. McKensie evaluated Dayton's current practice of probation and found it was not really working because theft in general continued to rise in the county. In 2000, he began to read articles on other different methods of discipline judges are using. He was particularly fond of the method that allows offenders to clearly know they have wronged the retailer and the community. McKensie found that other judges were using different forms of shaming similar to Japan. After completing his research, McKensie decided to implement a new discipline structure in Dayton that would make people who violate the rules, specifically shoplifters, pay dearly for their behavior. His method is as follows (see Figure 4.2):

- If a suspect either pleads guilty or is found guilty for theft or shoplifting from a retailer, the choice is to:
 - Spend 10 days in jail or
 - Spend four days walking in front of the retailer they stole from carrying a sandwich sign that reads:

I stole from [retailer's name] and I'm ordered to walk by Judge McKensie.

McKensie said that specifying on the sign that he is the one responsible for this person's punishment alleviates the retailer from responsibility and allows the judge to take full responsibility. The shaming method does not discriminate between juvenile and adult offenders. Individuals 14 years of age and older can still be made to walk. If a juvenile is ordered to walk and the parents do not agree with the decision, parents can appeal. There has been only one appeal since 2000. Once adult offenders are found guilty, they are banned from setting foot inside of the retailer they stole from for life. If the retailer occupies multiple locations, the adult offender is banned from every one of them. Once juvenile offenders are found guilty, they are banned until the age of 18. After the age of 18 they are allowed to return and this time to pay for merchandise they want.

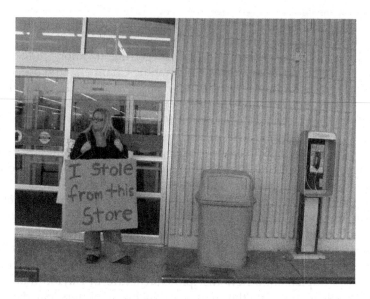

Figure 4.2 Example of the type of punishment Judge James McKensie issues to shoplifters who are convicted.

However, if they decide to steal again after the age of 18, they will incur a life ban if found guilty.

I asked McKensie what happens if the offender decides not to finish all four days and cuts it short. Not to worry, he told me; he fixes that problem as well. Offenders who decide to cut out a little early finish off their sentence in jail or are ordered to walk an additional four days. The judge said that some individuals do not want the ridicule that comes along with their public humiliation so they show up to serve their walking sentence wearing a ski mask to hide their appearance. According to McKensie, however, faces must be clearly visible. He believes that society needs to see the people who committed the crime, and the offenders must know they are being seen and often recognized by friends and family. If they are caught wearing any camouflage to conceal their identity, they will be asked to remove it or forfeit the walking, which in turn leads to jail time.

McKensie said that the community appreciates this method, as do the retailers. It is nothing new that retailers will have to raise prices because of thieves, which in turn places an added burden on the public. The judge believes that adults emulate how they grew up and that parents have a responsibility to teach their children to act appropriately. He went on

to say that the work ethic in America has changed. Many people want a check from the government or to steal from the public instead of working for what they need. The judge said he believes in his method of discipline because it provides a good example for the children in the community, which is easily seen when kids go shopping with their parents and see embarrassing consequences of shoplifting for offenders.

One thing I learned during our discussion together is that McKensie believes one of the worst things in the world is a thief. He wants to ensure that the society of tomorrow, the children of Dayton, Tennessee, will learn early lessons on good moral behavior and that the people involved in deviant behavior have learned their lesson. Yes, the offenders have definitely learned their lesson, at least in Dayton, Tennessee. An extraordinary statistic uncovered during the conversation is this:

> The judge reports that he has not had one person reoffend with regards to shoplifting since 2000.

The method of public shaming has proven its effectiveness again and again. So why do other judges not employ this discipline method nationwide to help retailer curb the theft problem? There is one simple answer, according to McKensie: some judges are afraid of being publicly ridiculed. Members of the American public refuse to hold one another accountable for bad behavior. There are so many crimes labeled as victimless or nonviolent with such low levels of punishment that it is more of an inconvenience than a deterrent for offenders. Shoplifting is one of those crimes. McKensie said that his method not only deters individuals from stealing again but also saves taxpayers money by not having to house the offenders inside jails.

In 2008 a new reality show aired on the Fox Network titled *Moment of Truth*. People are given a lie detector test prior to being on the show in which they are asked 21 questions; they are not provided with the results. When the show airs, the contestants are asked the same 21 questions live in front of an audience of family and friends. The more questions they answer truthfully, the more money they win. The contestants have the option to either keep the same answer they originally provided or change their answer. However, they do not know if the lie detector picked up deception during the initial answer; therefore, they are gambling if they attempt to lie. If they are caught lying once, they lose all their money. Many people lost their money because they lied,

and as of September 2008, no one had reached the $1 million mark for telling the truth.

Interestingly enough, more than 80% of the people on the show were asked if they have ever stolen from their employer or falsified documents at any time during their career. The response from the contestants was almost always yes. The thefts ranged from food to money. The falsification ranged from medical reports to family-owned business financial documents. People watching the show can hear and see the audience's responses. When the contestants answer yes to stealing from their employer (this is not one of the questions where contestants were caught lying; they readily admit to the dishonesty), audience members laugh. However, when they said yes to cheating on their spouses, audience members boo to signify their disapproval for that particular behavior.

This reaction by society tells us that stealing from employers is not a big deal but that adultery is. That is why employers have such a difficult time combating internal theft: it is accepted by society in general. The United States is not alone when it comes to employee theft; it exists on every continent. I remember speaking with a security professional from South Africa some years back about how culture affects deviance in the workplace. I asked him about workplace theft in Africa, and he replied that it is not much different from the United States.

Organizations must create a culture that does not tolerate counterproductive behavior (see Figure 4.3). Organizations must start from the inside out. A book titled *Absolute Honesty* by Larry Johnson and Bob Phillips provided six principles regarding how to create an ethical infrastructure.

1. Tell the truth, which deals with the reasons people are not honest, such as:
 a. Fear of retribution
 b. Fear of paying the price
 c. Fear of losing face
 d. Fear of being disliked
 e. Fear of losing competitive advantages

2. Tackle the problem, which focuses on dealing with issues at hand—not allowing problems to fester and clustering them into a forever-burning inferno.

3. Disagree and commit, which allow employees to have a voice; however, once a decision is made, employees are to support it.

Figure 4.3 Sample of a "Culture of Integrity" handout.

4. Welcome the truth, in which employers are allowed to have an open-door policy for employees. It creates an environment where employees feel safe to tell the truth and how to overcome defensive behavior.

5. Reward the messenger, which occurs when those who tell the truth are rewarded. It is positive reinforcement for employees to be rewarded for ethical behavior.

6. Build a platform of integrity, which creates an atmosphere of open communication and trust.

I took each of the principles and developed them into an integrity and ethics training program for use in a retail business setting. Each principle has an associated training module. Each module has a scenario that revolves around an ethical dilemma that must be resolved by the employees taking the program.

The program takes about 4 hours to facilitate. The employees are provided with a current copy of the code of ethics and a participant's guide for the culture of integrity program. The guide has areas that need to be filled out by the participants.

For the first principle, tell the truth, employees are taught about the reasons that truth telling is difficult. Most will be able to relate to at least

one of the reasons, which leads to discussion. A story is inserted about someone who did not tell the truth for one of those reasons and how to get past it. Another part of why people do not tell the truth is something called catastrophic chaining.

Employees start with a small event that is going to occur and blow it out of proportion by anticipating negative events. The negative events may or may not occur, but the anticipation precludes them telling the truth. For example, store manager Joe is going to have a visit by his supervisor. He has not completed some of the paperwork that was required by his supervisor. Joe is now under extreme stress for the visit because he knows his supervisor will want to see it. Joe believes that his supervisor will be very angry about his failure to finish a task. Joe also thinks that this will result in his termination. If Joe is terminated, he will most likely lose his house, and his family will be out on the street. Joe cannot substantiate any of his suspicions about what is to come, but in his mind the visit will end everything. Joe makes a decision that he will go to the doctor so he can get a sick notice to not come into work for the visit.

Joe's behavior is probably pretty consistent with what employees want to do if they perceive trouble is on the way. If Joe had a good relationship with his supervisor, he could have just told him that he did not get it done and would have it finished as soon as possible. This would have stopped all the chaos going on in Joe's head and would have allowed him to welcome the visit. The scenario for tell the truth is as follows:

> Give an example of a situation concerning yourself or your store where a negative experience turned out better than anticipated.
> What did you do?
> Why?
> What could you have done differently?

After participants complete the scenario, they are allowed to discuss their answers with the group.

The second principle, tackle the problem, is one with which many supervisory people have an issue. Many managers allow problems to fester until they are completely counterproductive. If they would have just dealt with the small stuff in the beginning, the massive tsunami may have never hit. The program teaches managers how to tackle the little problems step by step.

According to Johnson and Phillips, tackling the problem should occur in the following manner:

- Prepare what you are going to discuss.
- Present the issue to the employee.
- Focus on the present tense (do not go back through everything the employee has ever done wrong).
- Attack the problem, not the individual.
- Listen to and see other's point of view.
- Use the "I" approach instead of "you."
- Give constructive feedback.
- Search for solutions that best serve the company.
- Follow through and strive for closure.

It cannot be emphasized enough that managers should be trained to deal with problems effectively. If problems are nipped quickly there is a better than average chance that there will be no aftermath. The scenario that ties in with tackle the problem is as follows:

It is the end of the week, and you just completed payroll. You are excited because you made a sales plan and met your hours goal. Your top-producing employee came in late several times during the week. What do you do?
What would you say to the employee?
What is the benefit of addressing this situation?
What is the impact if you do not address it?

You will find that most managers know what the right thing to do is and during the training will also tell you that they do the right thing. However, as we all know that is not the case for most managers, especially when times are tough in the organization. It is imperative to address the effects of not dealing with situations such as this. Not only does it show that the manager does not follow policy for addressing tardiness, but it also negatively impacts other employees who do show up to work on time each day.

For employees to feel like they are part of something bigger, they need to have their own voice in the organization. Disagree and commit allows employees to be heard so they can feel like they are contributing to the greater good of the organization. Many managers have a difficult time listening but a very easy time talking. As loss prevention professionals, we all know that listening is key to getting information. The more time we allow employees to "free" talk, the more we learn about the culture in the store, region, or organization as a whole. This area is also where you will see compliance versus commitment. Employees

who are complying with organizational direction are doing it to keep their job and really do not believe in what they are doing. Employees who are committed do it because they believe it is the right thing to do.

The following describes reasons for which employees do not commit according to Johnson and Phillips. The participants are to put down a suitable resolution on how to avoid each of the reasons from occurring.

1. Perception of dishonorable intent: perception that someone is crossing the line.
2. Perception of unfairness: people know life really is not fair, but they want it to be. When it is discovered that unfairness has occurred, people want no part of it.
3. Perception of a sham: when employees have uncovered that their opinion really did not matter and their supervisor was just pretending to care about their voice, commitment is not in the cards.
4. Perception of being powerless: deception techniques used by supervisors that are detected by employees leave a feeling of indignity and helplessness.

For example, a regional manager is holding a store manager meeting to discuss the fourth-quarter strategy to boost sales in the region. She defines all of the items believed to be prohibiting the region from making their plan. She calls out a few stores that have done well and makes it a point to impress upon the others that it can be done. She asks the opinion of what the managers think can be done and says she is willing to try anything and is open to new ideas. Many managers chime in and give her ways of elevating the sales. A few days later the managers receive a fax that outlines the fourth-quarter strategy as a result of their meeting. Not one item or idea conveyed by the management team is on the strategy; only what the regional manager discussed is on it. The managers do not believe she cared about what they had to say and was just going through the motions (i.e., perception of a sham). The end result is a lack of commitment to the strategy.

There is a second scenario for disagree and commit:

Think of a time where you did not agree with a decision.
What were the circumstances?
What did you not agree with?
What could have been done differently?

Welcoming the truth builds authentic relationships. There are reasons, though, that people do not want to welcome the truth. The main thing that prohibits truth telling is defensive behavior. If the truthful information being provided will negatively affect another person, people are reluctant to tell. One of the main reasons is they are afraid of the other person's reaction. Just think of the husband and wife who have been married for years, when one ventures outside of the marriage. The guilt is telling the person who strayed that he or she owes the truth to his or her spouse, but the probable reaction that will be enacted as a result of the information can be overwhelming. The same is true with employee–employer relationships. Employees need to feel like they can tell their boss that they messed up. No one is perfect, and mistakes will be made. Those mistakes either will be disclosed because the supervisor is open to welcoming the truth or will be covered up because the conversations pose too much of risk.

The scenario that goes with welcoming the truth is for participants to identify their strengths and weakness. If they uncover that confrontation is an issue for them, the likelihood of telling the truth diminishes. If confrontation is not an issue, they are more likely to tell the truth because they are not afraid of the outcome. In this section, they also need to understand whether they are open to listening to the truth. Many managers will tell their employees that they have an "open door," but they really do not. They need to understand how others perceive their willingness to hear and deal with the truth.

Rewarding the messenger is a form of positive reinforcement that will not go unnoticed. If employees have finally found the courage to come forward with information, they should be applauded for their behavior. Because of the Sarbanes–Oxley Act of 2002, whistle-blowers are protected, but it does not have any provisions about rewarding them for telling. The rewards falls on the employer. I remember once a field manager came to me with information regarding his supervisor. The supervisor had put him down on his expenses as a lunch companion and inadvertently sent the report to him. After looking at the report, he noticed that his name was associated with a lunch transaction he was not part of. The supervisor was well-liked, respected, and pretty high up on the food chain. The field manager did not sleep for days because he was not sure what to do. He knew that he had a duty to act but feared the outcome of the situation. He finally came forward with the information, and after a lengthy investigation and interview the supervisor was terminated. I asked people involved in the investigation who were also

higher on the food chain to call him up and tell him that he did the right thing. As loss prevention people we tend to think a different way from most people. We do not need to be rewarded for bringing information to light because that is why we are employed. Other people in the organization often struggle with coming forward, and when they do it needs to be confirmed that they did a good thing.

The scenario that goes with reward the messenger is as follows:

> How can you create a culture where people are open with information necessary to build a culture of integrity, and how do you sustain that behavior?
>
> Is there anything you would change?
>
> You do not have to discuss, but write the names of the associates with whom you have not dealt.

The platform of integrity is the written protocol for how you intended to behave when it comes to ethics. The first part of this is to write an integrity statement that declares your beliefs. Before you start to manufacture the platform, though, you will need to assess the current condition of the organization when it comes to integrity. You can formulate questions based on the five principles to understand where the conditions are good or bad.

Declaring your beliefs is imperative to making the entire program work. Once you disclose how you really feel about integrity and follow it up with actions associated with what you stated, change will come. Employees will realize that this is for real and is here to stay.

5

External Theft

When analyzing the causes of shrinkage of inventory in the retail world there are four main causes to consider: (1) internal theft; (2) external theft; (3) operational errors; and (4) vendor theft. This chapter will discuss the cause of shoplifting, a type of external theft. External theft includes shoplifting, burglaries, robberies, and any other acts employed to deprive the owner of merchandise or product that would otherwise appear on the shelf for sale. For example, vandalism and the destruction of property in the course of a burglary deprive the owner of that product.

Shoplifting accounts for between 35.6% and 42.5% of retail store inventory shrinkage, depending on what survey or study you might be reading. However, the problem affects each business with intensity unique to that business. For example, a chain of discount department stores may measure its shoplifting problem to be 30.9% of the loss of all stores, whereas a chain of fashion jewelry stores realizes closer to 46.7% of its losses in shoplifting because of the value and price of the product. According to the University of Florida 2008 National Retail Security Survey Final Report, the average sources of inventory shrinkage show shoplifting at 35.6%. No matter which way you analyze it, shoplifting is a problem for all retailers.

What does a shoplifter look like? How do you tell if shoplifters have visited your stores? How do you recognize that a store has a problem? There is no stereotype to identify all shoplifters: they are not a certain color, they do not all wear the same outfit, and they do not all have the same physical characteristic, like green hands. The answer lies in watching behaviors and actions. Shoplifters look like you and me. They can be homemakers, children, doctors, lawyers, movie stars, politicians, and

even police officers. They can be rich or poor or anything in between. We do know that shoplifters usually feel entitled to the items they steal, rationalize why they should steal, and get an adrenalin lift when they get away with it. This is driven by their quick analysis of how hard the theft will be and the risk of getting caught.

There are four types of shoplifters: (1) professionals, (2) thrill seekers, (3) amateurs, and (4) juveniles. Professional shoplifters are driven by the need to steal as a means of income. Addicts fall into this category because they must shoplift and sell their stolen goods for drug money. One professional I had experience with was a 45-year-old male named Johnny, who put high-priced product into his shopping cart and wheeled it up to the customer service desk for a refund. Johnny generally presented a copy of a receipt from a legitimate purchase. He would ask to speak to a manager to lodge a complaint about the store or product and then would demand cash in return. Johnny had a very high percentage of success. As stores caught on to the large number of refunds Johnny was making in a certain region, they started sharing information. District loss prevention managers communicated and mapped out his progress; they could see that his store visits conformed to a pattern. Eventually, Johnny was caught. When police arrested him, they found maps of Ohio, New York, and Pennsylvania on which he had plotted locations for more than one discount department store chain. Johnny also had a detailed list of each shoplifted item and return he had made, totaling more than $315,000 in one year.

Thrill seekers are high school or college kids who steal on a dare from their friends or to gain entrance into a fraternity, sorority, or clique. They are lonely stay-at-home moms seeking a thrill. They might be doctors or lawyers who are bored with their work or relationships and are seeking that shot of adrenaline or the attention of a loved one. Thrill seekers generally are planning to steal when they enter the store. They have stolen before without getting caught, and they will do it again for the rush it gives them. Thrill seekers usually give themselves away because of nervousness prior to concealing the product: wandering around with no real purpose, licking their lips from dry mouth, becoming pale and shaky, and being keenly aware of who is looking at them instead of paying attention to what is on the shelves.

Amateur shoplifters are the hardest to catch because their decision to steal is normally not premeditated. These thieves may not display any signs of nervousness or suspicious behavior until they decide to commit the act. This type of thief includes anyone who is a nonprofessional and is

not driven by the need to sell stolen goods for profit and who is not driven by peer pressure to steal (Figure 5.1).

Juvenile shoplifters are more of a nuisance than a large threat to profitability. They are usually going to target candy or a small toy while visiting the store. Preteen girls who shoplift usually choose cosmetics or

FIGURE 5.1 Shoplifting is often not a premeditated act, so shoplifters are among the most difficult to detect.

jewelry. Apprehending this type of shoplifter requires the utmost caution and knowledge of state laws. Juveniles unaccompanied by an adult become the store's responsibility if they are apprehended. The very first call should be to their parents. Having associates who are aware of prevention tactics like good customer service are the best line of defense against juveniles who attempt to shoplift.

The very best prevention method is to have associates who are alert and well trained to recognize the signs that give away a potential shoplifter. Customers who refuse assistance, demand to be left alone, or reply to friendly greetings with rudeness should raise suspicion. In these circumstances, associates are well advised to continue to pay attention to the customer. Shoplifters want to alienate employees because they do not want to be recognized. Some additional theft indicators for juveniles include the following:

- Not handling merchandise and examining it to determine quality or price
- Nervousness, paleness, dry mouth
- Looking around for associates' whereabouts to avoid being detected
- Holding up merchandise such as clothing to block view of an accomplice
- Using a cell phone to describe merchandise or receive descriptions of what to steal
- Wearing unseasonable clothing, such as a raincoat with big pockets on a hot sunny day
- Carrying large shopping bags that are either not from stores in the mall or do not have a particular store design on them.

One might think this list of behaviors is developing a profile that fits shoplifters. Shoplifters do exhibit a set of behaviors that is hard to conceal. Merchants should be focusing on shoplifters' behaviors and accompanying bodily responses to the stress or adrenaline instead of on nationality, race, gender, or social status, because focusing on the former is much safer and more accurate.

Shoplifters are generally attracted to merchandise they cannot afford if they are an amateur and merchandise they can easily sell if they are a professional. For example, an amateur shoplifter will usually take jewelry, fashion sunglasses, fashion jeans and tops, leather coats, music and video CDs, and small electronics. This list is by no means inclusive and gives an idea only of what areas of the store to watch. Professionals will target razorblades, over-the-counter painkillers, infant formula, collectables,

diabetic test strips, and expensive appliances. They are in the market for items that can be sold at a flea market or pawn shop or on an Internet auction site. The best way to know what product is being shoplifted from your store is to take periodic physical inventories and analyze the largest quantities of product groups that are showing shrinkage. Remember the old angler's adage: "We fish where the fish feed."

There are two ways to address the shoplifting problem in a retail store: (1) prevent the shoplifting from taking place by removing the opportunity and increasing the risk of getting caught; and (2) catch shoplifters in the act and prosecute them to the fullest extent of the law. Let us first examine some prevention techniques. The first prevention tactic is likely the most important: customer service provided by the associates on the floor. Shoplifters do not like to be recognized; they do not want to be warmly greeted when they enter a store. Shoplifters shy away from employees and look for uninhabited, out-of-the-way areas of the store to conceal product. Sometimes they have to move selected merchandise to one of these areas to conceal it while an accomplice looks out. The next important prevention tactic is training associates on the proper way to approach customers and what to say to let suspected shoplifters know they have been detected. For example, consider an employee who observes a customer shopping for a brown leather wallet and then sees the shopper place the billfold in his pocket. The associate could approach the suspected shoplifter and say, "May I find a gift box for that brown leather wallet you have selected?" or "May I obtain a new brown leather wallet from stock to replace the one you selected? That one was on display and may need some cleaning and conditioning." Another approach when a customer enters the store is to say, "Hello, thanks for coming in. This display was just filled in with the newest product styles so you will have the best choice. I'll be right here to assist you."

These statements include no accusations. The associates simply used a good description of the product to give the shoplifter the message that they know what was taken, right down to the color and style. The associate in this case offers assistance and service to the suspect. Most amateur and thrill-seeker shoplifters will either surrender the product or leave very quickly without taking additional product. This is not likely to work with professional thieves and organized retail crime gangs.

Associates should be trained to work the sales floor in zones if more than one shoplifter is observed; in this way, they are spread out and can see many angles of the selling floor. In a specialty store setting, it is important to not get boxed into a corner by shoplifter accomplices so that the sales

floor cannot be observed. Developing the habit of keeping our backs to the wall and heads up so we can look out across the floor demonstrates to customers that sales associates are aware of what is going on around them. This is very much a valid prevention method (though this tactic is not always possible in a department store). Associates should also be trained to know when to call for help on the sales floor. For instance, a signal for associates in the office to come to the ladies' clothing department is to announce, "Office please pick up line 4 for ladies' clothing" (when there is no line 4) over the intercom. In department stores and specialty stores where there is a trained security staff member, associates should know how to call for help when shoplifting seems imminent.

Shoplifting prevention can include the use of technology to increase the shoplifters' chance of getting caught and to make it less appealing. Electronic article surveillance (EAS) involves tagging merchandise, especially the highest price or highest theft product. When the tag crosses the pathway of sensors, an alarm sounds, alerting sales associates or loss prevention. There are two main types of EAS technology. The first is acustomagnetic, which uses a metal-filled tag detected by the sensors. Sensors can be located in pedestals adjacent to the doorway, in the floor, or in the ceiling. The second type, shown in Figure 5.2, is called radiofrequency (RF) and is activated by a small diode attached to an antenna detected by the sensors. Various companies offer this technology; the best known are Sensormatic, a subsidiary of Tyco Inc., and Checkpoint Security Systems.

It is very important to remember that these systems are only as good as the people who work in stores. I have been in stores where EAS systems were installed, and the associates abdicated the protection and control of the merchandise to the system. They forgot about their responsibility to control the product and to respond to the EAS system once it was activated, which eventually made the stores easy targets for shoplifting. When the EAS system alarms, an associate must approach customers and ask them what they think activated the system. Never accuse a customer because the system sounded. It is best to say something like, "Excuse me, ma'am, we may have left an inventory control tag on your purchase. Please come back into the store with me, and I will correct the problem." By always treating the customer courteously and moving away from the main public area it will be easier to avoid embarrassing the customer. Keep in mind that this person you are interviewing is not a shoplifter, and more likely than not there will be a legitimate reason the system alarm sounded. Pacemakers and cell phones have been known to falsely activate EAS systems. What is most important about the system is the deterrent value. It

FIGURE 5.2 Antitheft radiofrequency tag.

is acceptable if the system alarms; you want customers to know it works. One deterrent is to make a big show of testing the system by setting it off when a known shoplifter or group enters a store.

More than ever before, retailers are using camera systems that record shoplifting activity. The benefit of a camera system and recording device is that suspected shoplifters are recorded in the act, and that evidence can be removed from the recording device by burning it to a CD-ROM and handed to the police officer who responds to the store when called. Today, analog cameras and video cassette recorders (VCRs) are being replaced by internet protocol (IP) cameras, digital video recorders (DVRs), and network video recorders (NVRs). The biggest differences in the IP cameras and DVRs are the increased clarity of the pictures and the increased efficiency of using high-speed Internet lines to connect the equipment to the corporate office so a store can be viewed remotely.

99

DVRs can store any amount of data relative to their memory size, most commonly 160 to 250 gigabyte hard drives that can store from 30 to 90 days of recorded video if the cameras are set up to record only motion. DVRs and NVRs record on the hard drive and do not rely on cassettes that must be changed like in VCRs. The DVR or NVR should be equipped with a CD burner and USB ports so that quick copies can be pulled from the operating software.

The number of cameras placed in a store will vary based on the square footage of the sales floor and how many departments need to be covered. The number will also be limited by the amount of money allocated to be spent on such a project. To justify placing a camera system in a store and to obtain financing, you have to show a return on investment. This is generally done by comparing the cost of the equipment and installation expenses with what can be saved by having such a system. Can shrinkage be reduced? What can be saved in avoiding lawsuits from a slip-and-fall incident in the store? Savings can be realized by allowing operations field managers to have access to remote video where they can view a store's readiness for business, signing program, and marketing campaign. They can discuss missed sales opportunities with management, can follow up on mystery shop scores, and can count people to determine conversion rates. The field management will give the best testimonials toward building your business plan to use camera systems. All of these will contribute to return on investment.

Camera and recording systems should be overt and visible on the store sales floor. The former should be concealed in smoke or mirrored domes. The monitor that shows the video can be placed in an office out of customers' sight or out in "public view." Some retailers use these systems very effectively by allowing customers to see themselves on the public view monitor as they walk into the store, which gives the message that they are being recorded. If set up in this manner, the camera system can be an external deterrent to shoplifting. If the system is less conspicuous, then it will be more useful to provide evidence than as a deterrent to shoplifting.

Additional deterrent physical security items include the use of signs posted in the store stating that shoplifting is not tolerated and that the product is protected. Here are some ideas for sign messages:

- Shoplifters will be prosecuted to the fullest extent of the law.
- This store's merchandise is electronically protected.
- Please help keep prices low; shoplifting makes merchandise cost more.

Many businesses will have guidelines on the content of these signs. The marketing department will also provide input for the signs' design and color scheme as well as their placement.

Mirrors in the store provide another shoplifting deterrent, as they alert shoppers that they are being viewed. Sometimes convex mirrors are placed up high in corners because they give the best view of the ends of aisles and corners of the store where shoplifting concealments are likely to happen. Some retailers have office areas near the front of the store adjacent to the cash registers, some of which have glass that appears to be a mirror from the outside to customers but is a window from which people inside the office can view the sales floor. Tile-sized mirrors can also be placed on the ceiling on the sales floor over high-theft product and where shoplifters like to conceal product.

Product deprivation tags are excellent theft deterrents because they are designed to ruin the product when a shoplifter removes them after it is stolen. One example is an ink tag affixed by a pin through clothing and secured with strong magnetic bearings that grip the pin. If the tag is tampered with, it releases a bright red or yellow dye that ruins the clothing and colors exposed areas of the perpetrator's hands. Other styles of tags are made of plastic and steel clamps that close down snugly on merchandise, such as on a pair of sunglasses where the tag grips the temple. Trying to remove the tag with a screwdriver, saw, pliers, or other tools could gouge the frame and ruin the sunglasses. Both styles of tags are removed with specially formed magnets that release the magnetic bearings from gripping the pin or metal clips.

There are several vendors that research creating theft deterrent solutions for retailers. Protex International (http://www.protex-intl.com) sells security coils and tie-downs for securing leather coats and cameras and similar expensive merchandise controls. Se-Kure Controls, Inc. (http://www.se-kure.com) provides a catalog of everything from mirrored and smoke domes simulating a camera system installation to alarm wraps for expensive electronic devices and software protection. Both are reputable vendors willing to meet with security practitioners to find a solution that is right for the business.

For all the energy and deterrent devices we employ to prevent shoplifting, these will not always work and the customer may become a suspected shoplifter. State laws are written to allow an agent of a retailer to approach suspected shoplifters to recover their merchandise. Before embarking on a shoplifter apprehension program of your own, it is a good idea to consult with your legal department to determine state laws where

your stores are in operation. This is important because apprehending shoplifters is a high-risk and high-liability endeavor, and the first time an attorney calls or writes a letter objecting to how a client was treated during a detainment at a retail stores, the legal department will become our best representative. It always works more seamlessly when the in-house corporate attorneys are able to review the shoplifter apprehension policy before it goes into effect.

Speaking of policies, never implement an apprehension program without first writing a policy that every store detective will be required to follow. If store management will be empowered to apprehend shoplifters, then the policy must be published in the store policies and procedures. Whether those policies and procedures are in a book or online, they must be accessible to those charged with the responsibility of apprehending shoplifters. Policies should be detailed, clear, and concise. The apprehension policy manual will be reviewed during court cases in more than one instance by both the prosecution and defense. For this reason it is imperative that the people apprehending shoplifters in your business should be trained using the current policy.

Apprehending shoplifters is an art. It must be practiced and perfected. My experience is that store detectives or floorwalkers who are good at catching thieves have a knack for reading people's behavior. They can tell by how customers are handling the merchandise, how they are looking around, and how they are walking that they are persons to observe. Theft indicators were previously discussed; store detectives should remember that shoplifters' hands, not their faces, do the concealing. Once suspects have found the merchandise they desire to steal, their actions are what the store detective must observe. Many shoplifting investigations have gone awry because store detectives either did not see the theft or stopped observing long enough to lose sight of the shoplifter and they ditched the product. Once the suspected shoplifter ditches or gets rid of the product, they have eliminated the evidence of the crime. If a retailer apprehends a suspect and does not recover merchandise they will most likely be sued.

Associates generally must fulfill five criteria before apprehending a shoplifter:

1. The store detective must see the subject select the store's merchandise off the shelf and be able to describe it.
2. The store detective must observe the subject conceal the merchandise and know where it is concealed.

3. The store detective must maintain visual contact with the suspected shoplifter as the suspect moves through the store.
4. The store detective must follow the suspect past all points of purchase to be sure it is not paid for.
5. The store detective must apprehend the suspect just as he or she exits the outermost door of the store.

Retail companies sometimes make minor adjustments to these guidelines such as allowing an apprehension just before the suspect exits but past all points of purchase, for example in high-crime areas where it is dangerous for associates to leave the store completely. In addition, a camera system is sometimes used to observe thefts, and eye contact must be maintained by the camera operator while using a radio to communicate with detectives on the sales floor to apprehend suspects. In any event, eyewitnesses must see the store's merchandise selected off the shelf and must be sure it was not brought in by suspects. These observers must know where the product is concealed to be correct in asking for it back upon apprehension. There must be a consistent observation to ensure that the product is not dropped before it is recovered. Passing all points of purchase helps to show intent to steal because shoplifters who have been caught will likely say they were going to pay for the goods. There is a good reason to follow each of the five rules; together they help develop a strong case and help limit liability.

When store detectives have followed the rules and it is time to approach the suspected shoplifters, they should be accompanied by store management or another loss prevention associate as a witness. The approach should be calm and low key, and store detectives should verbally identify themselves as an associate of the company. They should then ask for the shoplifted merchandise back by being as descriptive and concise about how many items, color, style, and brand name. They might also explain where on the suspects the merchandise is concealed so that it is completely understood that they have been caught stealing. An example of a greeting might be, "Hello sir, I am Karl, an associate of XYZ Company, and I work in the loss prevention department. I would like to recover from your possession a blue Polo dress shirt and one pair of white Nike sneakers. The items are in the orange shopping bag in your left hand." Once the store detective recovers at least one article of the merchandise, which is now the evidence, the detective should move the situation out of the public eye by escorting the shoplifter into the loss prevention office. At that

time the rest of the product can be recovered, and a larceny report can be filled out.

Depending on the retail business's guidelines for prosecution, the authorities should be notified, and the shoplifter will be released to the police upon arrival. When juveniles are apprehended, the parents should be called right away to retrieve their child. Store detectives assume responsibility for juveniles while they are in the loss prevention office. Witnesses must be present during the detention, and no interviewing should take place until their parents arrive. In the event that a parent cannot be reached or suspects will not cooperate so they can be identified, the next phone call must be to the police. Never release a juvenile without adult supervision.

Keep in mind that to win a shoplifting case store detectives must prove intent to steal. This is in the mind of the shoplifter—they intended to deprive you of your merchandise and take it with them. However, it is impossible for store detectives to know what suspected shoplifters are thinking. To prove this you observe their actions and detain them beyond all possible points of payment. In a department store with cash registers along the front of the store, that may not be until suspects leave the store entirely. In a department store with registers in each department, that might be once they leave the department where the product is on display. Young juveniles and older senior citizens may not understand the difference between right and wrong. This makes it much harder to prove they intended to steal. Involving the authorities in those cases should fall under the advice of the legal department of your business.

Shoplifters should be detained in an office near the sales floor of the retail store. The room should have a desk and some chairs and a door for privacy. Detentions must be reasonable, businesslike, and professional. To be reasonable a detention should be between 20 minutes and 1 hour; anything beyond an hour without good reason will generally be viewed by courts as unreasonable. A businesslike detention means that the interview and recovery of all merchandise is to be done in a calm yet confident voice. No yelling, table pounding, or other shows of emotion are advisable in this circumstance. Being professional means that the level of conversation be kept positive and focused on the investigation. No bribes or bargains should be sought or discussed. Remember that everything the store detective or floorwalker does will be open to scrutiny in a court of law. Recover the merchandise, have all required reports signed, including an admission of the theft, and release shoplifters to the authorities or on their own recognizance.

All recovered merchandise is considered evidence for court. In some jurisdictions an officer will take the evidence to the police station until court. If that happens, have the police officer sign a receipt and photograph the merchandise. In most cases the store will be responsible for keeping the chain of custody of the product until court. To maintain this, the merchandise should be place in a sealed plastic bag with a tag on it with the date, time, name of shoplifter, name of store detective, and description of the contents of the bag on it. The tag with this information could be a simple 3 x 5 index card. It should then be locked up in the store's evidence locker until the trial. After trial disposition, the merchandise can then be returned to the selling floor.

One way to increase shoplifter apprehensions is to offer an associate shoplifter reward program, in which the store pays a small monetary reward or gift card reward to associates who report suspected shoplifting to store detectives and management. Store associates will occasionally see a suspect take product and conceal it but are authorized not to apprehend the person but only to report it. One risk in this reward program is that store detectives must trust associates and do not observe a theft firsthand. If the program is communicated well and there are written guidelines for a reward program, it can work well. This will heighten awareness among associates and encourage them to do the right thing if they suspect a theft. When trying to increase the number of apprehensions you should avoid setting goals or quotas for store detectives that they must meet to stay employed. This will usually come out in court if a suspected and prosecuted shoplifter pleads not guilty and goes to trial. By the same token, never encourage your associates to meet a goal for rewards that they must earn. That program must be strictly voluntary.

Store detectives, floorwalkers, and even managers make mistakes; they are only human. Many retailers refer to this as a "bad stop," which infers the error of the business. I prefer to call apprehension activities where things go wrong an "attempted apprehension." When store detectives or floorwalkers come face to face with a suspect without merchandise, they should break off all contact and discussion with the individual and return to the store office. Before walking away, the store detective should thank the customer for their time. If it becomes necessary, store detectives only apologize for the customer's inconvenience; nothing less and nothing more is recommended. State law generally gives merchants the right to stop and talk to the shopper and conduct an investigation of missing product. In those cases an inconvenience has taken place. When an attempted apprehension occurs, it becomes necessary to have

all employees involved document their recollection in a written statement and to create a file for safekeeping.

Shoplifting incidents occasionally turn into robberies when perpetrators threaten bodily harm to store associates or to a store detective while being caught. This usually involves shoplifters pulling a gun or knife and telling the associates of the store to back off. In some cases, associates have been pushed out of the way or to the ground so the robber and accomplices can grab as much merchandise as they can carry and run out the door. Some state laws consider this an act of aggression enough to move the crime from a shoplifting incident to a robbery. In all instances of a shoplifter brandishing a weapon, it is advised that the store associate or store detective comply with robbers' demands and focus on cooperation to get them to leave the store. The police department should be called as soon as it is safely possible. Some stores may have panic buttons as part of their alarm system that can be used to summon police. To deter cash robberies, a drop safe, in which cash is dropped into the safe without using combination or key to open the door, can be an effective deterrent to robbery.

Teaching your associates some basic rules if approached by a threatening individual will help to maintain their safety and avoid a hostage situation from complicating an already stressful situation:

- Remain calm.
- Comply with the demands of the robber.
- Make good mental notes about what is observed.
- Never try to follow the robber from the store location, including not running out to get a license plate (make note of what you can see from inside).
- Call police immediately upon the robber exiting the store location.
- Start to write everything down that can be recalled about what was said, what weapon was actually observed, if any, and the physical description and actions of the robber.

When police arrive, do not run out of the store to give them the scoop. Upon receiving an alarm for a robbery, the police will approach the store with extreme caution and will assume that all people are potential robbers. They will likely have shotguns trained on the store exit doors until they can observe or communicate that it is safe to enter. They will begin the investigation once they are sure there is not a robbery still in progress.

Burglaries are another external theft factor for retailers. A burglary occurs when the store is empty and involves forced entry and removal of the store's assets. Most retail companies spend money on physical alarm systems that should act as a deterrent. Do not let any vendor try to convince you that an alarm system will prevent burglaries; I have learned from experience that an alarm system sign on the door will not stop them from happening. I have experienced burglaries where the telephone line was cut to the mall or plaza, rendering the alarm useless. The majority of burglaries I have investigated involve a hit-and-run method. The burglar throws a piece of parking lot curbing through the glass door and climbs through the hole while not setting off the door contact. If the store is equipped with glass break sensors, they will pick up the intrusion and send an alarm. Once the burglar is in the store, he or she will grab as much product as possible within the time the burglar feels safe that no police response will occur. Most burglars will visit the establishment and will know exactly what they are going to take and where it is located before the burglary. They will be watching for how often the police patrol the parking lot and will have timed police response in the store's jurisdiction.

Other alarm components will help to verify the break-in such as motion detectors and electronic beams. A strobe light and loud siren would be an additional psychological factor to help rush burglars out of the store, but all of these components do little to stop a burglary in progress or aid in catching burglars. A camera system will record the burglary and document the description of the perpetrators if they are not wearing a hood or mask. Some alarm systems have video systems built in as part of the integrated system, and this is a plus. In Dallas, Texas, a city ordinance has been passed that requires video verification of a burglary before the police respond. This is a growing trend to help free up the police from responding to false alarms. The best solution to this problem is video verification, whereby the alarm company can see the burglar when the alarm activates and can send an electronic photo file right to the police officer's car.

Burglary prevention and detection are not possible with basic alarm or video surveillance techniques. A few products in development will one day stop a burglary in progress. Smoke Cloak manufactures a smoke-emitting device that will fill a 1,200 foot room with harmless, thick smoke in 20 seconds. This prevents burglars from seeing well enough to make their way through the store to grab the product. If they become disoriented, they will be trapped and subsequently caught by police. This system has been successfully installed in Europe and South America in jewelry stores, convenience stores, and drugstores. Smoke

Cannon and Bandit Solutions are similar systems. Once these companies can satisfy fire marshals, landlords, and alarm companies that their device is safe and Underwriters Laboratories compliant, they will have better luck with getting installations approved. I have been in a room in which the vendor set the Smoke Cannon off with three trays of sunglasses. A mixture of sugar glycol with water and heat emit the smoke into the room. It did not leave a residue on the sunglasses. The smoke is harmless to breathe. The room will clear in roughly 40 minutes. I believe this will be a reliable burglary defense in the future along with louder sirens and brighter strobe lights.

6

Organized Retail Crime

It is Tuesday morning at 10:05 a.m., and Hillames Department Store has just opened. George has just walked into the ladies' sportswear department to check out who is working and where they are. He is interested in ladies' designer jeans and finer leather coats and jackets. He is very concerned about price and quality. George also pays close attention to whether products have any electronic article security tags or product deprivation tags. He does not see any associates, so he leaves the department after making some mental notes about where the quality goods are located. George exits the store and goes to a white Chrysler van at the far end of the parking lot. When he enters the van, he tells the other four occupants what he observed.

Ten minutes later, George and his friends Mary, Jane, Max, and Jim head back to the department store. They leave Don, their driver, in the van. In the store the five friends go back to the ladies' sportswear department and encounter the sales associate, who is hanging blouses on a display rack near the designer jeans. Mary approaches the woman and asks her where the ladies' cocktail dresses are. The associate and Mary head off across the department to the other side of the store. George looks around for other signs of associates, while Jane and Max pull all the designer jeans they can fit into their arms off the rack and stuff them into a foil-lined bag Jim is holding open on the ground near them. George does not see anyone and signals to the group that it is all clear. They move over to the leather coat rack, and again Jane and Max take all the coats they can grab off the rack—hangers and all—and bag them.

Just then, George signals that Mary is on her way back with the sales associate. Jane, Max, and Jim carry three overstuffed garbage bags out of the department in the opposite direction from Mary. Mary and George thank the associate for her help and explain they cannot buy a dress because George forgot his wallet. They leave the department in the same direction as their accomplices who are almost at the store exit near where Don and the van are waiting.

The group hits the doors and walks quickly to the van with the stuffed bags, which they load into the back. Don drives the group down the road to the next shopping mall.

Meanwhile, at Hillames Department Store the sales associate approaches the ladies' designer jeans rack to hang some new styles that have just arrived and is shocked to find the rack approximately three quarters empty. She runs to call the store's loss prevention team to report a possible theft, still uncertain where the merchandise could have gone. She never saw Jane, Max, or Jim take out the large, foil-lined bags and fill them. She was busy with a customer and has no idea that her department had been victimized by an organized retail crime (ORC) gang. In fact, she had never heard of organized retail theft, because the store had never educated its associates about ORC.

Organized retail crime, which includes multiple organized shoplifting conducted by a group or gang, theft from trailers or distribution centers, and in some cases counterfeiting, is estimated to be a $30 billion a year problem for retailers, according to the Federal Bureau of Investigation Task Force's report on organized retail crime. The most concerning thing about this crime is that it occurs repetitively, from shopping center to shopping center, city to city, state to state. Because members of local law enforcement do not link shoplifting offenses from one shopping center or city to the next, they rarely recognize the series of crimes committed by one shoplifting gang until the thieves are long gone from the area. In addition, ORC has an alarmingly high average cost per incident. The crimes are usually in large quantities of product and large amounts of cost dollars to the companies they effect. The actors who commit these crimes are known as boosters because they boost, or lift, product out of the store. Sometimes they also use a shoplifting tool called a "booster box," which is a box (or bag) with handles that looks like it comes from one of the stores in the shopping mall or center. The bottom of the bag or box is cut out to form a trap door. The booster bag is placed quickly over an item that they intend to steal, and as shoplifters place their hand under the bag, holding the merchandise in the bag, they lift it up and carry it away.

Law enforcement and retail communities commonly refer to three levels of boosters. Level-one boosters usually work alone and boost merchandise from stores in a geographic area in which they are familiar. They may be drug addicts or people fueling a gambling addiction. Level-two boosters usually work in groups that include a lookout and a driver. They may cross state lines to other areas with malls and shopping plazas. They can belong to a loosely structured gang or organization. Third-level boosters usually work in well-structured groups with each member having specific responsibilities. These gangs travel over large areas, across states. They are affiliated with organized theft rings that move large amounts of stolen merchandise to the fencing operations.

These crimes are considered organized because they are well planned out by more than one individual, more than one individual executes them, and the stolen product is resold by fences, who resell the stolen goods and do so knowingly to make a profit for themselves or for a political group. These people are unscrupulous pawnshop owners, swap meet attendees, Internet auction sellers, and gang members who sell to people on the street. The FBI has traced some proceeds from organized retail theft to funding for terrorist activities. They have also shown that occasionally the stolen merchandise is moved out of the country to South America.

Like boosters, law enforcement and retailers assign levels to fences. A level-one fence is mostly a small-volume reseller who moves between $1,000 and $10,000 worth of stolen product per week. These people are likely to oversee level-one, -two, or -three boosters. Level-one fences recruit and train boosters and maintain communications with the higher levels of fencing operations. Level-two fences move between $10,000 and $45,000 in stolen product and purchase stolen goods from level-two and -three boosters. They are usually intermediaries in the process of placing orders with the ORC operatives for stolen merchandise that either they or a higher-level fence wants to sell. Level-two fences are often responsible for repacking and reselling bulk stolen products such as baby formula. The FBI supports that level-three fences often appear as legitimate wholesalers or distribution businesses and move anywhere from $45,000 to $1,000,000 in product a week. They often mix stolen property with legitimate products. They are the most complex fencing operations and may fund special interest criminal activity or launder money for criminal groups. They are the ORC leaders who set the pace and orders for thefts that are taking place to provide them with product. Level-three boosters at this level help make ORC so profitable for the thieves who work together to steal from retailers because they are paying a percentage of what the product is worth to the thief. For example, if a thief were stealing razorblades in bulk and the blades are in a 12-pack worth $10 per pack, the thief might shoplift 20 packs of blades worth $200 on the retail market. The fence will pay the thief roughly a third of what the product is worth, so the thief will make $70 for the 20 packages of blades he or she gives to the fence. The higher the level of fence, the more he or she will pay for the stolen merchandise.

In 2004, Cook County Sheriff police detectives interviewed an admitted booster (called Joe here to protect his identity) and thus were able to identify how a professional thinks and acts within the organization (Safeway-Walgreens, 2004). (Full credit for making such an interview possible also goes to Walgreens and Safeway grocery.) Joe was 29, and his highest level

of education was ninth grade. When asked to give his occupation, he said he was a professional shoplifter. He had begun shoplifting eight years prior and had been caught three times. The highest sentence he had received was 3 months in jail. Joe said he targeted discount department stores and pharmacies primarily. He decided this partially because he thought it was unlikely that store associates would stop him at these types of stores, and he stayed away from stores that had security at the front door. Otherwise, he was not afraid of being captured and stole freely.

Joe said he did not want to be in any store too long, and almost never had he been chased out of a store. He believed strongly in not running out of a store with product because that would attract unnecessary attention. Joe felt like video surveillance was not a deterrent and was told by his mentor that the camera domes are mostly fake and empty. Joe said he would not look at a security guard if there was one in front of the store, and most of them would not have chased him because they were all over 50 years old. Uniformed police officers did not deter him because he was not going to be there long and was not attracting attention.

Regarding locked cases, Joe said he would try to break into them; however, if he was unable to get into them within 50 seconds he moved on because he wanted to be out of the store in 4 to 5 minutes. In drugstores the mirrors in the back were useful to Joe, so he could see the entire store to tell if someone was coming. Store associates did not bother Joe because if they asked to help him, he would ask them the location of the product he was looking for. This just led him more quickly to the product he wanted to steal. When security officers followed him, Joe would make them "double take themselves." Joe said the officers did not have a criminal mind like he did and did not think on the same level that he did. Joe feels he just has a knack for picking out plainclothes security in a store. He had never been apprehended by security officers, only by Good Samaritans who saw the theft and reported it or copied down the getaway car's license plate number, leading the police to pull him over. While in the store, he also used two-way radios to communicate with his group members in the parking lot, who acted as his lookout.

Shoplifting years ago was really easy according to Joe, and now there were hundreds of boosters competing with him for the same types of merchandise: small, easy-to-conceal items that are easy to steal and in demand at flea markets and swap meets. Joe shoplifted every day. A typical day for him was to visit a few stores. He went to drugstores mostly on Saturdays and Sundays; on these days the pharmacy section was closed and he specialized in diabetic test strips, which were usually in back

near the pharmacy. He thought small electronics were not worth stealing because they were upgraded so frequently.

Joe sold his merchandise to a fence he heard about from other boosters who are mostly drug addicts. Joe said a fence would generally pay one third of the retail value of the stolen merchandise. For example, if he took $1,500 to $3,500 worth of diabetic test strips to his fence, he would get paid between $500 and $700. Joe had used the same fence for 8 years. The fence owned a grocery store with another street location not open to the public where he stored all the stolen merchandise. Joe had been in this second building and had seen product ranging from cosmetics to medication such as Tylenol and Zantac to stacks of baby formula. The fence was likely to pay out $10,000 to $15,000 in cash for $30,000 to $45,000 worth of stolen merchandise a day. Joe said a steady stream of boosters visited the store to unload stolen goods.

Electronic article surveillance (EAS) systems with tagged merchandise in the department stores did not bother Joe. He said that he usually flipped the bag of merchandise up over the pedestals and the alarm would not go off. He had a unique way of leading off with one foot to activate the automatic door opener and flipping up the bag of tagged merchandise over the height of the system so it would not set off the alarm. If it did go off, he would run. Joe was particular about the type of installed system because the whole-door systems were not as easy to get by.

Joe usually used stores' luggage or a backpack to conceal the merchandise he would steal. He had tried to quit but started stealing again when he became addicted to drugs. Joe surmised that drug addicts comprised 98% of shoplifters. Burglaries had declined because people did not keep valuables out in their homes anymore and instead had in-home safes or used bank safe deposit boxes. When asked to name any retailers with security or procedures that were so tight he just would not try anything in their stores, Joe answered, "Not really; with we shoplifters, where there is a will, there is a way."

For professional thieves there does not seem to be one extremely effective deterrent. Joe expressed in his interview that locked cabinets or locking peg hooks in the health and beauty aids department and electronic areas slowed him up the most. However, even when encountering those he still attempted gallantly to break in. He viewed store associates as just a resource to lead him to the goods. Associates who were trained to engage customers and to stick around to determine their needs and to offer genuine service could discourage a thief like Joe. Recall that Joe did not like to stay in the store very long, so he might have moved on if the associates

were more friendly and helpful than he expected. Visible security did not intimidate this professional.

Real camera systems, though not a deterrent, do provide clear evidence of the concealment and theft of store merchandise, which can then be given to the police. In addition, by using camera systems, associates would be able to recognize boosters when they return to the store so they could react faster and could shadow the boosters until they leave. Camera systems are a good backup to floorwalkers to ensure product is not dumped before the booster leaves the store. ORC task forces usually do not apprehend known theft gang members on the first offense when they are operating at a mall. The members of the task force usually follow the boosters to the vehicle and watch a number of thefts as the boosters keep returning to the same vehicle to unload the stolen merchandise. Police officers are then alerted, and they help with the arrest in the parking lot of the vehicle under surveillance when the group returns to empty the merchandise. This is the best way to impress upon law enforcement authorities that the crime involves more than one incidence of shoplifting and more than one retailer. It usually involves more than one mall and city. Local law enforcement agencies are just beginning to understand the severity and nature of these thefts.

THE EXPERT'S RESPONSE

To get the most reliable information, I had a conversation with Frank Muscato, Organized Retail Crime Investigation Supervisor for Walgreens Pharmacies and a recognized expert on ORC detection, apprehension, and education. Mr. Muscato had a full career with the Dallas Police Department in 1993, when he was working with Wal-Mart on large investigations of video cassette thefts that were being stolen by organized gangs. Wal-Mart invited Frank to help create their first ORC crime investigation unit. In 1995, Frank created the LP Legislative Team to help influence legislative efforts in all 50 states where Wal-Mart operates. In 2004, Frank left Wal-Mart to assist Walgreens in their newly created ORC Team where the pharmacy chain was experiencing increasing external theft issues.

At Walgreens, Frank is deeply involved in advising store management, investigating crimes they report, liaising with local law enforcement, and educating all involved on how to recognize and shut down ORC theft operations.

Frank explained that pharmacies and big-box retailers, including grocery stores, suffer similar thefts of razor blades, over-the-counter (OTC) drugs, health and beauty aids (HBA), fragrances, infant formula, and small electronics. Boosters find a lucrative and low-risk enterprise by traveling from store to store to steal small amounts from each and then selling the stolen property to fences, online, at flea markets, or any way they can. When boosters get caught in shopping malls targeting stores for clothing, they sometimes switch to pharmacy and grocery chains because they are mostly free-standing stores and not in a mall environment. ORC booster gangs may go back and forth depending on the needs of their fences and the ease of the thefts. Frank says that it is hard for law enforcement to realize that ORC boosters are committing large, felony crimes because the boosters will know the state law where they are operating and steal under the felony limit in each incident, therefore appearing to be minor thefts. For instance, boosters who were recently caught were found to be carrying a list of the felony limits in the states they were traveling. A booster will go into stores in Georgia (where the felony limit is $300) and steal razor blades totaling $250 to remain at the misdemeanor level. They will then travel to South Carolina, (where the limit is $1000) and steal $800 in merchandise, again to stay within the misdemeanor limit in case they get caught. In many states, if a booster gets caught with a misdemeanor violation, they may only be issued a citation to court and be released. They will then simply travel to the next store and continue boosting,

One of the most important methods in combating this type of thievery, according to Frank, is to educate law enforcement at all levels. There are roughly 975,000 law enforcement personnel in the United States, yet perhaps only 4000 of those officers know, understand, are aware, or have been trained to recognize the connectedness of ORC gang communications, offenses, and interstate travel. Retailers have become much better at communicating and cooperating to protect themselves and apprehend ORC gang members. Frank will receive calls from loss prevention supervisors at Walgreens or from his peers at other retailers to get involved in the investigations when an ORC gang has hit stores in their area. He will immediately become engaged and may contact law enforcement in the city or try to talk with the ORC booster or gang member who was apprehended. He will interview them to learn as much about the operation as possible, such as who the other members involved are and possible fence locations. Together with law enforcement they will assemble a case and attempt to prosecute everyone involved to the fullest extent of the law.

Frank says today's retailers have a much improved relationship and cooperation with law enforcement and it is increasing as retailers continue to educate and form partnerships with their local authorities. Almost every major retail chain has some type of ORC team devoted to the investigation of, and education about ORC. At some point we must and will get the upper hand in dealing with ORC theft groups.

As mentioned earlier, department, specialty, small-box, and big-box stores are favorite targets of ORC gangs. These groups are active in all of the contiguous 48 states at one time or another; three of the largest are in Southern California, Miami, and New York City. Transient theft rings travel from state to state in groups of three to ten people. There are nearly 2000 transient theft rings in existence today; three years ago, the number was closer to 1400. Inner city gangs now tend to gravitate toward this type of theft because it is more lucrative and less risky than other types of crime. Many of these actors have extensive and diverse criminal backgrounds.

Besides the transient theft rings, retailers have to focus on habitual offenders and financial crimes artists. The ORC investigation teams, similar to those described by Frank Muscato, consist of multiple members of his team, local law enforcement, and occasionally other retailers' loss prevention ORC team members. One of the key success factors of Frank's approach to ORC is a strong relationship with law enforcement in every jurisdiction in which they operate. If the police have not joined in the ORC blitz, as they are called by some of the specialty retailers, the police are on notice that investigation or "blitz" teams are working in the area and to be ready to respond.

Once they begin operating at a shopping center, the ORC blitz team is strategically positioned looking for professional shoplifting activity. One of the most reliable signs is focusing on behaviors. Transient theft gang members have a stoic expression and act very intense and businesslike; in contrast, the dynamics of customer behavior in the shopping center is light-hearted and includes laughter, flirting, and even arguing about the best buy. Observing behavior of a transient ring leads to watching the theft take place and the handing off the goods to a mule who is then followed until they empty the merchandise into a vehicle. Figure 6.1 is an example of what a booster van full of stolen merchandise would look like to law enforcement agents.

The ORC blitz team will observe three or four thefts and follow the mules back to the vehicle each time. Law enforcement is called to the parking lot and the officers witness the evidence of the thefts. This can take

FIGURE 6.1 Example of booster van full of stolen merchandise.

many hours of surveillance so that all members of the theft ring and all vehicles involved are identified. The desired outcome is to apprehend the whole transient theft ring, recover all the stolen merchandise, and secure all the vehicles involved. If an apprehension is attempted too early, the likely result will be only one booster with one booster bag of merchandise. Figure 6.2 is an example of what booster bags would look like.

The police will usually make the arrests on shopping center property since these transient theft ring members may flee police, become violent, and employ countersurveillance techniques. Boosters have been known to wear layers of clothing so, while escaping, they can change hairstyles and alter their appearance quickly, running back into the mall or stores where it is very easy to get lost in the crowds. When shopping mall's security departments are involved, it is for the added surveillance of the camera systems. This allows for more effective tracking of transient theft rings members who are very skilled at countersurveillance techniques.

The key is learning to educate law enforcement officers and trainees on apprehension of ORC theft gangs and provide instruction at state police

FIGURE 6.2 Example of booster bags.

training academies. One of the best ways retailers can contribute, even if they do not have the funding for an ORC task force or investigations unit, is with intelligence. Many stores have camera systems that record theft activity or can report thefts from their stores. There is an ORC specialty report compiled every 2 weeks of the top 25 U.S. shopping centers that are being victimized by ORC theft gangs. This report is a collaboration of 10 specialty retailers that contribute the information.

To address the ORC problem, more sophisticated retailers have begun to form their own ORC task force, headed by a senior manager or director in the loss prevention area. The task force includes one loss prevention analyst and four field regional loss prevention managers who work together to identify and investigate organized crimes committed against the specialty stores. The task force also works closely with other retailers' ORC teams to exchange information and support their efforts.

Task force leadership trains local police on how to identify counterfeits of designer products. With the help of a company's wholesale division, the task force has the ability to created product identification cards that fit neatly into police officers' notebooks to help them determine

whether merchandise in the field is counterfeit. These cards might show the defining characteristics of a purse or a pair of sunglasses.

For a few retailers these efforts have resulted in hundreds of thousands of dollars of product being confiscated in New York and on the West Coast. They have also helped to build cases for the arrests and prosecutions of people selling stolen goods.

Task force founders and leadership may also lead quarterly meetings of an ORC round table, which includes approximately 60 attendees from retailers, including Stein Mart and Walgreens Pharmacies, to law enforcement representatives, including those from the FBI, the Warren County, Ohio, Prosecutor's Office, and various police departments. Many successful apprehensions of ORC gangs in the Ohio, Indiana, and Kentucky tristate area have resulted from intelligence shared and cooperation generated during these meetings.

Another aspect of the ORC task force is the use of software to scour Internet auction sites for company products being sold in large quantities, especially after known burglaries or large ORC gang thefts. This identification of e-fences often makes it possible to trace the goods back to the thieves.

An ORC task force may also use technology such as Vigil Active, a Web auction monitoring software that automates the review of product auctions on such sites as eBay and Craigslist. This Web site monitoring software can organize analysis of all Web auctions for a business's product by using key words. By setting up search parameters using trade names or brands, it is possible to isolate and review all the auctions for any given brand on eBay. For example, searching for all auctions of Swiss Army Watches will return a listing of each Swiss Army Watch auction ranked from 25 pieces down to 5 pieces. The user sets the parameters for searches. The power of this software is the time it saves analysts in tracking down trends of large sales. Large-quantity sellers may be fences, recent recipients of burglarized product, or store employees who are removing the product to sell on the Internet. The software may also uncover counterfeited product being sold on the Web.

Another way retailers are involved in the fight against ORC is the National Retail Federation (NRF)-sponsored Joint Taskforce on Organized Retail Crime. Composed of roughly 20 of the country's top retailers from all sectors, the force is dedicated to the education of law enforcement, shared intelligence between retailers and law enforcement, and investigation of ORC.

Loss prevention professionals can take some steps to band together and impact organized retail crime by educating in these ways:

1. Educate executive management in your business about ORC and gain much needed support to develop a program to combat this crime.
2. Help store associates understand what ORC is and how the crimes are carried out. Make associates aware of your company's policies on how to react to what they see.
3. Communicate with other retailers about the existence of ORC boosters or gangs active in your area. Tip each other off when you have been affected.
4. Join and make use of the Law Enforcement Retail Partnership Network (LERPnet), a national data repository for major retail incidents and a secure Web portal for retailer and law enforcement.
5. Learn everything you can about ORC. The more loss prevention leaders learn about these crimes, the stronger we will be in the fight to lessen its impact.
6. Influence your federal, state, and local legislators to pass laws that increase the penalties and lower the dollar limits of offenses to qualify the crimes for higher penalties. Push for repeat offenses and involvement with fences to carry stiff sentencing.

7

Organized Retail Crime
An Industry Approach

As discussed in the previous chapter, organized retail crime (ORC) is a growing problem for most retailers. The National Retail Federation (NRF), an advocate agency supporting retail as a business with education and lobbying efforts, conducts surveys among its members and its 2009 Organized Retail Crime Survey revealed the following:

- More than nine out of ten retailers (92%) reported that their companies were victims of ORC during the past year, up eight percent from 2008.
- When asked about how they would rank ORC as a threat to their company on a five-point scale, nearly one-third (29%) of retailers gave organized retail crime a "four" or "five" rating, identifying the problem as severe or significant. (On average, retailers gave ORC a rating of 2.87.)
- The average retailer spends around $215,000 per year on labor costs to fight ORC.

What efforts has the retail industry made to react more effectively to organized retail crime? Professional associations such as American Society for Industrial Security (ASIS), National Retail Federation, and the Retail Industry Leaders Association have worked together to find solutions to ORC. They work to educate retail businesses, management, and loss prevention and asset protection practitioners on how retail theft gangs work. The professional associations lobby in state and local legislatures to

garner support for bills that will create and strengthen laws around organized retail crime and fencing. They also strive to increase and support liaison relationships between retail establishments and law enforcement. In the fight against ORC we will have no success unless law enforcement at all levels—local, state, and federal, including the Federal Bureau of Investigation (FBI) and the Immigration and Customs Enforcement (ICE)—work together. Raising awareness and having strong legislation are essential to impacting ORC.

The FBI estimates that retailers lose $34 billion annually to organized retail crime. I received this information from FBI Supervisory Special Agent Jerome Barker, the Cincinnati Division Criminal Enterprise Program Coordinator, in July 2006. He did a joint presentation to Cincinnati and tristate retailers and law enforcement as part of a joint effort by Walgreens Pharmacies, Stein Mart department stores, and other specialty retail companies to help create a partnership. Both sectors seemed very willing to participate.

In the previous chapter, we have discussed levels of fences and its profitability. ORC ring leaders have made frequent, large contributions to secular terrorist charity organizations such as the Holy Land Foundation and the Sulaiman Abdul Aziz Rajihi (SAAR) Foundation. These organizations are believed to funnel cash to terrorist groups such as Hamas and Hezbollah.

The retail trade business loses $64,600 every minute to ORC. Many retailers, both specialty and mass merchandise, consider themselves most unlikely targets. Consider that many specialty retail stores have started carrying high-fashion and high-retail brands like Versace, Prada, Burberry, and Dolce & Gabbana. Increases in high-fashion brands in stores correlates directly with reported thefts. Camera surveillance in some cases provides evidence for groups of four or five working together. Thus, even small specialty stores are not immune to ORC. It is rising at an alarming rate because thieves find easy access to the product and an abundance of specialty and chain stores, combined with low or no fear of punishment. This results in high profit and low risk for ORC gangs.

Organized retail crime groups are winning the battle, and law enforcement is not. However, thanks to incident reporting sites such as the Area Law Enforcement Retail Team (ALERT) and the Law Enforcement Retail Partnership Network (LERPnet), police officers are more organized and receive more information than ever before. These Web sites allow both retailers and law enforcement officials to communicate on incidents and track occurrences.

In years past, shoplifting gangs existed only in larger metropolitan areas. Antishoplifting signs, tagging, or even electronic article surveillance were the only necessary tools to keep people honest. These tactics will not work with organized thieves, as discussed in the previous chapter. Camera systems will not deter organized retail thieves, because most do not care whether they are recorded. Camera systems with a recording device will provide the necessary information and even evidence to law enforcement. They will provide photographs of perpetrators to post on Web sites for communicating with the authorities or among stores of a chain so they can look out for organized theft rings that might visit their stores.

Retailers are now initiating relationships with trade organizations such as the Joint Retail Task Force, an NRF entity whose member retailers and law enforcement agencies work together investigating organized retail theft, educating businesses, and introducing key legislation through lobbyists and members of Congress in favor of tougher laws against major thefts. This organization has worked hard to develop training courses for law enforcement on what ORC is all about and how it works. They come alongside member retailers that want help in identifying ORC and training on how to reduce it. The organization is trying to influence universities and even community colleges to prepare students for loss prevention and security management careers. For example, Eastern Michigan University now offers a degree in loss prevention management.

Those involved in retail loss prevention can be proactive by educating employees and communities about organized retail crime, providing expert testimony on legislative bills, and being a resource for state and federal authorities. For example, Target Corporation's asset prevention department has made a very smart business move and provides an extensive forensics lab for the law enforcement community in Minneapolis, Minnesota, in which evidence for some of the most serious crimes is analyzed. Not only does a program like this give back to the community, but it also enriches the relationship between the retailer and federal, state, and local authorities. Similarly, a specialty watch and accessory chain funds a forensic computer analysis lab for police to gather evidence on all types of computer crimes. In building a partnership with a cyber investigations task force by donating equipment and software in the Hamilton County area near Cincinnati, this chain will help to foster cooperation in investigating fencing operations on Internet auction sites and in fraudulent credit card schemes.

Loss prevention is about being proactive, and supporting analytical research is one way to understand the trends affecting loss prevention,

for example, by helping fund research on the National Retail Security Survey conducted by Dr. Richard Hollinger and his staff at the University of Florida's Department of Social Studies. Other studies have been carried out, but I feel like this annual survey effectively shows the trends and the most effective solutions that retailers report. Retailers, as well as myself, have contributed to this survey. We report shrinkage trends in dollars lost and causes of shrink. We report solutions such as analytical software or camera systems that help reduce loss. Over the years, the survey has had mixed participation numbers, so it is very important that retail loss prevention and asset protection leaders respond to it.

From an educational perspective, there are roughly 675,000 police officers, which includes 250,000 crime prevention officers, in the United States. Collectively, retailers employ more than 30 million people. If all those employees understood the organized retail theft problem and knew what to do if they saw an organized theft gang, the theft problem could be strongly addressed. All too often, professional shoplifters report that associates in stores will walk right by or even lead them to the product they are looking for. But because they are too busy and spread too thin to spend much time giving good customer service, engaging the customer, and it's easy to just wait until the sales associates move on to another department to assist another customer. Pay and benefits relate directly to how much they care about their job. There is a lot to be said for providing store associates with excellent pay and benefits and treating them with respect and dignity. The culture of a business certainly has an effect on whether its associates will care enough to take the time to service customers rather than just point at a product and walk away. It is up to those in loss prevention and asset protection to be the catalyst for treating associates well and inspiring the culture of integrity.

Organized retail crime has attracted the attention of law enforcement in larger markets where retail theft gangs are active. Supporting law enforcement in making sure boosters and fences are sentenced jail time is the best way for retailers to help solve this problem. Remember, if great customer service is absent, deterrent equipment or signage will have little effect on a retail theft gang. Catching and prosecuting them will affect their criminal record and possibly will get them off the street with jail time—time they will not be stealing from organizations. Two examples of companies who are doing an excellent job at engaging law enforcement at the federal and local levels are Walgreens Pharmacies and Frank Muscato, manager of its organized retail crime task force; and GAP, Inc. and Nelson Harrah, who leads its ORC mitigation efforts.

ALERT (http://www.usalert.org) successfully demonstrates a partnership between retail and law enforcement to target organized retail crime, check fraud, credit card fraud, counterfeiting, and identification theft through sharing information related to these crimes. This organization was created by the Shelby County, Tennessee, Sheriff's Office and is maintained at minimal cost to law enforcement because it is supported by subscribing retailers. Information sharing is conducted in accordance with all local, state, and federal laws as well as in compliance with all company and agency policies and procedures. Some of the information includes habitual offenders, shoplifting, internal theft, fraudulent refunds, counterfeit merchandise, counterfeit currency, check fraud, credit card fraud, and identity theft. Roughly 900 members are part of this communication reporting network.

An initiative of the federal government in support of law enforcement is the 2006 Department of Justice Reauthorization Bill. Section 1105 details the provision on organized retail theft, which requires the attorney general to establish an organized retail theft task force within the FBI. The mission of the task force is to quickly identify hot spots of ORC activity across the country and to deploy agents and resources more efficiently to apprehend and prosecute these criminals. The panel is directed to work closely with the retail community to create a national database or clearinghouse operated in the private sector to identify where organized retail crimes are being committed. Appropriations for fiscal years 2006 through 2009 for law enforcement education, training, and support were conservative in amount. The law authorizes $5 million annually for law enforcement participation and federal agent training to investigate and prosecute these crimes.

LERPnet evolved from this mandate and the partnership of the FBI with the retail community. NRF and other trade organizations joined forces to create and launch this national data repository for major ORC incidents. It has been fully operational since April 2007. Retail subscribers pay a setup fee of approximately $200 per user and $1,200 annually to belong to the network. This tool will help provide a nationwide resource and will encourage collaboration like never before and will allow law enforcement to see patterns and investigate crimes connected to other cities, counties, and states. Thousands of incidents have been reported by close to 50 retail participants coming from all sectors. Reports include organized retail theft, burglaries, robberies, counterfeiting, and auction site activity fraud.

LERPnet will provide retailers and law enforcement with information, data, and analysis tools to prevent, detect, and respond to ORC crimes. It will enable members of the retail loss prevention community to work together toward common goals. It has developed a confidential forum and secure technology platform for the exchange of information and data. It is recommended that you consult with your legal department to examine the agreement that is presented for signature upon joining. You will want to ensure that your company understands the limitations and potential liability with this tool if it is improperly used.

The Cargo Theft Prevention Act of 2005, signed in March 2006 by President George W. Bush, is also significant to fighting ORC. This law includes in it a prescription for a cargo theft database and increases the penalties for cargo theft. An example of this theft involves a trailer of Levi's jeans hijacked from a carrier and moved into storage for a month to "cool off." An FBI sting interrupted the theft scheme before the jeans could be reshipped to New York City to be sold in the garment district. Many cargo thefts occur at the manufacturer's warehouse, in cross-dock operations, at import–export storage sites, on loading docks, and from trucks moving between these sites. This law now includes cargo theft as a separate reported category in the Uniform Crime Report (UCR). The act increases the prison terms to 3 years for anyone convicted of stealing cargo with a value of less than $1,000 and to 15 years for thefts greater than $1,000.

The FBI estimates that cargo theft costs businesses between $16 and $30 billion domestically and $30 to $50 billion worldwide compared with annual losses in vehicle thefts, which are estimated at $6.3 billion a year, and jewelry thefts from jewelry firms, estimated at $111 million annually. While the cargo theft problem is spread over shipping firms, warehouse firms, and wholesalers, retailers are not immune to its effects. Every retailer relies on the shipping industry, whether related to imports coming overseas or by truck from wholesaler to their stores. If the hijacked retail merchandise is in transit from a retailer's distribution center to its stores at the time of the loss, it will be shrinkage for the stores scheduled to receive the product. The product would be in the inventory of the stores upon delivery. Even if the theft is discovered and adjustments are made to the store inventories, the overall loss will be felt by the company's bottom line.

At an organized retail crime round table held in Mason, Ohio, in 2006, representatives of the FBI's Organized Retail Crime Task Force explained some of the challenges they face in identifying ORC. What makes it difficult to determine the extent of the problem includes the manufacturer and retailer shrinkage tolerances that allow some crimes to go unreported.

They look at it as a cost of doing business. An example of this is within an Italian company where they manufacture most of what we sell. It is the Italian philosophy that product be open and available to the customer to try on and touch. This same service orientation facilitates higher theft rates, and some of that does go unreported. Other drivers of nonreporting are costs of insurance, costs of prosecution, and embarrassment. Since before this act was passed the Uniform Crime Report did not have a separate category for cargo theft, it may have been hidden as robbery, burglary, or motor vehicle theft.

One theory is that shoplifting data are grossly underreported. Supporters of this line of thought argue that some retailers apprehend shoplifters but do not prosecute. In the course of protecting stores, in situations in which organized theft gang members are apprehended and the merchandise is recovered, the gang members are released. The security agent may not recognize the perpetrators as ORC members or professionals. With no police involvement there is less of a chance that their thefts will be reported appropriately as organized retail theft.

Many law enforcement agencies do not report shoplifting for the annual UCR. If the crime is not regarded by the reporting agency as worth reporting, we are missing valuable information toward identifying the seriousness of the crime. Studies suggest that only 1 in 50 shoplifting incidents leads to the offender's apprehension or prosecution. You can see with these concerns at the federal level that retail loss prevention departments have some serious reckoning over what to do about the problems. This demonstrates why it is so important for retailers to work together and communicate about their group effort to cooperate with the authorities.

Retailers should also consider the following concerns:

- The difficulty of prosecution for some retailers and in some jurisdictions. Is the cost of prosecution worth it? Should a retailer tie up the local courts for shoplifting incidents of $100 or less?
- The trade-off for a small penalty just is not worth it, for example, out-of-state investigators who have to return on travel expenses to testify at each hearing.
- Many retailers do not have resources directed at investigation of ORC, and it goes undetected.
- Organized retail thefts are not understood by every retailer in the industry or go undiscovered. The NRF 2009 Organized Retail Crime Survey stated that "nine out of ten retailers (92%), report their companies were victims of organized retail crime during

the past year, up 8% from 2008" (Rodriguez, 2009). In this same study the respondents said they believed that 49% of executive management did not understand the complexity of the problem.

- Some thefts are attributed to internal theft incorrectly. Not having observed retail theft gang activity in their establishments, large portions of missing merchandise may be attributed to internal theft, especially if recent internal investigation activity occurred at the establishment.

Law enforcement has its own challenges, including those being prosecuted failing to show up in court. Some professional shoplifters may not have proper citizenship papers or may be fleeing from agents of the Immigration and Naturalization Service, which would weigh heavily in their decision to show up for court. Some law enforcement agencies equate thefts to petty shoplifting as opposed to criminal enterprise. Occasionally, federal resources must shift toward working terrorism cases.

Trends in legislation include increasing state felony levels to make organized retail crime less lucrative. In addition, members of Congress have recently addressed the problem on a federal level with three very recent pieces of legislation. On July 15, 2008, Representatives Brad Ellsworth of Indiana and James Jordan of Ohio introduced H.R. 6491 to amend Title 18, United States Code, to deter and punish individuals and enterprises that engage both nationally and internationally in organized crime involving theft and interstate fencing of stolen merchandise from retailers. In the Senate on August 1, 2008, the Combating Organized Retail Crime Act of 2008 was introduced by Senate Majority Whip Richard Durbin of Illinois. This bill would toughen the criminal code regarding organized retail crime by better describing offenses and capturing conduct of individuals engaged in organized retail crime. It would require the U.S. Sentencing Commission to consider relevant sentencing guidelines enhancements and physical retail marketplaces such as flea markets and online auction sites to review the accounts of sellers for suspicious activity and report it to the Department of Justice. It would also demand that high-volume sellers on the Internet display a physical address, post office box, or private mailbox registered with a commercial mail receiving agency. A third piece of legislation, the E-Fencing Enforcement Act of 2008, was introduced in early August 2008 in the House of Representatives by Bobby Scott of Virginia. The act is designed to protect online consumers from purchasing stolen and potentially dangerous merchandise. As of the time of this writing, H.R. 6491 was referred to committee and has not been acted on further.

Senate Bill 3434 also made it to committee and stalled there. In September of 2008, there was a hearing by the Judiciary Committee Sub-Committee on Crime, Terrorism, and Homeland Security and no further action was taken. Through 2009 and 2010, no further action has been taken on any of the three bills. Legislation still remains a big opportunity.

There are many other opportunities to make tougher laws for ORC criminals. We encourage retailers across North America to join the fight against this most serious crime. Research your state's progress in passing laws that make organized retail crime more severe, curb fencing at all levels, and help keep prices low for retail customers.

Many states have passed successful legislation to fight ORC. Texas passed a law making it illegal to use bogus universal product codes (UPC) labels and counterfeit receipts in the commission of a crime against a retailer. States also have addressed repeat theft offenses by making the third theft conviction a mandatory felony; however, Texas increased the felony theft level to $1,500.

Over the past 10 years, almost all state legislatures have raised the dollar value that warrants a felony offense; exceptions include Florida, Illinois, Indiana, and Vermont. Some of the recent increases in felony amounts include Alabama (from $250 to $500), Wisconsin (from $1,000 to $2,500), and Wyoming (from $500 to $1,000). Inflation is one reason for this; as prices for product increases, legislatures are increasing felony levels to keep serious crimes properly defined by prosecutors and state statutes. Penitentiaries are full, and the most serious crimes receive judicial consideration for incarcerating another inmate. By raising the felony level the legislatures are reducing the crime severity. Only Maine has reduced the dollar amount of felonies to $1,000.

The NRF is working on several areas of legislation with lobbyists to help retailers combat ORC. It should be a crime to try to defeat electronic article surveillance equipment by using foil-lined bags and in 31 states (with two additional states pending passage of legislation), merely possessing these bags is considered being in possession of criminal tools. Use of bogus receipts or UPC labels to return stolen product or to cause product to be scanned at a lower price is a crime in 25 states (again, with two additional states pending passage of legislation). Property-fencing legislation was passed in 27 states (with three additional states pending passage) to control swap meet and flea market sellers of certain types of bulk merchandise, such as razorblade cartridges or infant formula, and requires receipts for proof of where such sellers acquired the product. Only two states have laws concerning theft by Internet jurisdiction, and

two states have laws pending. The Internet is one of the easiest ways to fence product using auction sites, and fences feel safe from detection due to the amount of protection they enjoy from the owners of the auction sites. This is an area where state and federal legislators can make impact and retailers can show their support.

Legislation passed in ten states (with one state pending) targets ORC boosters by making shoplifting a felony if boosters steal from three or more retailers within a certain period of time, regardless of dollar amount. Laws addressing theft using emergency exits as a getaway have been passed in six states and are pending in two others. Credit card skimming, where organized criminals steal not the credit card but the information on the magnetic strip to use on bogus cards, is a growing problem and victims do not know they are victims until they receive their next bill. Legislation has been passed in 28 states to address this type of crime.

State laws are more frequently being passed to mandate felony status when two or more people have been caught shoplifting. When a property fence is involved, it is characterized as an organized theft. Laws like this have been enacted in Washington and Alabama. In thefts with intent to resell the product, some states have enhanced penalties for felony level. The law creates a prima facie case for intent when multiple items of the same product are stolen. For instance, 20 packages of razorblades and multiple boxes of diabetic test strips have been found on flea market tables. One admitted booster said those were among the easiest items to conceal and walk out of a drug store or discount store with. Another state law that has passed in Ohio, Kentucky, Alabama, and Missouri condones reverse stings, which allow undercover police officers to represent property as being stolen to a fence. Delaware, Massachusetts, Maryland, and Michigan currently prohibit these stings.

The year 2009 proved to be a step in the right direction for retailers and law enforcement to combat organized retail crime. Many states are deciding that their current laws are not stringent enough and therefore are passing legislation to increase penalties for those involved in ORC-related activity. These newly crafted laws allow the following:

- Prosecutors to have additional tools to prosecute
- Law enforcement to file charges more specific to the type of crime being committed
- Retail crime to be made a less desirable venue for criminals
- Awareness for this growing epidemic

What follows is a brief recap of some of the states that took a stand against ORC in 2009 by either creating entirely new legislation or amending portions of their existing statutes to better accommodate ORC:

- Arizona-SB 1059: Arizona amended Sections 13-1501 and 13-1805 of their existing statute. Title 13, Chapter 18, Arizona Revised Statutes was amended to included Section 13-1819 to read Organized Retail Theft, Classification, which defines the act of ORC. ORC also became a class 4 felony.
- Kentucky-HB 369: Kentucky amended its organized crime law to address organized retail theft. It heightened the penalties for those who engage in ORC to be charged with a class C felony if the persons are acting as part of a criminal syndicate.
- Ohio-SB 320: Ohio revised their existing Racketeer Influenced and Corrupt Organizations statute, better known as the state RICO statute, to add ORC as a predicate offense. This particular piece of legislation was remarkably clever because it allowed for the aggregation of offenses that did not necessarily meet individual incident felony dollar levels but did occur within a certain time frame.

When state RICO statutes are revised to include ORC and when those engaging in ORC-related activity are prosecuted, the state or presiding jurisdiction is allowed to reap all the benefits afforded by the original statute. Therefore, criminal forfeiture, civil action, and civil penalties are some of the benefits for prosecuting under the new statutes. With the states marching forward on their quest to minimize ORC, we did not want to fall short federally. The reintroduction of three very important bills was also completed in 2009:

- Federal pending legislation for 2009 includes H.R. 1166: The E-Fencing Enforcement Act of 2009 deals with e-fencing or reselling stolen goods on the Internet.
- H.R. 1173: The Organized Retail Crime Act of 2009 is a comprehensive solution to ORC and the resale of stolen or illegally obtained merchandise through Internet auction sites, flea markets, pawn shops, swap meets, and illegitimate storefronts.
- S. 470: The Combating Organized Retail Crime Act of 2009 enhances sentencing guidelines, requires market places to file documentation with the attorney general for suspicious activity, and revokes seller accounts for selling illegally obtained goods.

131

These pieces of legislation were crafted and introduced because of partnerships among retailers, law enforcement, prosecutors, and retail associations.

Title 18, Section 1030 of the U.S. Code is a law addressing persons accessing networks and government databases without permission. It is tied to ORC in the protection of consumer data, which is present on all credit card magnetic strips. It also protects databases such as the National Retail Federation, Department of Justice, consumers' unions, and financial services by making it a crime to look for personal identity information on their databases. The bill is in the House Judiciary Subcommittee on crime, terrorism, and homeland security. This bill creates enhanced penalties for crimes committed via a computer. It establishes violations as a RICO predicate. ORC and E-fencing are on the radar screen of judiciary members and staff.

In mid 2006 a specialty retail chain created an organized retail crime task force, led by a former police detective (whom we will call Spike Kessel) specializing in cyber crimes. One of the first things he did was organize a group of retailers, namely, Stein Mart, Walgreens Pharmacies, and one bank in an effort to meet with the FBI, local law enforcement, county prosecutor's office, and the Secret Service. The meeting was attended by more than 150 participants from these offices. Communication and education are the most effective tools a retailer can use to affect organized retail crime. Today, Kessel's team has impacted more than 23 individuals for prosecution or indictments for over $250,000 in product. That is a great start, but there is more to do.

In June 2008, Millie Kresevich testified before the Ohio State House of Representatives legislative hearing in anticipation of Ohio lawmakers sponsoring a bill regarding ORC penalty enhancements and protections for consumers. She explained a three-step process (see Figure 7.1):

- Step 1: Preparation of the testimony involving the following steps:
 - Attend a hearing first to see what it is all about and to understand the order of the proceedings and how testimony is introduced.
 - Develop a partnership with law enforcement; you need good law enforcement representation with you at the table. Know law enforcement's exact position on the issues. If willing, ask law enforcement to provide letters of support to be presented during the proponent testimony.
 - Read the state's current legislation first—what are the main reasons you need new legislation or an amendment to the

Three-Step Process to Testifying on LP Issues at a Legislative Hearing

Step 1- Preparation

- Attend a hearing first to see what it is all about and to understand the order of things.

- Partner with Law Enforcement; you need solid law enforcement representation with you at the table. Know law enforcement's exact position on the issues. Ask law enforcement to provide letters of support to be presented during the proponent testimony.

- Read the state's current legislation first – what are the main reasons you need new legislation or an amendment to the existing law? If amending, does the added verbiage regarding the proposed legislation coincide with the existing verbiage for the current law? Does the proposed legislation enhance the existing law or create new elements that must be proven, making it more specific, but also more difficult to prosecute. If so, change wording to secure easier buy-in.

- Know how to address the audience. There are specific appropriate ways to address the members of the House, Senate, and Chairman.

- Know your co-presenters. Understand how their testimony will flow. Obtain a copy of the written testimony from co-presenters prior to testifying and review. If providing statistical information, ensure that everyone providing testimony is giving the same numbers.

- Are you being duplicative of others' testimony, or are you each taking an issue? Discuss topic distribution, but be ready to speak on all areas. Don't allow the testimony to be geared toward one specific type of business. Allow the approach to be a global perspective of unified retailers.

- Prepare answers to the questions likely to be asked. Know your issues' pitfalls. Partner with your retail association because they are the experts.

- Know your opposition. If possible, attempt to retrieve written documentation regarding the opposition's point of view. Conduct research geared toward refuting the opposition's stance on the topic. This is where the biggest obstacle will be; therefore, careful preparation and accurate information are a must. Know the entities and their arguments.

Step 2- Presentation

- Written testimony is usually required prior to the verbal portion of the hearing. Search the Internet for existing testimony to see how the document should flow. If speaking on behalf of your organization (for example, by using company letterhead) run it by your legal department prior to submission. Allow enough time for changes to be made if necessary.

- Use examples, but also speak globally for all retailers. Be careful about overdoing the war stories. One specific example is sufficient enough to get the point across.

- Speak slowly and clearly, but with passion and conviction – you need to engage your audience and get them to care as much as you do about the issues. Avoid terms specific to LP that others may not understand.

Step 3- Understanding the Prosecutorial Perspective

Ask yourself questions such as:

- What do your state prosecutors think of the proposed legislation?

- Did you get their buy-in first?

- Will they use it if made into law?

- Are there objections?

- If there are objections, is it the entire community or just one individual? Attempt to find someone within the prosecutor community that you may be able to get on board.

- Be prepared to answer objections with relevant information.

- If successful, ask this individual to (a) write a letter indicating support, and (b) testify as a proponent for the legislation.

 - Speak with a filing prosecutor or one in the training division.

 - Provide evidence from other states that have successfully prosecuted under similar legislation.

Figure 7.1 Three-step process to testifying at a legislative hearing. (© 2008 Millie Kresevich & Julie Viljoen.)

existing law? If amending, does the added verbiage regarding the proposed legislation coincide with the existing verbiage for the current law? Does the proposed legislation enhance the existing law or create new elements that must be proven, making it more specific but also more difficult to prosecute? Change wording to ensure an easy endorsement of your views.

- Know how to address the audience. There are specific ways to address the members of the House, Senate, and chair.
- Know your copresenters and who else will be at the table. Understand how their testimony will flow. Obtain a copy of the written testimony from copresenters prior to testifying and review. If providing statistical information, ensure that everyone providing testimony is giving the same numbers.
- Are you being duplicative of others' testimony, or are you each taking an issue? Discuss topic distribution, but be ready to speak on all areas. Do not allow the testimony to be geared toward one specific type of business. Allow the approach to be a global perspective of unified retailers.
- Prepare answers to the questions likely to be asked. Know your issues' pitfalls.
- Partner with your retail association because they are the experts.
- Know your opposition. If possible, attempt to retrieve written documentation regarding the opposition's point of view. Conduct research geared toward refuting the opposition's stance on the topic. This is where the biggest obstacle will be; therefore, careful preparation and accurate information are a must. Know the entities and their arguments.
- Step 2: The presentation:
 - Written testimony is usually required prior to the verbal portion of the hearing. Search the Internet for existing testimony to see how the document should flow. If speaking on behalf of your organization (by using the letterhead on the written testimony), run it by your legal department prior to submission. Allow enough time for changes to be made if necessary.
 - Use examples, but also speak globally for all retailers. Be careful about overdoing the war stories. One specific example is sufficient enough to get the point across.

- Speak slowly and clearly, but with passion and conviction— you need to engage your audience and get them to care as much as you do about the issues. Avoid terms specific to loss prevention that others may not understand.
- Step 3: Understanding the prosecutorial perspective (if criminal law proposal) and ask yourself questions such as:
 - What do your state prosecutors think of the proposed legislation?
 - Did you get their buy-in first?
 - Will they use it if made into law?
 - Are there objections?
 - If there are objections, is it the entire community or just one individual? Attempt to find someone within the prosecution community that you may be able to get on board.
 - Be prepared to answer their objections with relevant information.
 - If successful, ask this individual to (a) write a letter indicating support and (b) testify as a proponent for the legislation.
 - Speak with a filing prosecutor or one in the training division.
 - Provide evidence from other states that have successfully prosecuted under similar legislation you are trying to pass.

This chapter has dealt with the responses of business, law enforcement, and legislative initiatives to dealing with ORC. While there are many approaches to dealing with this crime, there are almost as many obstacles to be worked out by both retail businesses and law enforcement agencies. Retail loss prevention practitioners should also be activists in educating, collaborating, and even pushing for legislation. This approach has not been the norm in loss prevention departments and must not be left for three or four retail trade associations to take on alone. We must all be involved and engaged in this fight.

8

Operational Causes of Loss and Awareness

OPERATIONAL ERRORS DEFINED

When I was a loss prevention manager trainee at a regional mass merchandise discounter named Hills Department Stores, training on the causes of operational inefficiencies was an important part of understanding shrinkage reduction. As a review of what constitutes shrinkage in a retail store environment, we must first look at how to determine a shrinkage figure. Shrinkage is defined as the difference between the physical inventory of the store and what is on the books at the time that inventory is taken. If there is less merchandise on the physical inventory than the book accounting of the store, then it is indeed shrinkage. However, if there is more merchandise than the book accounts for, then an overage has occurred. Most companies set goals at having zero shrinkage and zero overage.

While the term *overage* may sound less damaging than *shrinkage*, large overages are just as problematic. If one retail store is over in inventory, more than likely another is short the same amount, or the distribution center is feeling the shrink because of paperwork errors in a transfer. Another adverse effect of overages involves the bounce-back effect. That is, the very next physical inventory count will result in shrinkage of the same amount as the inventory evens up. An example of this would be an improper count of merchandise at 600 units instead of 300 units in one

physical inventory, making it appear that more of the product was on the shelf when in fact it was not. From an accounting standpoint, headquarters adjusts the books from 300 to 600. On the very next inventory count this same store tallies 300 units again when the books say 300. This will result in a bounce-back shrinkage. Now, these numbers are illustrative, but in real life that 300 on hand would fluctuate by received goods, sales, returned goods, and transfers. The point is that the model stock count would be influenced by that incorrect inventory causing the overage.

Operational inefficiencies can contribute to both shrinkage and overage. Two of the other three causes of discrepancies in the inventory— external theft and internal theft—will cause shrinkage almost exclusively. Vendor issues have a potential to cause overage but usually result in shrinkage. Vendor issues usually involve outright theft from the store during a visit or billing for more merchandise than is actually received in the store, resulting in shrinkage.

THE IMPORTANCE OF IN-STORE OPERATIONAL AUDITING

Operational inefficiencies or errors can happen in the receiving of merchandise, price changes, improper tagging, inventory adjustments, and damages. Operational errors are the easiest cause of shrinkage to remedy. They are entirely controllable with a strong program of associate awareness and auditing. Training at store level and by field managers who visit the stores will round out the program to ensure that errors are avoided; to the extent that they do occur, they will be caught early with a good audit program before they amount to much. This type of auditing for operational errors should be done at store level in a retail environment where stores are large enough to support a loss prevention manager at store level. If the store does not have a loss prevention staff, store managers can take on some of the responsibility. This type of auditing is not the same as operational and loss prevention audits completed, as discussed in the next chapter. In-store auditing is an excellent strategy to help high shrinkage stores to reduce and correct operational errors at the store before they contribute to shrinkage.

The internal auditor is generally charged with detecting deficiencies and reporting them. In loss prevention, the auditing function is responsible for detecting deficiencies and correcting them. The ultimate goal of

this type of auditing is to ensure the profitability of the business. Creating awareness by training associates in the store when errors are discovered and corrected will help associates understand the right policies and procedures. It will make them aware that someone is checking their work. Communications are improved within the store when these errors are reported to management. It is important to consider quality of the audits as much as quantities performed; however, a consistency of repeated and expected audits must exist. Consider the dam effect when conducting audits: concentrate efforts in problem areas. Plug the hole in the dam where the largest amounts of profit dollars are flowing out of the lake so you are not drowning in shrinkage while plugging an insignificant hole.

Here are some theories to consider when analyzing shrinkage results and in-store audit results that will help determine what action to take for improvement of the overall program addressing operational errors. If you have high shrinkage and high operational error detection, it may be a sign of poor or improper training taking place in that store: loss prevention awareness is down, and error correction is not occurring. If you have high shrinkage and low operational error detection, look for no awareness, unreported errors when found by associates, and a lack of follow-up on basic programs in the store. Low shrinkage and high operational error detection indicate that there is loss prevention awareness to report errors and no individual follow-up by management. Training is adequate, but management is not getting to the root of problems. Low shrinkage and low recovery of operational errors are the goal. When a store is running at optimum, there are a lot of awareness, frequent and efficient training of associates, peer pressure to do the right thing, and following of policies, procedures, and programs of the company.

CORRECTING THE PROBLEMS

Receiving errors are made when merchandise is improperly accepted or missing altogether from the store. A two-tier approach should be implemented in these cases. First, incoming shipments to the store should be tracked on a Shipment Receiving Log (Figure 8.1), where the receiving manager logs the date and distribution number, number of cases of product, and whether the shipment is split or complete. A split shipment means that two of four boxes arrived on Tuesday and the other two boxes are expected later in the week. If the store point-of-sale (POS) system gives information as to product in transit, the store may be able to reconcile right

MERCHANDISE RECEIPT LOG

(Make additional copies when needed)

Store Number _____

Store Name _____

DISTRIBUTION NUMBER			CLOSED LOOP MATCH		MISSING DC SHIPMENT FOLLOW-UP					
					Received inventory but not on closed loop report.		On closed loop report but never received.			
From Shipping Label	Number of Boxes Rec'd	Date Rec'd	On Report Y/N	Date of Closed Loop Report	Date Contacted Inventory Control	Explanation	Distribution Number	Date Contacted Inventory Control	Explanation	

Figure 8.1 Example of a log to track receipt of shipments.

then that the correct number of boxes was received. If not, the shipment receiving log will be used to reconcile shipments against a "Closed Loop" report that is received monthly and reports shipments for the month.

When receiving associates accept the boxes of product from the delivery person, they should always check that the boxes are addressed to the correct store location. I cannot tell you how often I have heard that one store location in a shopping mall got product from another location, and the product is most often not reported, so it is not added to inventory. It is also very important that receiving associates check the integrity of the shipping carton for damaged sides or corners where tiny holes in the box could be used to remove small pieces of merchandise. The carton should be sealed with original tape and not resealed, as any resealing could point to a theft problem while in transit. Associates should be trained that any discrepancies in the condition of the box or number of cartons received should be reported to the inventory control department at headquarters.

Few companies conduct detail counts of every item in the received cartons because of the strain that it places on productivity of management and sales associates in a retail establishment. If a trailer full of product to a department store arrives, the product is placed in stock on the sales floor or back-stocked within 24 hours of receipt. Practical experience shows that if product shipments are audited before leaving the distribution or manufacturing center by the responsible loss prevention staff and audit proficiencies exceed 90%, there will be little adverse effect on inventory results. Where shrinkage occurs is in the carelessness when store management does not log shipments or does not recognize a weekly shipment was missed and went unreported. Figure 8.2 is an example of using scanning a bar code to check-in a shipment box.

Mass merchandise department stores and specialty retailers that have embraced radiofrequency information devices (RFIDs) may benefit from having sensors at the receiving dock door that automatically scan the cartons of product that pass through the door and instantaneously account for all product received. The RFID system would then communicate with the POS system and update the stock status for the store's inventory. This system would eliminate the need for manual shipment logs and individual inspection of cartons. There are variations of RFID that involve labeling case packs with intelligent tags rather than each individual piece of merchandise. Case pack labeling would still be a more accurate way to control shipment receiving than the manual log because of the elimination of human error.

FIGURE 8.2 Example of scanning a bar code to check-in a shipment box.

Detailed receiving of product—if that is the preferred process—involves opening every carton and using shipping documents enclosed by the shipping distribution center of all product by stock-keeping unit (SKU), description, and retail price. Errors in quantity or product style can be documented on the shipping documents or in an audit log by the auditing associate. In either case the documentation should immediately be used to request adjustments for the shipment.

Price changes are a fact of life for just about every retailer in business, as merchandise becomes aged or shopworn. Price changes involve the adjustment to the new retail in the POS system and book inventory for the retail store. Most total retail solution accounting systems, such as Oracle and SAP, allow both systems to be adjusted simultaneously from the head-quarters on a SKU-by-SKU basis. If price changes are taken on store-level documents, those documents should be compared with the quantity, SKU, description, and retail of the actual merchandise quantity, SKU, and retail to ensure that everything matches. Audit personnel should follow behind store department associates to audit their work. Price-change audits should be documented in a paper or electronic log. Data entry of the actual price change should be audited, as errors can amount to thousands of dollars if entered into the computer incorrectly. Consider a price decrease of 100

pairs of sunglasses from a retail of $250 to $210, a retail difference of $40. If when the data is entered one zero of the quantity is left off, the resultant error would be a shortage of $3,600. Thus, 10 pairs of sunglasses are adjusted at inventory to a retail of $40 less, and 90 pairs are not adjusted the $40 and are expected to sell at the previous retail of $250. As each of the 90 pairs sells, the store would lose $40. By doing price-change audits, loss prevention can help ensure the integrity of the prices of the merchandise. When errors are found and corrected before the sales take place, operational errors are eliminated from causing the store inventory shrinkage.

Product recalls occur when the merchandise becomes outdated or headquarters decides that it should be pulled back and redistributed to outlets or stores in other parts of the country. Another cause of product recalls involves safety issues with the public interest at heart. The process for a recall differs in these scenarios, but the need for auditing and verifications remains important in each. In a doctor of optometry's office there are contact lenses and soaking solutions for sale. Because these products fall within the oversight of the U.S. Food and Drug Administration and are use medicinally, they have expiration dates. When the product expires it must be pulled from the display shelf and active use. The product is stored away until a recall from the corporate office is issued, and the expired product is then sent to a warehouse for destruction and disposal.

Now assume that the doctor's office has done its part and has pulled expired product and has locked it away until a recall was issued authorizing the product to be sent in. Also assume that the corporate office recognized its responsibility to recall all expired product quarterly and issued product recall documents to the office. Office associates will pull the product and either match it by item number or SKU to the recall sheet and enter a quantity. If the product is not well controlled by the inventory system, recall forms might have to be printed manually and the SKU and quantity of each unit written in manually. The associates would then box up the expired merchandise and place a copy of the completed recall documents with store number, product list, and management's signature on the document into the box. This will act as a packing list, even if the warehouse or corporate office gets an electronic copy of the recall for inventory-keeping purposes. The associates are responsible for placing an accurate address of the warehouse on the box and taping it securely closed. The shipment is now moved to the shipping area to be sent out on common carrier.

The audit process for product recalls should include examining the prepared shipment for signs of tampering, such as cut tape where access was gained to the box. The address on the outside of the box must be to

the company facility where the recall is to be sent for processing. Compare address destinations with those of associates in the store. The recall should be opened by the auditor and the recall authorization checked to make sure it is filled in correctly and completely with quantities that are to be recalled. The audit involves verification of the number of each style and individual included in the box. Errors in quantity claimed on the recall authorization will result in a loss to the store if there are fewer units in the box than are represented on the recall authorization.

Some department stores miss a recall altogether. The store does not pull the product indicated on the recall, so it is sent to the distribution point. When the next physical inventory is taken, that product missed on the recall may show up as shrink because the product is removed from the store's inventory model stock once the recall is closed. The product neither gets removed from physical inventory through the recall nor is recognized as valid inventory for that store.

In 2008 an economic recession affected many industries including banking, real estate, fuel, auto, and retail. At least three retail department store chains—Sears, K-Mart, and Walmart—considered resurrecting their layaway departments to entice customers to shop with them and be able to pay off their selections without incurring the high interest rates of credit cards. Layaway departments usually hold merchandise for the customer with a deposit down and their agreement to pay off the merchandise on layaway by the date due to pick it up. Some retailers charge a nominal fee to use this service. My recommendation based on real-life experiences is to avoid having a layaway department altogether. I have been involved in acquisitions of companies that offered layaway services and were holding million dollar outstanding balances where the merchandise was missing, supposedly picked up by the customers when final balances were not paid. You can be assured that if the remaining balance is not paid in full once the merchandise is picked up, the retailer is much less likely to collect that balance as time goes by.

Company operations will ultimately make the decision to support layaway, even at a risk of loss, because it keeps the loyal customers returning. Causes of operational errors resulting in a loss of merchandise and consequently shrinkage for the company involve associates not collecting the final balance and improperly storing away unrecorded merchandise and recording the wrong price. Additional considerations of internal theft may contribute to unreconciled journal entries with no merchandise in stock. The same auditing program can be used both to determine operational errors and to detect dishonesty.

The auditor should plan to conduct cross-referencing audits on a percentage of the actual product in storage. Start with customer records in the layaway department that show the date the layaway is due to be picked up and the balance due. There should also be a breakdown of all the merchandise in the package for the customer. Randomly pull layaway customer records and look for the merchandise to be in storage. Pull the merchandise boxes, unseal them, and audit item for item what is in the box against what was recorded on the layaway transaction. Be sure to record the last name of the customer, layaway account number, and balance due in either a manual audit log or on a computer. The next audit would involve pulling layaway merchandise boxes and tracing them back to the customer record. Looking for appropriate balances on the record and comparing what was rung up with what is in the box are the main audit functions in this exercise. Errors in ringing up the product will show up as long as it is checked in detail. A third check would involve looking for customer records that have not had payment activity for weeks or have never had a payment. A search for those boxes may turn up dishonest associates.

Allowing associates to hold merchandise for customers to purchase at a later hour or even later date is very risky and should be avoided if possible. If it cannot be avoided, a POS list of hold product should be maintained and checked frequently against the date the hold is due to be picked up and paid for. Hold merchandise is more likely to lend itself to internal theft rather than operational inefficiencies. The most effective control for hold merchandise—if it is unavoidable to have holds—is to limit the time frame that merchandise is kept off the selling floor and in hold storage. Merchandise held off the sales floor cannot be purchased by customers. Retailers lose thousands of dollars by associates retrieving the merchandise on hold and giving it to the customer while forgetting to ring it into the POS system and to collect payment from the customer. A last concern for holding merchandise is that it becomes a staging area for dishonesty. Store associates can set up merchandise they want as though they will pick it up on pay day and leave it until it is forgotten. Dishonest associates will watch it to see if management notices the lateness of the due date and, when fairly sure no one is paying attention, they will remove it from the store without paying for it. This is easiest when taken as they are leaving for the evening or by passing it off to a friend who visits during the day.

145

THE VALUE OF STORE INSPECTIONS

In the 1980s a retailer repeated the phrase, "What goes uninspected deteriorates." I find that to be true even today in our high-technology business environments. Those inspections just might look a little different when we use Internet protocol (IP) cameras connected to a network video recorder (NVR) sending video back to our office desktop of any store we want to pull up. If we are not fortunate to have camera systems in each store, then inspecting the old-fashioned way, by walking around and visiting each of the departments of the store, will do. The value of inspections is fourfold: (1) developing associates; (2) improving morale; (3) improving communications; and (4) improving performance. Associates are motivated because they are being taught standards as you inspect a log book, examine their display work, or explain how to sell a product properly. Consistency develops throughout the store. Morale improves when associates have direct contact with the leadership. Relationships strengthen when employees see managers who will not ask them to do something that they would not do themselves. Managers can follow up on delegated tasks only when they get out onto the sales floor to check on a project. Things now get done that did not before. Communication improves as people understand what is expected of them. Decision making is easier when managers see firsthand what is going on in the departments. Training improves. Overall performance improves because managers have to spend less time putting out fires. Discipline improves with inspections when policy violations have occurred or operational errors have been committed. Proper documentation allows for better performance evaluations.

VALUE AWARENESS FOR EMPLOYEES

Included in this discussion are the retail store cash registers, referred to as the POS system, although some customers of a store will attempt to remove product by deceiving the cashier, which by its nature fits in with external theft. However, this type of deception can be avoided entirely by training cashiers on complete value awareness, which is nothing more complex than helping your cashiers realize the value of the product they are recording in the register for the customer. Cashiers are retailers' last defense to ensure the full value of the product is paid to them. Value awareness training can be conducted in group meetings with cashiers over three or four 15-minute meetings before the store opens each morning or

as one large presentation at a storewide meeting. While it is unproductive hours paid to cashiering staff, it is well worth the return on investment if the store saves a few thousand dollars a week in corrected sales.

Consider this example of value awareness at work to understand what the benefits are. Mary is a cashier in a department store, and she is approached by a man and woman in their thirties with two children and a cart full of store merchandise to be checked out. They look innocent enough—your typical family buying some basic home goods and toys. The first item Mary scans is a hamper for $24.95, followed by a package of hangers for $7.88, a thermos for $4.99, and two handheld games from toys for the kids at $3.95 each. The total comes to $45.72 plus tax, right? Well, not quite, because while the family of four leaves the store with purchases, so does another $1,200 that was not rung into the POS system or paid for. Mary never opened the hamper box to look inside, even though it was obviously taped over like it had been previously opened. She missed eight pairs of ladies' jeans worth $207.92, two leather jackets worth $300, five sweatshirts worth $200, and two ladies' dresses worth $350. Because she never lifted the hamper box from the cart, Mary could not tell that it was loaded with additional product. Mary also just scanned the thermos without opening it to look inside. If she had, she would have found $142.08 worth of ladies' costume jewelry and scarves. By weight this additional product would have been very hard to detect by lifting it. Mary had to be taught to make the necessary verifications. This family of four might very well be innocent and are in for a big surprise when they get home and discover the additional product in these two containers. This hamper box and thermos could very well have been loaded up by professional thieves and left on the shelf for the mule to come in and remove. Our unsuspecting family came along meanwhile and picked up the planted boxes not realizing the hamper they wanted was left on the shelf, almost as if it were the display item. If the family were actually involved in a theft, without our cashier being well trained at value awareness, the store would suffer the loss unless a store detective witnessed the family filling the box and thermos with the extra merchandise.

In loss prevention our philosophy encourages the use of prevention techniques to save profit dollars and not to rely on the chance the store detective staff will catch the potential loss. All associates of a retail business must be prevention minded to safeguard the profitability of that business. To that end, it is necessary to cover all the bases when teaching value awareness to cash register staff, including having a basic knowledge of how much things retail for, what items can be concealed in what

items, and the importance of opening and searching merchandise containers. Cashiers should know that a ladies' leather coat is going to be in the price range of $99.00 to $325.00 and not $19.95. They should know that a microwave oven is more likely $85.00 to $239.00 and not $12.99. Customers will change price tags on product of value if the store's tags are not self-destructing when removed from the product to which they are affixed. Even the type of ticket used is a prevention tactic. Many retail chains have now upgraded to scanning the universal product code (UPC) on merchandise and do not rely on price tickets. They concentrate on ensuring that the shelf signage is accurate to reflect what the bar code will scan. Discount retailers are more likely to have adhesive tickets on the product, and those tickets must be scored so they do not peel off in one piece. The adhesive should be tested to make sure it is strong. The same goes for clothing tags, which should be affixed with a plastic "swift attacher" threaded right into the clothing and through the ticket hole. Again, that tag should show signs of being removed if someone tries to remove it.

Here is an outline of what we used at Hills Department Stores, a discount department store chain, to teach value awareness risks to all associates. All associates were trained because they were all cross-trained to work in the register areas at peak business hours and rush hours:

PREVENTION OF LOSSES AT THE POINT OF SALE

- Management trainer explains the types of losses to be prevented at the point of sale.
- Review and explain codes A thru E of the value awareness program.
- Tour the store sales floor with groups of not more than 10 associates following the outline of department and items listed in the value awareness program.
- Review the procedures to be used in dealing with problems found at the point of sale as outlined in the value awareness program.
- Ask for and answer any questions for the benefit of the group.
- The value awareness program is designed to help you, the cashier, in detecting and preventing losses. Theft by deception (switching tickets) and concealing merchandise are two methods of dishonesty that are increasing at an alarming rate. Our best protection against losses at the registers is well-trained and alert cashiers.
- To help you become aware of how to prevent losses at the registers, we are going to tour the store and discuss the following types of potential losses.
- Note: The following examples A through E, referred to as codes will identify situations to be explained to you as we tour the store by department and item.

Code A: Higher-priced items where the ticket has been switched with a lower-priced ticket.

Example: $79.97 chainsaw switched to $9.97
$254.97 snow blower switched to $24.97
Code B: Merchandise used to conceal other merchandise inside.
Example: Duffle bags may have four pair of socks in them
Lunch pails and thermos bottles for concealed jewelry and merchandise
Code C: Cartons used to conceal merchandise inside.
Example: Aquarium box emptied and filled with clothing
Toy storage chest filled with toys
Hamper boxes to look for concealed clothing and other product
Code D: Trading expensive merchandise with less expensive merchandise by switching the containers.
Example: Trading a $69.99 bottle of cologne with a $9.99 bottle of cologne by switching boxes.
Placing a $39.97 full leather football into a $19.99 rubber football box.
Code E: Switching sizes or items in merchandise sold as sets.
Example: Fishing rod and reel combinations by placing an expensive reel with an inexpensive rod.

- After review of the codes, management leads the tour pointing out potential risks in each department, identifying the code that pertains, and letting associates know the real value of the items. At the end of the tour the manager answers any questions that come up. The manager would explain that if cashiers observe a problem they should contact the appropriate departmental personnel for review. Once the problem is verified and correct value established, we would offer to sell the merchandise to the customer at the correct price or in the correct container.
- Never accuse customers of switching tickets or concealing merchandise because they may have found an item on the shelf in that condition and not realize it has been altered. Our primary goal is to be aware of and spot the problems to prevent losses at the point of sale. When associates caught any of the previously given codes and got them corrected, they were given a small cash award in their next paycheck. This is an excellent way to get the awareness of your cashiering staff to be at its best. The small cash award for preventing losses at the registers is a small price to pay for big dollars saved from rolling out the front door. While this method of operational training was used in the 1980s and '90s, the idea is still very valid. Today a virtual tour of the store can be communicated on large screens on a high-speed, computerized training system to get the same effect.

Operations and loss prevention training are the responsibility of the loss prevention practitioner because we have the best understanding of how these areas work together. In the retail environment almost all operational functions have risks associated with them that need to be considered. For example, if I am training an office worker to count daily receipts, I would show how to keep the coin and cash separated, how to use the bill-counting machine properly, and how to fill out deposit

slips. I would also explain that if the counting room or office was not locked and had traffic moving through it, the risk of losing cash would be very real. I would also state the importance of keeping the receipts in full view and locking deposits in the safe to avoid the risk of theft. Another example is training the opening manager to unlock the store, turn off the alarm system, and turn on some lights. Take that a step further, though, to searching maintenance workers before they leave after working all night for any hidden merchandise in their lunch box, and keep the store front locked so unwanted visitors do not remove product before the store opens for business. Loss prevention policies can be combined with just about every operational function, so it is worthwhile for loss prevention practitioners to take loss prevention training seriously and to use it to their advantage.

9

Developing an Effective Operational and Loss Prevention Audit Program

An operational and loss prevention audit program will measure proficiency for each segment of the business audited, will uncover high-risk transactions that might develop into fraud investigations, and will expose weaknesses that can be remedied through employee training. A vice president of loss prevention once told me that auditing store operations and raising awareness of loss prevention would not be effective in uncovering theft because these methods would in themselves help prevent store thefts. He thought was that audits are rote and repetitive and if effective, prevented instead of detected.

Today, auditors who are doing their job correctly, are using available technology, and are being meticulous about their job will uncover the red flags or high-risk transactions. In my experience as a consultant and loss prevention professional, I recall a time in which 15% of the audits performed at one company uncovered fraud necessitating an investigation. Training may have taken place where weaknesses were found. Proficiency ratings were communicated to management in an audit cover page. Most importantly, however, the company wisely used the chance to stop the fraud and catch perpetrators.

AUDITING BY PRIORITY

Let us now look at how to determine where to audit (e.g., stores, corporate offices, supply chain) and in what order. The retail business will reflect shrinkage reserve on the profit and loss statement; where actual physical inventory results for the year exceed the reserve is where most loss prevention departments focus their audit programs. After the Sarbanes–Oxley Act of 2002 passed in response to the massive corporate fraud scandals of 2001 and 2002, publicly traded companies began formulating audit committees that operate independently of the corporate board of directors. Responsibilities include monitoring and auditing corporate governance and ensuring that all fiduciary reporting is accurate and approved by the company's chief executive officer (CEO) or someone in an equivalent position of power. Thus, audit committees would likely require an internal audit department, which may examine all functional departments at corporate headquarters— accounts receivable and payables, purchasing, treasury, finance, inventory control, and new store construction—and uncover material weaknesses or more serious errors that could contribute to reporting company profitability mistakenly on inspected reports.

In many companies, internal audit teams also conduct store audits. Some larger department store chains have a store audit department to carry out financial and operational audits. In smaller specialty retail stores, the responsibility for store auditing generally falls on loss prevention. Even in a business conducting operational audits in store locations, the loss prevention department may want to develop a very focused audit that tests prevention and control policies. The present chapter concentrates on the loss prevention department, which is charged with operational and loss prevention auditing at the store level.

Sarbanes–Oxley laws do require a certain amount of auditing of store controls. Although individual store results cannot affect the bottom line, stores in aggregate can affect the bottom line if they are operating improperly, are violating policies, or are involved in fraud on a large scale. For example, in a now defunct drugstore chain, the CEO led aggregate fraud that was committed at the store level. He would have two or three trailers of store merchandise moved to a store, and the employees there would take their physical inventory. Once the store had an inventory result, the trailers would be moved to the next store on the inventory schedule and be counted in that store's inventory. The CEO was inflating the inventory of the chain of stores so he could qualify for larger loans to buy more

merchandise. The business eventually went bankrupt, and the CEO is still serving a prison term.

Loss prevention team members may serve supply chain warehouses, distribution centers, and manufacturing centers by auditing physical security processes, merchandise security controls, and preshipment verifications. The internal audit department will likely review inventory control processes and manufacturing processes.

Loss prevention departments should check for adherence to policies and protocols that are already in place, not for potential but not yet in place policies that will serve as a "gotcha" and will both skew the audit and anger a number of departments in the process. When determining what to audit in your stores, it is necessary to be guided by the policies and procedures that ensure control of the store's financial, physical, and personal assets—that is, those geared toward prevention of dishonesty, protection of your people's well-being, and maintenance of the store's merchandise inventory. Developing questions that test the proficiency of the store's adherence to those policies is one of the first ways to build the audit.

Federal guidelines such as state wage, hour and hiring guidelines, federal immigration and naturalization laws concerning fitness for work, the Health Information Portability and Accessibility Act (HIPAA), and Credit Information Protection must be considered, because if they are not followed they will result in heavy fines or business interruptions. In addition, think about what questions your operational business leaders have: are they policy oriented or just administrative? If leaders recommend questions not grounded in policy, then you may want to leave them off an audit and find some other method of testing them.

CONTENTS OF AN AUDIT

A basic retail audit document can be composed of any number of sections with between eight and infinite questions per section. A complete loss prevention and operational audit covers at least the following eight areas.

- Asset review: Depositing all receipts, daily balancing to the point of sale (POS), measuring management's compliance to oversight of daily controls, gift certificate and gift card controls, and corporate supply credit card controls. This list of examples is inclusive, but it is important for each business to decide from an operational perspective what is most important.

- Exchanges, holds, discounts: This area reviews hold policies for customers and associates, exchange controls and inventory management of merchandise returned on an exchange, customer and associate discounting, and all associate transactions relevant to policies and procedures.
- Inventory control: A complete review of all receiving, transfer, recall, and inventory balancing procedures as well as physical inventory-taking practices and associate awareness of inventory results. Inventory adjustments are reviewed for accuracy and timeliness in preparation. Proper authorizations must be ensured whenever adjustments are made to the business's on-hand inventory.
- Voids, returns, passwords: This area of the audit reviews all voids and returns over a given period (3 to 6 months is usually a good slice of time) for adherence to policy. Prior to an audit, the auditor will use any available exception reporting system to capture the returns and voids for 3 months to a year, depending on volume of the store, to make locating them quick and easy. Returned merchandise is researched and possibly located, if it has not sold, to ensure proper return to stock and to verify its validity. Passwords are reviewed to make certain they are being changed monthly and that responsibilities assigned for each associate's level of security fits each person's job description.
- Physical security: This area of the audit is mainly concerned with the doors, fire exit hardware, alarms, key control, emergency procedures, and trash controls. Incident reports are also reviewed for additional risks the store should be addressing.
- Manufacturing lab: This section is added if a location has a product manufacturing or repair laboratory on site. It deals with assessing how policies and procedures are followed in accounting for physical (product) inventory, damages, and breakage of inventory. Some quality control inspections are completed, and associates' adherence to safety standards is assessed.
- Human resources: This audit section reviews the hiring practices of the stores including reference checks, preemployment assessment testing, and all other background testing. A review of I-9 form completion is mandatory, and corrections must be made immediately. It is important to verify that personnel records are kept securely and not left out and available for anyone to read. Verification of new hire orientation, including a loss prevention message about honesty, can be made.

- Medicare, HIPAA review: Medicare and HIPAA are both government control areas that must be adhered to by any business that files on behalf of customers for Medicare or is in control of personal health-care information. This section is used in organizations that include some type of health-care provider, like dentists, optometrists, and audiologists.

These eight sections show specific areas that are grouped together to suit a specific program. There is no limit to the number or types of sections that can be included in an audit of a retail store. These examples help visualize what an audit could look like. Each business should build audits around what is important in supporting it toward making its goals and fulfilling its mission.

SCORING AUDITS

To score an audit it is necessary to weight questions based on importance to profit loss prevention. For example, the question, "Are bank deposits made in accordance with company policy?" would be worth up to 10 points if a company had high missing deposit dollars from month to month. If a store suffers internal theft of deposits or a robbery of one or more deposits in transit to the bank, it would be a direct loss in profit. In the same audit, a question, "Does the safe contain only authorized funds?" would be worth 2 points because a store would be able to operate profitably if there were money left behind by a customer in the safe.

Management should decide whether the overall score is more important to the field manager than individual breakdowns of sections of questions. One option is to score each question at 1 point, thus eliminating arguments around why questions are weighted differently. Select the method of scoring that best fits your business.

The audit cover letter and scoring page should be taken seriously. These are the documents that report the location of the audit, manager of the store, date of audit, reason of audit, and scores for each section reviewed. A total score is indicated, and written narrative of findings is included so the recipients get the auditor's objective conclusions of the strengths and opportunities for the store. This reporting document should be sent to a vice president-level leader along with regional and district management. A copy is generally sent to a director of audit and the internal audit department.

THE TRAINING BENEFITS OF AUDITS

Many years ago, when I first started in retail mass merchandising, it was a big deal when the auditor showed up at my store location. Every staff member was worried that we were doing something wrong and that was why we were being singled out for an audit. The store manager would be sweating bullets, and managers would be on their best behavior. The one thing I remember that helped make the audits more tolerable is that auditors would quickly set everyone at ease by taking time to explain policies or procedures or how to complete a particular task. The auditors were trainers and never left the store until they were sure that someone in that store understood how to properly complete the operation for any audit question they were deducting points for. After one or two audits, we really looked forward to the auditor's visits because we knew we would be learning the right way to do the job if we did not know it.

I cannot tell you how often I hear retailers admit that they dread the auditors coming because they come in teams, spend a week poring over every record and paper they can get their hands on and typing into their computers with a frenzy, and then leave. No one hears anything for a week or two, and then the ceiling falls in when the regional manager comes in to scold everyone for the bad audit score. No one learns anything. If you want to make an impression, take the time to teach, motivate, and explain everything. Never leave a store unit until you are sure that someone in that building knows how to execute the policies and procedures. Take an hour or two to explain the audit results, and talk with the store manager. The payback is better follow-up scores, better-trained people, more highly motivated people, and bigger profit for your company.

AUDIT INTEGRITY

If you are setting up the audit department or are leading an existing audit department, then teach by example. Educate auditors on how to use audit sample sheets to track work product. When completing audits, have a system for how samples are pulled from storage data and reviewed. A system for when to pull data from the point of sales system and when to dig into file cabinets. A sample tracking document will help guide the audit work and make answering questions easier.

The worksheet is the only part of the audit that should be completed on paper by hand, as gathering the required number of samples for each of the audit sections will be an asset when later answering the audit questions electronically. In a retail store, it is essential that auditors come in 1 to 2 hours before store opening to run daily and monthly reports from the system and to obtain any information reports from the POS system before the day begins to avoid interrupting business. Next, they should pull sample returns, exchanges, and daily transaction records for each week that will be reviewed. Once the sample worksheets are used to guide the audit, auditors should use a portable electronic device (e.g., laptop, tablet, handheld personal digital assistant) that can be carried through the location while answering questions. Paper audits are discouraged, since they will have to be transfered later to the computer and will thus hold up the review process with store management.

Employing auditing software to keep a uniform reporting environment is recommended. Professional auditing firms use software tools and programs such as Lotus Notes and Access. A number of effective audit management tools are available to loss prevention departments. Some are Web based, and the software resides with the provider. Others, like Loss Prevention Management Software (LPMS)–Audit, are purchased and reside on the company's server. The system is updated with audits completed in the field each time loss prevention personnel connect to the corporate network. I think this system is most versatile because it allows for working offline (i.e., it does not rely on Internet connections) to complete an audit and is easy to administrate.

Completing an audit correction action plan is important to ensure accountability to correct the audit deficiencies. While still at the store location, auditors need to help management identify the most important items to correct first—where they will get the biggest return for their time invested in creating new habits within the store. It might be the top five items that are selected. What supports the goals of the store and of the company? That is where the correction plan should concentrate. This audit correction plan should then be sent to the store manager's immediate supervisor and the next level up with a copy to the auditor and the director of audit compliance for the company. If the store has not earned a passing score, a follow-up audit should be conducted approximately 90 days from the first audit. On this audit, only the opportunities and action plan items may be reaudited.

HOW TO USE AUDIT SCORING EFFECTIVELY

A passing score for an audit should be 80% and above. Operational and loss prevention audits should be easily accessible, not kept secret. Since audits are based on stores' policy and procedure, conducting one should be easy, right? One would think so. However, my experience has been that audits are a challenge because really operating a store—with all of the day-to-day difficulties—is complex. Workload plus payroll constraints minus sales-to-hours guidelines equals not everything getting done just the way it should be done. Because of this, consider equating audit scores to your company's standards of performance (SOP) for a scoring system. For instance, if on performance reviews an SOP of 3 means that an associate meets the expectation, then on an audit a 3 would equate a score of 80% to 89%. If a 4 rating indicates that the associate exceeds expectations, then on an audit a 4 would mean 90% to 94%. The range of 95% to 100% would equate to a 5 on a review, indicating that an associate far exceeds expectations. At the other end of the spectrum, 70% to 79% would correlate with a 2 on a review, meaning that the associate meets most expectations; below a 69% would equate to an associate failing to meet expectations. If store managers are rated on this type of system, then they will understand how the audit score they just received relates to their performance.

EXCEPTION REPORTING

Using exception reporting to lead the way on an audit is a smart way to proceed. A number of companies, such as XBR, a product from Datavantage, and Fraud Watch, a product from SAP, offer POS exception reporting. They operate in one of two methods: (1) pull data from a T-log file created from the company's POS system; or (2) analyze the transactions selected by the administrator or work in conjunction with the T-file and glean analytical data on a constant basis by mapping transactions. It is important to be aware that no matter what application you select, each one can be developed to analyze transactions specified by your company. It is very important to keep the software releases up to date and properly working.

Exception software will give insight into high-risk transactions and red flags in returns, exchanges, voids, discounting credit card transactions, no-sales, potential for dropped sales, gift card sales and returns,

and more. How these data are presented in reporting is pretty much up to management and the needs of the business.

An exception reporting system is set up so ad hoc reporting can be done by all loss prevention personnel with access to the system and user rights or a license. Previously designed reporting by the system administrator that are always in a rigid format are available along with the ability to set them up to auto send to designated recipients on a daily, weekly, or monthly basis. The most useful return on investment for an exception reporting system is the time a loss prevention department saves when an analyst uses the corporate computer to identify potential theft situations. The exception reporting will take the high-risk transaction right down to the cashier at store level so that it is evidence of what was rung into the POS system.

For example, Cathy, the analyst in the corporate headquarters of a large retailer, runs exception reporting on high-dollar cash refunds for the entire company. She is able to see the chain average as a percent of sales for the chain, each region, and even down to store level. Cathy notices that region 12's average cash refunds is 7.8%, much higher than the chain's overall average of 2.5%. So Cathy scrutinizes cash refund dollars, sales, and number of transactions in all stores in this region and finds that store #112 has refunds at 9% whereas many of the other stores are closer to the chain average. Cathy can now pull up all the cash refunds for store #112 and view each cashier's performance for the month specified. A line on the report will have the cashier's associate number, name, sales, total refund count, refund dollars, cash refund count, cash refund dollars, and percent to sales. From this list, Cathy can now pick which cashier is driving the high percentage for the store.

As she looks through this store's report, she comes across cashier 7255, with $1,250 in cash refunds and $1,350 in total refunds and a cash refund average of 93%. Cathy selects cashier 7255 to see all of her refunds and is able to print these reports or save them for future reference in the investigation. Cathy starts an investigative case file for this store and is able to access each individual refund from the POS system including details of what was returned, the customer information captured, if any, and method of tender. She can also determine if there was an original sale transaction for each refund in the exception reporting system. After pulling all of these data, Cathy may call several customers to determine if they received acceptable service during their visit to this store. Usually she can also determine if they still have the merchandise or received a refund. If the store has a camera system

that integrates with the exception reporting system, Cathy can pull up each transaction on video within seconds and verify if a customer was present. At this point Cathy can turn the investigation over to a regional loss prevention manager for further review, interviews, and disposition.

The return on investment (ROI) given by exception reporting software justifies its purchase. Additionally, this software will more than double the quantity and recovery dollars of investigations for a year. From an operational and loss prevention audit perspective, using exception reporting software is an excellent time saver in cutting to high-risk transactions, saving hours of manual research by an auditor. In today's environment where we are asked to do more with less this is just the tool you need.

When hiring loss prevention associates for the auditing function, it is necessary to find individuals who are meticulous and detail oriented. An analytical mind and consultative outlook are always good traits, but it is more important to find people who are technically capable than merely skilled in auditing. A college graduate from accounting, business, or even criminal justice disciplines can be trained in audit skills the way your business prefers. We discovered that high-capacity performance store managers make excellent auditors because of the wealth of knowledge they bring to the table about how a store operates. The loss prevention auditor position is an excellent stepping stone to another business unit or more responsibility in the loss prevention department. By recruiting the right people for the job, you will be able to enhance the professionalism and reputation for effectiveness of the loss prevention department.

FRANCHISE AUDITING

Franchises are prevalent in the food services industry, including McDonald's, Chipotle, Panera Bread, and KFC. In specialty retail there are a few franchise operators. Individual business owners operate franchise businesses and pay a royalty and advertising fee in exchange for use of the company name, company-generated advertising, and the goodwill the name generates to draw in customers. Each franchise is set up based on a legal contract with the corporate entity—an agreement between the franchise (or corporate entity) and the franchisee (small business owner) on how they will do business together. Franchise stores report sales

monthly and pay royalties as a percentage of the sales to the franchisor corporations.

It may be useful for corporations with franchises to develop an audit function dedicated to checking how franchised stores operate, focusing on accurate financial reporting as well as on helping business owners develop successful business habits. Audits may be offered as a self-help tool, where the owner could choose whether to accept recommendations to implement controls. Franchisors should use these types of audits as an opportunity to enrich business relationships, to identify financial control issues, and to improve the efficiency of the businesses. Identification of risk management issues and teaching loss prevention techniques would be a nice benefit of the program also.

The franchise audit program also reveals fraud through sample refunds, voids, petty cash, write-offs, credit memos, cash sales, no-sale transactions, discounts, credit card transactions, price overrides, and looking for register overages or shortages, altered documents, skimming, swapping checks for cash, missing documents, duplicate billing, false customer data, special orders, and shipments to nonstore locations. Because corporate franchise audit teams are part of the corporate business, they cannot solve franchise owners' problems or conduct their investigations but just deliver the evidence with suggestions for how the owners can deal with the losses. Because each franchisee is a seperately owned business, they must solve their own problems.

A franchise audit team consists of two audit and compliance personnel. Because this is a financial audit, it takes two full business days conducting a review of two years' worth of sales data. Approximately 90 different aspects of the business are reviewed. This is one way the loss prevention department can show additional value for the company and can be viewed as a profit-generating unit based on the royalties and advertising fees that are returned to the bottom line. Most of the time loss prevention is seen as a cost center because such a department does not contribute to the company's profit.

FIELD OPERATIONS AUDIT COMMITTEE

To make the operational and loss prevention audit department very effective and to make sure it fits into the mission and goal of your business, it is important that leadership from critical areas of the company is

involved. A field operations audit committee (FOAC) would help achieve this goal. Different from the audit committee that reports to the board of directors, the FOAC is composed of operations leaders and decision makers and representatives of the legal department, associate relations or human resources, risk management, regulatory services, Sarbanes–Oxley compliance or accounting, and loss prevention. This committee has as its purpose the following:

- Updating and keeping all existing audits current, seeking and providing feedback on what each functional area would like to add or remove because of policy changes.
- Soliciting information on changed policies or upcoming initiatives that could require revisions or completely new audits to be created.
- Loss prevention gives updates to the functional areas on audit productivity and proficiency averages.

The director of your audit program should be charged with organizing and planning of the FOAC. That person calls the meetings and plans the agendas to be discussed and is also responsible for managing the workload that the committee agrees to implement. The committee should meet quarterly or biannually, depending on the needs of the business. This is the best way to keep all the functional areas, communicating through the year because their priorities will be their departmental goals. Between meetings, assign individual workgroups to handle details like reviewing audit revisions or creating audit questions and similar work. Approving and finalizing should be reserved for the FOAC meetings.

In conclusion, now more than ever businesses need some form of audit of the facilities they operate, especially since the passing of such laws as Sarbanes–Oxley and because of regulatory issues. Being a strong partner to the operational leadership and supporting the business mission and goals give loss prevention increased value to the bottom line. By developing effecive auditing programs that uncover fraud and reveal opportunitites to be more proficient operators, loss prevention can ensure they are not left out when the business leaders are allocating loss prevention budget dollars.

10

From the Ground Up
How to Build a Loss Prevention Department

Most loss prevention practitioners will enter an organization that has an existing loss prevention or asset protection department—not that these departments function flawlessly and that no improvements can be added. It is a much larger undertaking to enter a company without any sort of existing loss-prevention department. The seasoned practitioner will need to utilize all of their expertise and experience to make is successful. Some seasoned loss prevention professionals are willing to go to smaller organizations such as a convenience-store or drugstore chains if they feel they have the chance to move up to director or vice president quickly. This section of the book will help those starting a new department from scratch, which is rare, or those who have been hired to restructure an existing department into an effective and efficient organization.

WHERE TO BEGIN? A STEP-BY-STEP PROCESS

The first thing to remember if you are going to start or reconstruct a loss prevention department is that not everyone in the organization will know what it takes to have an effective program. The key to success is to break down this enormous project into a step-by-step process that is easier to manage than trying to tackle it all at once. Create an outline of the most important steps that must be accomplished, and include people who

would be an asset to the plan to whom you could go to for advice. This is your support network. These are the specialists with knowledge that can be assembled to bring your project to life.

For the purpose of discussion, it is assumed that a seasoned and proven loss prevention practitioner is charged with this project. The first objective is to write a business plan for the department. It is extremely important that the mission, vision, and goals of the loss prevention department parallel the company's same goals. If the loss prevention department is not working to support the aims of the business at large, it will be doomed to failure. Most retail organizations are in business to make a profit and are funded by operating stores that take in money to create a profit. Loss prevention supports this by reducing the drains on profit called shrinkage. It will be counterproductive if the stores are being operated by management committed to building a customer base and to creating an exciting atmosphere where customers can touch and try on the accessible merchandise and loss prevention team members are working to lock up every piece of merchandise and accuse as many customers of theft as possible.

Along with a business plan and mission for the loss prevention department, it is necessary to build a budget to fund the activities chosen to support the business. If investigations, auditing, and training will be primary functions of the department, then budgeting for field associates—most likely loss prevention managers—will be necessary. Budgeting for salary, benefits, cars, equipment, and travel expenses, among other things, will take care of staffing. You will also have to budget in development for the associates, meeting expenses, and communications. If the loss prevention presence in the company will be small, perhaps the budgeting will be for services from a company like LP Innovations, Inc., which can conduct audits and investigations in stores as needed. Where does the funding come from? Unless loss prevention is self-sufficient at selling something or raising the funds in some way, funding will usually come from the operating margin of the stores. This is why support of the overall goals of the company is so important.

Part of the business plan includes the strategy to accomplish your business objectives and goals. If shrinkage reduction is a goal, purchasing electronic article surveillance (EAS) equipment and tags—for example, acousto-magnetic, radiofrequency, and radiofrequency identification (RFID) devices—might be necessary to control inventory. Comparing equipment and testing it to validate its effectiveness are extremely important before choosing a vendor. Conducting a request for proposals (RFP) period where vendors visit and compare system and pricing will help

determine the very best system for your organization's circumstances. A large purchase for a large number of stores will likely need approvals from top management including the chief financial officer (CFO) of the company. If so, be prepared to prove return on investment (ROI)—that is, the savings to the company, or the return expected after spending capital on buying the equipment and tagging all the product. You must figure in all costs associated with the purchase including labor to maintain the systems from day to day, depreciation over 3 to 5 years, and how much shrinkage reduction at cost will pay for the systems and tags.

Whether building or refurbishing a loss prevention department, it is necessary to be masterful at planning and execution—that is, getting loss prevention managers to effectively get all the work done that is necessary. Planning involves determining how many working days out of the year that a loss prevention manager has to actually be in stores to conduct audits or investigations. Take the year—365 days—and eliminate all weekends, office days, vacation weeks, and holidays; then look realistically at what your field people will have available for influencing and shaping those physical inventory figures. That is the actual working time they will be in stores conducting audits, investigations, and training. This is invaluable information when determining how many stores loss prevention managers should be assigned at the district and regional levels.

Department store chains with store allocations that cover a loss prevention representative in every store have an advantage because there will be someone working on the mission, goals, and values of the department daily in every store. Some retail chains have a loss prevention manager who covers two stores in proximity if both are experiencing challenges with shrinkage. This gives store-level associates increased experience in planning their use of time and emphasis for each of the stores. District loss prevention managers might have 12 to 15 stores in a district, depending on store volumes. Regional loss prevention managers may have from 5 to 10 district managers.

Specialty retail may have only district or regional loss prevention managers, who take a larger quantity of stores with smaller volume and focus on stores that need them the most. They have to budget their time to make every minute count. Some specialty retailers might see value in having a manager cover a few stores in proximity and focus on awareness or internal investigations and report to the district or regional person. Extremely important are good organizational and planning skills to help

guide these employees in the right direction. Most retailers use physical inventory results to determine what stores get priority for visits.

Some organizations take a more expanded approach and use exception reporting as an indicator of top-priority stores. Exception reporting reveals "low-hanging fruit," or employees who are stealing from the organization and who are easiest to recognize. These individuals simply do not care or are just plain sloppy in their thievery methods but usually do not get caught. They have been stealing for who knows how long and getting away with it. They probably do not even realize that the company now has a loss prevention department and that their secondary income will soon come to an end. These individuals will stand out when exception reporting is used.

Measuring results is the next step in building a lean and effective department. Leaders of the loss prevention department should understand where the small successes and small failures are taking place because this helps in keeping perspective and in making adjustments to the overall plan. Reviewing the inventory results and providing the comparisons between inventories to show the trends at the store, regional, and chain level with the executives will help them understand how far you've come. Reporting on investigations, recoveries, auditing, proficiency scores, training opportunities, burglaries and robberies, restitution collected, and business abuse hotline responses are all examples of categories you want to report information on because they affect profit. You want to keep on top of the categories that are measurable and provide those metric to those who need to know. Keep in mind, using measurable categories such as case count, to set quotas is an ineffecive method. Even more important than the metrics of the department are the personal phone calls to operations management requesting feedback on how the loss prevention department is performing: "Are we meeting the expectations for helping solve field managers' problems? What more can we do?" Stellar customer service from loss prevention demands that no calls go unanswered. Responding to all calls for advice, investigation, and training creates winning loss prevention departments. In loss prevention, the customers are the stores, the field operations management, anyone in the corporate office who needs our expertise, as well as customers who frequent the stores.

Setting a vision and developing leaders are two extremely important functions of the department's leadership. Without a vision for where the department is going, associates will lack direction. It is really important to set performance objectives that align not only with the company's

objectives but also with where the department is headed. A lofty vision might be to reduce shrinkage and increase professionalism. This vision is lofty because its focus, individually, are completely different. But if approached correctly, they can each be achieved. Part of a loss prevention department's future is developing leaders for tomorrow. Associates need to know that their leaders want them to advance and be successful. Many of the most successful departments promote from within whenever possible, have little to no turnover, and are constantly developing their associates for future leadership roles.

Do not get so specialized that the silo effect sets in and associates are left out of mainstream business. Do not be afraid to get involved in functions not related to loss prevention in the company. For instance, conducting audits of hiring practices or franchise business financial audits may not be directly related to shrink reduction, but they add value to the department. Franchise audits on financial reporting that uncover unreported sales and returns royalties to the bottom line make loss prevention look more like a profit center than a cost center. Are we loss prevention persons who happen to do some business, or are we business associates who happen to specialize in loss prevention? I would rather be the latter. When senior management notices the value that loss prevention brings to the table, you can be assured that you will be invited to the table of many projects that should have loss prevention perspectives added, such as designing the store of the future. To be invited, loss prevention leaders need to be well versed in all the functions in the business and be seen as a collaborator with all areas.

Motivate and encourage associates to be effective and successful. If you are the leader of the department, be the biggest cheerleader when your associates do something great. Build them up when they get that first big investigation recovery. Send a reward when they surpass the shrinkage goal. Call them personally on their birthday or anniversary with the company. Let them know you empathize with what they go through daily to achieve the goals. Do not expect that others within your new organization will somehow know all the achievements being made every day. Especially in a newly formed department, wins need to be broadcast publicly and frequently. The announcement needs to be targeted at specific individuals, such as those funding your endeavors.

Presentation for displaying your wins is critical. You will likely be invited to executive meetings with other department heads, during which they will provide an update of what is going on in their respective areas. It is imperative that you outperform others because you need money to grow

your department. The only way you will get the money you need to be successful is to show that good things are starting to happen. To measure success, you will need to have a starting point. Go back to the prior year and retrieve any available statistics—for example, shrinkage, internal and external cases, audits. The good thing is that out of the three different areas, shrinkage may be the only statistic available because people not in loss prevention usually conduct the inventory. Therefore, if there were no cases or audits for the prior year and there are three cases and two audits for the current year, progress is being made. A good rule of thumb is to use PowerPoint to show your wins. This allows you to use graphs so the message is clear that the organization is definitely moving in the right direction.

Always ensure when hiring a new associate to seek out input from others in the department and from associate relations and possibly the legal department after interviews are conducted. Always reserve the final say for yourself. As leader of the department, always be sure to have the final interview of all new hires. The hiring process is the best place to determine if new associates will fit in with the culture of the company and with fellow associates.

RESET LOSS PREVENTION EXPECTATIONS

Initiating loss prevention in an organization can be like going from warm weather to cold weather without realizing the change is going to occur. Employees need to be slowly acclimated to a new culture that embraces ethical behavior and proper controls. Transitioning from a culture that did not adhere to strict policy and procedures to one that has many checks and balances can be a shock, not to mention very overwhelming. The newly formed loss prevention department needs to define its game plan and carefully organize the rollout. When expectations are reset for any type of situation, the desired result is that the old behavior will cease and the new teachings will become part of everyday life; however, old habits are sometimes hard to break.

To be successful, start with the most important parts of the program. Before the establishment of a loss prevention department, employees had most likely been getting away with everything. They need to understand that dishonesty of any nature no longer will be tolerated. Do not take for granted that employees will automatically understand the many faces of dishonesty, so provide a few examples, such as stealing money or product as well as falsifying company documents or cheating to increase store statistics. As you are discussing the new expectations with the group—even

the executive group—pay attention to body language as you start to expand on the cheating portion. If employees begin to squirm in their chairs, this may be a good indicator that cheating is widely accepted in the organization.

Do not forget to tie in the requirement from the Sarbanes–Oxley Act that cheating in the workplace be reported to Wall Street. The act brought compliance and financial integrity to the forefront of many publicly traded corporations. Businesses are now expected to have outside auditors who check controls, an audit committee, and top executive certification of financial results reporting. Information technology (IT) departments must have integrated compliance controls to assure that proper verifications are being made and that no material weaknesses are known exist.

After you cover the main points of being honest, you will want to discuss how employees' daily lives will change. This is the part where resistance will begin. Most employees are probably not stealing from the organization necessarily; therefore, telling them not to steal will not cause any extra work. However, when you begin to discuss all the new checks and balances that managers will need to adhere to, they will be thinking of how much more time it is going to take. When assigning additional work to employees, it is paramount that you discuss the "what's in it for them" and consequences for noncompliance. If managers receive bonuses for profit, they will be able to relate to a discussion of how the new controls will increase profit and reduce losses. If payroll hours are somehow related to profitability, you can discuss how they will be able to have more payroll hours when the new controls allow their store to become more profitable. Set clear expectations on how long employees and management have to implement the new practices within their stores. Give them a reasonable amount of time to implement the new guidelines, but be very clear on the consequences for not following the directives. Be sure that someone will be able to monitor the progress—using something as simple as a checklist to be mailed to a supervisor—or employees will be less likely to comply.

FACING THE CHALLENGES

When it comes to starting any kind of a new department, there will always be roadblocks, which can include executives' unreasonable expectations and not having enough money to do the things you need to do. When you take over an existing department, the expectations are usually less than

starting from scratch because executives will already understand loss prevention and its function. They expect good if not great results, but they are usually reasonable. When an organization does not have existing loss prevention, some of the expectations can be unreasonable because they do not understand how policies must change to bring along prevention awareness and build a culture of integrity. Some organizations expect that by the next inventory cycle, results will have improved immensely. For those of us who have ever taken over a bad store or bad region, we know that it is not likely that the store or region will improve after one cycle. Because we are indirect influences, it takes time to get everyone on board with the new program. You will not get people's bad behaviors to change overnight. You will be lucky to get them to change during the inventory period for the following cycle to reflect the results.

The same is true when starting a loss prevention department: its effectiveness will probably not be noticed right away. That is why having frequent and candid conversations with executives about what you are doing is the way to validate the department's worth. Explain the process and that the overall results might not be immediately evident. Executives are looking to see if they made the right decision by starting a loss prevention department, and reducing shrinkage is one way for them to see that they did. They must also be patient and realistic in their expectations, though. Take time to build the proper relationships with the executive team when you first come on board. You want to display your expertise and business sense, but you do not want to come across like an arrogant know-it-all. They are less likely to be unreasonably critical of your efforts if they trust you and understand your plan. Ensure that they understand the approach you are taking and how you plan to reach the goal. Do not be afraid to have discussions regarding readjusting the goal if it is unreasonable. Some new people feel like they need to agree to fit in, but they are setting themselves up for disaster if they know what they agreed to do is unachievable.

Dan Mania, security director of Delaware North, is someone who knew he needed a loss prevention department. Delaware North is a global leader in hospitality and food services with operating companies in the lodging, sporting, airport, gaming, and entertainment industry. I met Mania in 2007 when he contacted me regarding an article I had published in *Security Management Magazine*. The article was about creating a culture that is not conducive to employee counterproductive behavior. Mania asked if I could come and speak to his security personnel from across the nation regarding the topic, and I agreed. He does not have a retail loss prevention background, but he is well versed in all aspects of security. He

also understands the correlation between employee behavior and organizational actions. Delaware North has retail venues within their lodging, sporting, and airport locations. Because the retail venue revenues pale in comparison with those of the casino and resort establishments, the focus has never been on establishing loss prevention for the retail side of the business. Mania saw this need shortly after he came on board and continued his quest until he finally was able to get a position approved for a loss prevention manager. I asked him to discuss his plight with getting the organization to understand the need for loss prevention:

Q: What made your organization realize it needed a loss prevention department?

A: Simple question—complex answer. We are a food and beverage concessions and retail company at heart with some fierce competition in our markets. As a result, we face a daily battle to innovate and become ever more competitive. It would be inaccurate to say that we woke up one morning and "realized" that we needed a loss prevention department. For a long time, the company has understood and recognized the importance of efficient operation and minimizing avoidable loss, but more recently our competition in the marketplace has helped us place a greater focus on the value of loss prevention. Also, recent strategic planning and internal management development studies convinced our management teams at all levels that focusing on loss prevention across the organization was simply the right thing to do.

Q: Why were retail losses not a concern before?

A: They were, but only recently did the company feel that it was appropriate to manage avoidable loss from a strategic, corporate perspective. In the past, to some extent, we viewed shrink as a "cost of doing business." Essentially, we permitted our operating groups to accrue a certain amount of loss because it was "unavoidable." For a variety of reasons, our philosophy has evolved, and we now believe we can do better for ourselves, our partners, and our customers if we measure and manage risk to our margins and profitability via strategic loss prevention.

Q: What process did you follow to finally get approval for the position?

A: I do not believe in doing anything "just because." I believe in data and in facts. To some extent, my approach is low key and subtle, but in the end I think I pick and choose battles that I know I can win. I pushed for a more strategic approach to loss prevention

171

during our corporate strategic planning process. I slowly, but steadily, introduced data from our industries and our competition to help raise awareness and understanding. I developed presentations for management at every level to help raise awareness and understanding, and I took every opportunity to express my opinions. In time, I think momentum behind the idea of strategic loss prevention built, and the company began to look at it as the tremendous opportunity that it represents. Finally, I sponsored a group of managers during an internal training and development program that analyzed shrink and the potential impact of a loss prevention program on our company. I wanted to take the opportunity to objectively show executive management that my approach was worth a try. In the end, the group recommended the creation of a corporate loss prevention leadership position, and executive management agreed.

Q: What are the expectations for the individual you hire?

A: I expect the new corporate loss prevention manager to bring the right acumen, experience, and approach to this critical role within our organization. The company is taking a "show me" approach, so the key will be to demonstrate value and ROI. Of course, this is a process, and it will take time. Success will not happen overnight; rather, this is a long-term venture that will require significant organizational change in many ways. The organization will be patient, but it will be incumbent upon us to demonstrate value. I expect the new loss prevention manager to start with the basics. First, within the company's cultural and technology framework, we need to ensure that we are accurately measuring the scope of the problem. Then we can develop a game plan to attack it. I don't expect the new LP manager to show up on the first day with that game plan in detail, but this person should bring the experience and acumen to the table to be able to develop it in time.

Q: What do you believe will make or break the position?

A: If the interview team and I do our job, we will find the best fit with the fewest personal and professional obstacles to success. Executive management understands the need and supports the role, but the key will be to show that our sole interest is in improving the business. Our goal is to make our company more efficient

and more profitable. If we hire the right person, in time, he or she will earn the support and attention for our loss prevention agenda. Once that happens, we will have a tremendous opportunity to positively, and strategically, improve business operations and profitability at every level.

Mania's story is not unique in trying to justify the need to establish a loss prevention department to an organization. Although he had a bit more stacked against him than most because his business is not all retail—the smallest portion is retail.—his approach to justifying the need was the right way to do it. He did not go into a board meeting and tell the executive team that the shrink numbers are bad and that is the reason the organization needs a loss prevention manager. His approach was very methodical. He did his homework before he said a word. In addition to a small portion of the business being retail, Delaware North has a very large security department that could be construed as having loss prevention personnel. Mania had to ensure that the organization understood the difference between security and retail loss prevention.

After Mania completed the necessary research on loss prevention, he began to present his findings to the executive team. He conducted research by talking to people in the field of loss prevention, by reading articles on the subject, and by researching similar businesses to see what they are doing to prevent retail losses. He did not leave any stone unturned because he wanted to have all the answers before the questions were ever asked. The presentation of the research was critical to accepting the information. One key thing Mania learned through his research is what the competition is doing with regards to loss prevention. He learned that one of Delaware North's competitors had an established loss prevention department that was able to show favorable reductions in shrinkage over time. This information was crucial because every organization wants to stay on top of its competition.

One thing Mania had that some loss prevention people lack is patience. He had to have a great deal of patience. It took a long time and much hard work to get the position approved. Because of all his hard work and gathered information, Mania was able to provide the executive team with a full understanding of what retail loss prevention really is and would be for the organization.

MAKING IT SUCCESSFUL

Following the steps does not mean that the department you formed or refurbished will be successful. It may mean that you now have a functioning part of the organization, but is it really doing what you envisioned? Is it making the stand you hoped for? Is it producing the results that are expected? Think of it as a home remodel. You have a vision, and you want it to come to life. You may have seen the end result in magazines or on TV, but you were never exactly sure how to get it there. You solicited the help of some professionals who have already done it, but the challenge of succeeding still remains. You took all the precautions and followed all the necessary steps in the hopes that your remodel will be perfect. The only way to gauge that is to the see the reaction from others as they walk in. If they are mesmerized by your work, you have accomplished your task. If they walk in and say, "Nice job," you have performed mediocre. If they do not react at all, you know what that means. The same is true of your newly created department. You want executives in the organization to be wowed by what you are doing and what you are going to do. You want to be sure they are certain the investment is well worth it. This is no time to just get by, because you will not be able to make your department grow on getting by. To fully understand how to make a successful loss prevention department, I solicited the knowledge of Paul Jones, global director of asset protection for eBay and former vice president of asset protection for the Retail Industry Leaders Association. He has more than 20 years of retail loss prevention experience.

Jones believes that to know whether you are successful, you must be able to define it. This is where knowing the organization will be helpful. Some organizations are very results driven, whereas others pride themselves on having a stable culture. Understand how the organization operates and what makes other departments successful in the eyes of the executives. Jones gave the following ways of defining success relative to loss prevention:

- Maintaining shrink.
- Reducing controllables such as safety expenses, worker's compensation, loss prevention costs, lawsuits.
- Human and emotional capital; improving the functional relationships so you are an invited business partner.
- Part of success is to gain credibility as a business leader, not just a functional expert. Loss prevention needs to sit at the table with

senior leaders and participate in full business conversations and be seen as credible.

Jones believes that one of the main factors of being successful is implementing measurements. You start by hiring the right people, getting them to believe in you, and being seen as an authentic person. When you hire the right people, working with those people allows you to develop a strategy for success. Then you motivate them in the execution process, remove hurdles, and have robust conversations along the way. The conversations should focus on the hurdles and results.

The theme of relationships once again surfaces. The "us versus them" stigma must be completely removed for loss prevention to be viewed as a business partner. Without this partnership, it is virtually impossible to have success—not because you are not delivering the desired results but because the people who are assessing those results do not particularly care.

A big part of the job is to discuss the wins and hurdles and to ensure that loss prevention is elevated to a business discussion, not just a topic discussed during inventory, Jones explained. Unsuccessful loss prevention leaders wait for an event to initiate a conversation regarding loss prevention. One role of loss prevention leaders is to market their department internally and make certain they are providing value to the organization.

The marketing portion of the job—where the leaders are separated from the doers—is where most will fail. The leaders will not be involved with the day-to-day functions of the audits and investigations; rather, they will be at the table with the other leaders of the organization discussing how integral and invaluable the loss prevention department is to the success of the organization. The appropriate marketing is easier said than done. Loss prevention leaders need to be salespeople who want to ensure their customers keep coming back because they like what they see and get. As with anything, the better it looks, the more desirable it is to others. Some loss prevention leaders do not have outstanding results but are extremely successful in the eyes of the loss prevention community and to their executives. That is because they have marketed what they are doing properly.

Jones described his success using a multipronged approach to marketing. Just because one thing works does not mean it is the only thing that can be used. There are many different avenues for communication. See what the organization currently is accustomed to and follow it.

E-mail is one good way to communicate items such as internal newsletters, which provide high-level overviews of what is going on in loss prevention. Of course, you want to describe the wins and provide necessary

information. Nothing should be put in this letter that executives might not know is going on. For instance, if there is an internal investigation that will provide critical key opportunities, make sure the people who need to know about the investigation are aware before you release any documents pertaining to it.

Another part of the marketing strategy is to have formal senior executive team meetings. Jones recommends that these meetings be held two times per month to discuss what is going on in the department, again with a high-level overview. Executives like to have graphs and visuals that drive the point home; therefore, either printed documents or a PowerPoint reflecting the wins should be given at least once per month during the meetings. Most executives expect loss prevention people to be analytical, so you are providing only what is expected.

Meetings and newsletters are pretty standard ways of communicating. Jones also found that organizing a shrink steering committee (SSC), composed of department heads who make decisions regarding shrinkage, is effective in helping executives view the loss prevention team as a business partner. This approach is effective because it makes executives who are not necessarily thinking about shrinkage routinely responsible for it and for discussing it during meetings. As we know from earlier chapters, employees who have a vested interest in the organization will usually perform better and have fewer instances of dishonesty. The same approach is used with the SSC. Employees who are now directly involved with a facet of the business they had nothing to do with before will be more concerned about the results. This concern will turn into action in the departments they manage. For instance, if an executive from the merchandising department is on the SSC and one of the main contributors to shoplifting is the location of product in the store, this executive will listen to why it should be moved. If this person is not directly linked to shrinkage, the answer will usually be that the organization is not merchandising for shoplifting; it is merchandising for customers and sales.

NECESSARY TOOLS AND WHERE TO FIND THEM

It would be nice to have all the information you need at your fingertips for any new venture you start. However, finding the resources you need, especially when it is something that was previously nonexistent, can be an ordeal. Because loss prevention is so specialized, it is difficult to locate all the information you may need in one area. For those who have never

started up a loss prevention department but are now challenged to do so, having the information they need readily available would make the journey much easier. Thanks to the Loss Prevention Foundation (LPF), resources have been compiled to make life much easier for the loss prevention community.

The Loss Prevention Foundation is a nonprofit organization that assists the loss prevention community by providing educational resources including two certification programs for loss prevention: loss prevention qualified (LPQ) and loss prevention certified (LPC). Foundation members have access to many online educational resources that can help advance their career and broaden their perspective on loss prevention as a profession. The following sections provide resources that are extremely useful to anyone in loss prevention. They were taken directly from the foundation's Web site. The information is split up into the following categories:

- Associations
- Online publications
- Loss prevention resources
- General resources
- Search sites

Websites are provided to help you in your loss prevention journey. Many of the publications such as *Loss Prevention Magazine* are in print as well. Some of the associations require individual or organizational memberships, and others do not.

ASSOCIATIONS

General Associations

- Retail Industry Leaders Association (RILA): http://www.retail-leaders.org
- National Retail Federation (NRF): http://www.nrf.com
- American Society for Industrial Security (ASIS): http://www.asisonline.org
- Consumer Electronics Association: http://www.ce.org
- Electronic Retailing Association: http://www.retailing.org
- National Association of College Stores: http://www.nacs.org
- The Association for Convenience & Petroleum Retailing: http://www.nacsonline.com

- Retail Tobacco Dealers of America: http://www.rtda.org
- International Council of Shopping Centers (ICSC): http://www.iscs.org
- Association of Online Retailers: http://www.shop.org
- International Association of Property Crime Investigators: http://www.iapci.org
- Association of Certified Fraud Examiners: http://www.acfe.com
- Jewelers' Security Alliance: http://www.jewelerssecurity.org

Food Industry Associations

- Food Marketing Institute (FMI): http://www.fmi.org
- General Merchandise Distributors Council (GMDC): http://gmdc.com
- National Grocers Association: http://www.nationalgrocers.org
- International Food Service Executives Associations: http://www.ifsea.com
- The Association of Food, Beverage and Consumer Products Companies: http://www.gmabrands.com
- International Dairy, Deli, Bakery Association: http://www.iddba.org
- Distilled Spirits Council of the United States: http://www.discus.org
- Produce Marketing Association: http://www.pma.com
- National Association of the Specialty Food Trade: http://www.specialtyfood.com

Drug and Pharmaceutical Industry Associations

- National Association of Chain Drug Stores (NACDS): http://www.nacds.org
- Cosmetic, Toiletry, and Fragrance Association: http://www.ctfa.org
- American Pharmacist Association: http://www.aphanet.org
- National Community Pharmacist Association: http://www.ncpa-net.org
- National Council for Prescription Drug Programs: http://www.ncpdp.org
- Generic Pharmaceutical Association (GPhA): http://www.gpha-online.org
- Consumer Specialty Products Association: http://www.cspa.org

- American Association of Colleges of Pharmacy: http://www.aacp.org

Restaurant Industry Associations

- National Council of Chain Restaurants (NCCR): http://www.nccr.net
- National Food Service Security Council (NFSSC): http://www.nfssconline.org
- National Restaurant Association: http://www.restaurant.org
- Green Restaurant Association: http://www.dinegreen.com
- International Hotel & Restaurant Association: http://www.ih-ra.com

Safety Associations

- National Safety Council: http://www.nsc.org
- American Society of Safety Engineers (ASSE): http://www.asse.org
- National Association of Safety Professionals: http://www.nasp-web.com
- Occupational Safety & Health Administration (OSHA): http://www.osha.gov

Supply Chain Security and Logistics Associations

- International Cargo Security Council (ICSC): http://www.cargosecurity.com
- Maritime Security Council: http://www.maritimesecurity.org
- National Defense Transportation Association: http://www.ndtahq.com
- Council of Supply Chain Management Professionals (CSCMP): http://www.cscmp.org
- American Association of Port Authorities: http://www.aapa-ports.org
- International Warehouse Logistics Association: http://www.iwla.com
- Material Handling Industry of America: http://www.mhia.org
- Worldwide Business Research–Logicon: http://www.wbresearch.com
- Supply Chain Council (SCOR): http://www.supply-chain.org
- American Trucking Association (ATA): http://www.truckline.com

- Warehousing Education & Research Council (WERC): http://www.werc.org
- National Wooden Pallet & Container Association: http://www.nwpca.com
- International Foodservice Distributors Association: http://www.ifdaonline.org

Crisis Management Associations

- Business Continuity Planners Association: http://www.bcpa.org
- Disaster Preparedness and Emergency Response Association: http://www.disasters.org
- Association of Contingency Planners: http://www.acp-international.com

Diversity Organizations

- Network of Executive Women (NEW): http://www.networkofexecutivewomen.com
- Women's Business Enterprise National Council: http://www.wbenc.org
- International Organization of Black Security Executives (IOBSE): http://www.iobse.com

Audit Organization

- The Institute of Internal Auditors (IIA): http://www.theiia.org

Government Organizations and Agencies

- Federal Bureau of Investigation (FBI): http://www.fbi.gov
- Central Intelligence Agency (CIA): http://www.cia.gov
- Transportation Security Administration (TSA): http://www.tsa.gov
- Department of Homeland Security (DHS): http://www.dhs.gov
- U.S. Drug Enforcement Administration (DEA): http://www.justice.gov/dea
- Food and Drug Administration (FDA): http://www.fda.gov

- Bureau of Alcohol, Tobacco, Firearms and Explosives (ATF): http://www.atf.gov
- United States Secret Service: http://www.secretservice.gov
- Federal Emergency Management Agency (FEMA): http://www.fema.gov
- U.S. Environmental Protection Agency (EPA): http://www.epa.gov
- Centers for Disease Control & Prevention (CDC): http://www.cdc.gov
- U.S. Bureau of Industry and Security: http://www.bis.doc.gov
- U.S. Customs and Border Protection: http://www.customs.gov
- U.S. Computer Emergency Readiness Team (CERT): http://www.us-cert.gov
- U.S. Department of Transportation (DOT): http://www.dot.gov

ONLINE PUBLICATIONS

Loss Prevention Publications

- *Loss Prevention Magazine*: http://www.losspreventionmagazine.com
- *Security Management*: http://www.securitymanagement.com
- *Integrated Solutions for Retailers*: http://www.ismretail.com
- *LPinformation Magazine*: http://www.stores.org
- *Security Director News*: http://www.securitydirectornews.com
- *Asset Protection Executive*: http://www.apemag.com
- *Security Magazine*: http://www.securitymagazine.com
- *Security Manager*: http://www.securitymanager.net

General Retail Publications

- *Retail Forward*: http://www.retailforward.com
- *Retailing Today*: http://www.retailingtoday.com
- *Chain Store Age*: http://www.chainstoreage.com
- *Women's Wear Daily*: http://www.wwd.com
- *This Week in Consumer Electronics*: http://www.twice.com
- *Retail Net*: http://www.retailnet.com
- *Convenience Store / Petroleum*: http://www.cspnet.com
- *Convenience Store News*: http://www.csnews.com
- *Mass Market Retailers*: http://www.massmarketretailers.com

- *Morning News Beat*: http://www.morningnewsbeat.com
- *Retail Merchandiser*: http://www.retail-merchandiser.com
- *RetailWire*: http://www.retailwire.com

Food Industry Publications

- *Progressive Grocer*: http://www.progressivegrocer.com
- *Supermarket News*: http://www.supermarketnews.com
- *Grocery Headquarters*: http://www.groceryheadquarters.com
- *The Gourmet Retailer*: http://www.gourmetretailer.com
- *Food Industry News*: http://www.foodindustrynews.com
- *Beverage Industry*: http://www.bevindustry.com
- *C-Store News*: http://www.c-store.com
- *Petroleum & Convenience Store News*: http://www.npnweb.com

Drug Store Industry Publications

- Chain Drug Review: http://www.chaindrugreview.com
- Drug Store News: http://www.drugstorenews.com

Restaurant Industry Publications

- Chain Leader, Insight for Restaurant Executives: http://www.chainleader.com
- Nation's Restaurant News: http://www.nrn.com
- Restaurants & Institutions: http://www.rimag.com
- Restaurant Business Magazine: http://www.restaurantbiz.com
- Food Service: http://www.foodservice.com
- Quick Service & Fast Casual Restaurant News and Information: http://www.qsrmagazine.com

Supply Chain and Logistics Publications

- Cargo Security International: http://www.cargosecurityinternational.com
- Supply & Demand Chain Executive: http://www.sdcexec.com
- Global Logistics & Supply Chain Strategies: http://www.glscs.com
- Supply Chain Management Review: http://www.scmr.com
- Logistics Management: http://www.logisticsmgmt.com
- DC Velocity: http://www.dcvelocity.com

- Food Logistics: http://www.foodlogistics.com
- Inbound Logistics: http://www.inboundlogistics.com
- Logistics Today: http://www.logisticstoday.com
- Logistics Management: http://www.logisticsmgmt.com
- Supply Chain Digest: http://www.scdigest.com
- Traffic World: http://www.trafficworld.com
- Transportation Security: http://www.transportationsec.com
- Modern Materials Handling: http://www.mmh.com
- Logistics Online: http://www.logisticsonline.com
- RFID Solutions Online: http://www.rfidsolutionsonline.com
- American Shipper Magazine: http://www.americanshipper.com
- Seaports Magazine: http://www.aapaseaports.com
- Seaports Review: http://www.seaportspr.com
- Journal of Commerce: http://www.joc.com

Safety Publications

- The Safety Sentinel: http://www.naspweb.com
- Hazmat Management: http://www.hazmatmag.com
- Compliance Magazine: http://www.compliancemag.com
- Occupational Health & Safety: http://www.ohsonline.com
- Safety & Health Magazine: http://www.nsc.org

Crisis Management Publications

- Disaster Recovery Journal: http://www.drj.com
- Homeland Defense Journal: http://www.homelanddefensejournal.com
- Homeland Security Daily Wire: http://www.hsdailywire.com
- Continuity Insights: http://www.continuityinsights.com

National News Organizations

- The Wall Street Journal: http://www.online.wsj.com
- USA Today: http://www.usatoday.com
- The New York Times: http://www.nytimes.com
- Forbes: http://www.forbes.com
- CNN: http://www.cnn.com
- Reuters News Wire: http://www.reuters.com

Leadership Publications

- Chief Security Officer: http://www.csoonline.com
- Chief Information Officer: http://www.cio.com
- Chief Executive Officer: http://www.the-chiefexecutive.com
- Chief Executive: http://www.chiefexecutive.net
- Chief Financial Officer: http://www.cfo.com

Diversity Publications

- Diversity Plus Magazine: http://www.diversityplus.com
- Enterprising Women: http://www.enterprisingwomen.com
- Professional Women's Magazine: http://www.professional womanmag.com
- Minorities & Women in Business: http://www.mwib.com

RESOURCE LINKS

Loss Prevention Resource Links

- Contact, Inc.: http://www.contactinc.com
- LP Jobs: http://www.lpjobs.com
- Wicklander-Zulawski & Associates, Inc.: http://www.w-z.com
- Hospitality Lawyer.com: http://www.hospitalitylawyer.com
- Loss Prevention Research Council (LPRC): http://www.lpresearch.org
- National Association for Shoplifting Prevention (NASP): http://www.shopliftingprevention.org
- National Crime Prevention Council: http://www.ncpc.org
- Security Info Watch: http://www.securityinfowatch.com
- Smart LP—Resources for Retail Loss Prevention: http://www.smartlp.com
- Retail Loss Prevention eXchange: http://www.rlpx.com
- Security Technology & Design: http://www.securityinfowatch.com
- LP Information: http://www.lpinformation.com

Food Loss Prevention Resource Links

- Food Safety: http://www.foodsafety.gov

- FDA—Retail Food Protection: http://vm.cfsan.fda.gov
- FDA Recalls: http://www.fda.gov
- Food Service Central: http://www.foodservicecentral.com
- U.S. Census Bureau Monthly Foodservice Sales Data: http://www.census.gov
- U.S. Census Bureau Advance Monthly Sales for Retail & Food Services: http://www.census.gov
- USDA/FDA Foodborne Illness Education Information Center: http://www.nal.usda.gov
- Food Defense Resource Center: http://www.aibfooddefense.org
- Food for Thought—Industry Reports: http://www.fft-international.com
- Food CIO Forum: http://www.foodcioforum.com
- Food Info Net: http://www.foodinfonet.com
- Western Association of Food Chains: http://www.wafc.com
- Associated Grocers, Inc.: http://www.agsea.com
- Western Family: http://www.westernfamily.com

Drug and Pharmaceutical Industry Resource Links

- U.S. Pharmacopeia: http://www.usp.org
- Pharmaceutical Technology: http://www.pharmaceutical-technology.com

Restaurant Industry Resource Links

- Restaurant Page: http://www.restaurantpage.com
- U.S. FDA "Bad Bug Book": http://vm.cfsan.fda.gov
- State Health Departments: http://www.restaurant.org

Safety Resource Links

- OSHA Ergonomics: http://www.osha.gov
- National Institute for Occupational Safety and Health: http://www.cdc.gov
- Online Source for Recalls: http://www.recalls.gov

Supply Chain Security and Logistics Resource Links

- Western State Cargo Theft Association: http://www.wscta.com
- Cargo CATs (Los Angeles County Sheriff's Department): http://www.cargocats.us
- C-TPAT Minimum Security Criteria: http://www.cbp.gov
- Transportation Research Board (U.S.): http://www.trb.org
- Compliance, Florida Department of Transportation: http://www.dot.state.fl.us
- Commercial Motor Vehicle and Cargo Theft, Office of Motor Vehicles: http://www.dot.state.fl.us
- National Transportation Library (U.S.): http://ntl.bts.gov
- Eye for Transport: http://www.eyefortransport.com
- Procurement and Supply Chain Benchmarking Association: http://www.pasba.com

Crisis Management Resource Links

- National Hurricane Center: http://www.nhc.noaa.gov
- Pandemic Flu: http://www.pandemicflu.gov
- Pandemic Planning by State: http://www.pandemicflu.gov/usamap
- The Pandemic Network: http://www.pandemicnetwork.com
- DHS State Homeland Security Contacts: http://www.dhs.gov
- Homeland Security Exercise & Evaluation Program: http://www.hseep.dhs.gov
- National Institute for Occupational Safety & Health – Emergency Response Resources: http://www.cdc.gov/niosh/topics/emres/
- National Institute for Occupational Safety & Health – Emergency Preparedness for Businesses: http://www.cdc.gov/niosh/topics/emres/business
- Disaster Guides for Standard Safety Information: http://www.redcross.org/disaster/disasterguide/index.html
- DRI – The Institute for Continuity Management: http://www.drii.org
- Continuity Central: http://www.continuitycentral.com
- Disaster Resource: http://www.disaster-resource.com
- Overseas Security Advisory Council: http://ds-osac.org
- Office of the Coordinator for Counterterrorism: http://www.state.gov
- Terrorism Knowledge Base: http://www.tkb.org

- Global Incident Map: http://www.globalincidentmap.com
- Global Emergency & Disaster Information Service: http://visz.rsoe.hu/alertmap/index.php?smp=&lang=eng
- Avoiding Armageddon—Global Security Simulator: http://www.pbs.org
- Virus Bulletin: http://www.virusbtn.com
- Onestorm—Family Hurricane Planning: http://www.onestorm.org

Additional Government Resources

- Directory of State and Local Officials: http://www.fda.gov/ora/fed_state/directorytable.htm
- Bureau of Labor Statistics: http://www.bls.gov
- Bureau of Transportation Statistics (U.S.): http://www.bts.gov
- National Institute of Standards & Technology: http://www.nist.gov
- American Red Cross: http://www.redcross.org
- Ready.Gov Business: http://www.ready.gov/business/index
- World Health Organization: http://www.who.int/en/
- All CERT publications: http://www.cert.org/nav/allpubs.html
- StateScape—Legislative Policy Tracking and Analysis: http://www.statescape.com/resources/statelinks/statelinks.asp
- First Gov - U.S. Government portal to government information, services and online transactions: http://www.usa.gov/
- Code of Federal Regulations: http://www.census.gov/svsd/www/advtable.html
- U.S. Census Bureau Population Data: http:// factfinder.census.gov/home/saff/main.html?_lang=en
- Computer Incident Advisory Capability (U.S. Department of Energy): http://www.ciac.org

GENERAL RESOURCES
Leadership Resource Links

- Leadership Now: http://www.leadershipnow.com
- Security Executive Council: http://www.csoexecutivecouncil.com

Diversity Resource Links

- Diversity Inc.: http://www.diversityinc.com
- Diversity: http://www.diversity.com

Sarbanes–Oxley Resource Links

- Sarbanes–Oxley: http://www.sarbanes-oxley.com/
- Sarbanes–Oxley Compliance Toolkit: http://www.sox toolkit.com/

PCI Compliance Resource Links

- PCI Compliance.org: http://www.pcicomplianceguide.org/
- PCI Security Standards Council: https://www.pcisecuritystan-dards.org/
- PCI Internet Security Guide: http://www.internetsecurityguide. com/pci/pcicompliance.shtml

General Resource Links

- RAND—National Security Research Division: http://www.rand. org/nsrd/terrpanel/
- Hoovers: http://www.hoovers.com
- The World Fact Book: https://www.cia.gov/cia/publications/fact-book/index.html

Internet Scams and Hoaxes

- Scambusters: http://www.scambusters.org
- Hoaxbusters: http://hoaxbusters.ciac.org

SEARCH SITES

- Web Crawler: http://www.webcrawler.com
- ZABA Search: http://www.zabasearch.com
- ZOOM Info: http://www.zoominfo.com
- Technorati: http://www.technorati.com

- All The Web: http://www.alltheweb.com
- Kelly Search (U.S. Suppliers Search): http://www.kellysearch.com

SUMMARY

Because loss prevention is a tight-knit community of professionals, it is evident which organizations have highly successful departments. These departments are often featured on programs such as MSNBC when there is a need for a public discussion of theft. These departments have broken away from just being involved in their own organization and have distributed their wisdom so that others take note. It is not difficult to have a loss prevention department that performs statistically but that is seen by employees as a necessary evil. It is much more work to establish a department that is recognized as an integral part of the organization, as well as vastly knowledgeable, by society at large.

11

Investigative Practices of a Loss Prevention Department

INVESTIGATIONS DEFINED

Investigations can be defined as the relentless pursuit of the truth concerning who, what, where, why, how, when, and how much is involved in the commission of a crime. Investigations have a twofold purpose: (1) to identify the perpetrator of a crime; and (2) to identify the evidence that proves the intent of the perpetrator of that crime. Of course, there are other definitions, but I like these because they reveal the inquisitive nature of the investigator. In a retail business setting the most successful investigators are those who are inquisitive and driven by proving the details of the investigation. According to the National Retail Security Survey conducted by Dr. Richard Hollinger and Amanda Adams, graduate research associate in the Department of Criminology, Law, and Society at the University of Florida, retailers generally attribute 42% of their inventory shrinkage to internal or employee theft. In this same survey retailers estimate that it accounts for $15.5 billion in losses just from this single crime category. Employees are responsible for a higher percentage and dollar loss than shoplifting, operational or administrative errors, and vendor theft (refer to Figure 3.2 in Chapter 3). Assuming that retailers are supposed to entrust the store and its contents with the associates, this presents a very complex relationship between business owner–operators and their associates concerning trust.

UNDERSTANDING THE PARTS OF MANAGEMENT

This chapter deals with the investigative practices of a loss prevention department. Before we discuss investigations, it is important to understand that the philosophy of loss prevention is to prevent theft and policy violations that could result in the loss of assets, including associates because they may make a poor decision and may be terminated. When associate theft occurs, we look upon it as a failure of management. Management could have prevented the need for an investigation by enforcing the policies, training associates about the procedural controls, and creating awareness about the loss prevention department exception reporting and auditing. Management with good integrity is expected to make positive examples and model the way for associates.

According to the Association of Certified Fraud Examiners' 2010 Report to the Nations on Occupational Fraud and Abuse, there exists a strong correlation between a perperator's position of authority and the losses incurred by fraud. All too often even management may be involved in theft (Figure. 11.1). The Report to the Nations projected that 36.7% of theft was committed by employees and 17.1% was committed by owners

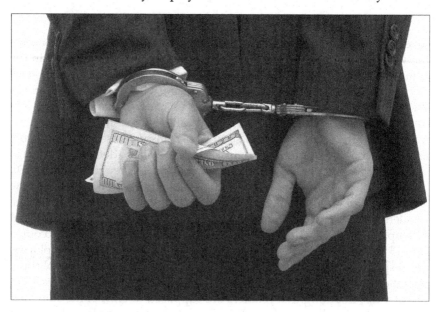

Figure 11.1 Many times management is involved in fraud and internal theft.

and managers/executives. An investigation was initiated in a specialty retail store in the mall when loss prevention analysts uncovered an Internet auction site tied back to a store manager who was selling high-fashion jewelry and accessories for deeply discounted prices. The investigators located the manager's store and noted that it had jewelry and accessory shrinkage. During the interview the manager confessed that he would take two or three pieces of merchandise every time he worked by placing them in his insulated lunch box because he was sure that no one would search it. This manager had been stealing for the last 2 years and confessed to taking more than $205,000 in merchandise; his Internet sales confirmed this. This store had a policy in effect that required all associates including management to have bags, briefcases, and lunch containers searched before leaving the store. This store was not conducting the required searches, in violation of company policy. When this happens, it is still a failure of management. Field management team members have responsibilities to control their stores and to lay down the policies and expectations as much as store managers.

Every time an investigation is concluded, the investigator must provide some training to make sure the manager or field manager left in charge understands where the policy violations were and what controls were violated that could have prevented the bad choices of associates who were investigated and eventually terminated for theft. Following are suggested fraud prevention tips investigators may discuss:

- Numbered and controlled manual receipts
- Proper balancing of receipts to tender amounts on a daily basis
- Trash controls
- Balancing monthly bank statements
- Proper balancing of credit card transactions
- Monitoring exception or high-risk transactions
- Verifying refunds controls daily
- Monitoring bank deposits daily
- Use of mystery shop program
- Use of closed-circuit TV for surveillance
- Employment application controls and verification
- Regulatory compliance

How does your retail business obtain information about dishonesty? Investigators may find all the investigations using their own devices, but if so they are missing a lot of potential investigations. My research examining investigative case data year after year indicates that tips or the need

for investigations came from the following, listed in order of highest frequency of occurrence:

1. Regional managers calling their regional loss prevention managers to report theft
2. Store managers calling their regional loss prevention manager (RLPM) to report theft
3. Use of exception reporting software to aid loss prevention analysts to find theft
4. Anonymous reporting on a toll-free business abuse hotline
5. Uncovered by the RLPM while conducting an operational and loss prevention audit
6. Store inspections turning up evidence such as empty blister packs in a secured stockroom

In a culture that emphasizes an open-door policy for associates to feel welcome to discuss issues with their manager without the threat of retaliation and the right to expect confidentiality if they want it, this is how the reporting of theft might look. In a culture that is not as open or does not emphasize communication as much, the use of a hotline might be at the top. What is important to take away from this is that there are a lot of ways to find out about theft. Be open to as many lines of communication as possible.

CONDUCTING INVESTIGATIONS

There are many good reasons to conduct investigations internally instead of hiring a third-party vendor or investigative firm. One of the most compelling is the Fair Credit Reporting Act (FCRA) guidelines, which require disclosure of investigations being conducted by a third party to the subject of the investigation. Before any employment action is taken, such as counseling or termination, the results of that investigation have to be disclosed to the subject of the investigation. You can see how that would not be in the best interests of the results of the investigation or the company. Similarly, when conducting a criminal background check using a third-party reporting agency, we must have associates' authorization to conduct the criminal background check and notify them of the results and the company's intent to take employment action before any is started. Most companies get consent for all inquiries into their criminal background along with all other prehire reference checks, drug testing,

preemployment testing, and educational background during the application process. Just be careful to consult with your legal department because the FCRA requires specific wording and specific format requirements on the preapplication authorization form.

During an in-house investigation where a criminal background check is necessary to learn about suspects' history, the appropriate authorization form must be signed before the criminal background check can be started through the third-party consultant. Once the background check is obtained, a copy of the resulting report and copy of subjects' rights under the FCRA must be submitted for their review. Additionally, a letter explaining whether the company will be taking employment action must be submitted to persons in question. Subjects of the investigation have the right to provide evidence that the background check is not correct and prove that their background does not have the alleged blemishes. After a reasonable time has passed, the company may proceed with the intended employment action.

Once a decision is made that an investigation is needed based on the information provided or evidence uncovered—and we will assume the investigation will be done by proprietary investigators—it becomes necessary to look for more evidence and proof that a crime was committed and that there was a perpetrator who committed the crime if one is not already identified. Investigations may also be done to uncover policy violations, such as sexual harassment and sharing a computer pass code, but we will continue this discussion as if it is a theft investigation. It is necessary to establish the credibility of persons making allegations. Go beyond the accusations to ensure that the information is not motivated by personal conflict between the two parties. A fact-finding interview should be done. This is a little less formal than an interview with a suspect but is structured enough to obtain the truth. First, verify the accusing associates' full name, address, position with the company and date of hire. Ask open-ended questions to allow subjects under investigation to give the whole statement including the details that make it clear to them that a theft did take place and who the thief is. Getting a written collaborating statement of the facts as the accusing witnesses see them will help ensure that the facts do not change later in the investigation. Sometimes accusers will be very comfortable with verbal accusations but do not feel good about writing out the accusation. Their internal conscience works against them when it comes to writing accusations out if they are not true.

Next, look for physical evidence of the theft by examining the store sales floor for some theft indicators such as empty clothing racks with

empty hangers on them. Another piece of physical evidence would be the paper trail with shipping receipt documents, price changes, sales transaction records, discarded price tickets, control logs, damage slips, and even discarded price tickets—any items that prove the product was in the store at some time and went missing. Some retailers have a very good handle on what merchandise is believed to be in the store. They can use a product's stock-keeping unit (SKU) or universal product code (UPC) to verify it in the inventory-keeping system in their computers. They can identify every sale, refund, transfer, and receipt of that particular SKU and determine if that item should still be on the shelf in the store. Finding written documents proving or disproving allegations of theft of funds can include expense account statements including restaurant receipts, mileage calculations, and unauthorized claims for expenses that would not normally be approved. In cases of expense account fraud, look for blank restaurant checks filled in by hand.

When investigating credit card fraud, the obvious evidence is the credit card receipts that might show multiple sales to one credit card and multiple refunds to one card over a few days or all on one day in a week. Sometimes store associates will be involved in counterfeit credit card schemes. Counterfeit credit cards can sometimes be recognized by the first four digits not matching the issuing company's code identifying the type card. Exception reporting software such as Aspect LP Software, Triversity Fraud Watch Software, and XBR from DataVantage can help identify credit card fraud. One very valuable exception report is a daily list of credit card returns that show the original sale transaction on one card, for instance, a Visa card and the corresponding refund transaction tendered on a Master Card that happens to have the refunding associate's name attached. The scheme is to find a big sale on a credit card and then refund it into associate's debit card account, thereby filling it with cash to be withdrawn.

Return fraud is one of the most serious internal theft schemes that affects every retailer and often accompanies other types of theft committed by the same associates. Associates often feel a false sense of security from being able to cover up the theft of cash from the register till by creating a fraudulent refund in a customer's name. The customer may not have visited the store recently. Refund fraud comprises approximately 42% of the investigations I have reviewed over the past few years. In one such investigation, a store manager of a leased optical shop within a larger department store would remove cash from the host store's cash register and create a cash refund as the reason for the missing money. The optical

shop point-of-sale (POS) system, which ran separately from the host store POS, was not updated with the refund. What uncovered the thefts was a report by the host company showing stores that were experiencing large cash deductions from the leased shop business. In this case, cash deductions did not immediately tip off the investigator to examine refunds. Cash theft, end-of-day balancing errors, and petty cash loans were also potential symptoms of this problem. The store manager was found out by the host store cash office supervisor who told the investigator that the optical shop had a lot of cash returns for which the manager took loans as she did not have the cash in her POS system in the department. The optical shop had very low returns of any type because this manager was not recording them in her register in violation of policy. The investigator never thought about refunds being the cause. The store manager confessed to $16,000 in fraudulent cash refunds, petty cash vouchers, and stolen merchandise. After the investigation, controls were put in place to require the host store manager to verify refunds for the optical shop manager. An exception report was developed on cash deductions from the host store charged against the business. Other controls that might work when the POS system for the store revision also includes using exception reporting to look for high percentages of cash refund to sales. Calls to customer to verify returns should be done by the manager in charge and verified by auditors. Proper signature requirements must be enforced. Original sales receipts must be attached to the refund to show where the product was previously purchased.

Purchase orders can be a source of paper evidence when investigating a misappropriation of funds case. The scheme involves a purchasing office associate who sets up bogus accounts and receives kickbacks for steering business to a particular dishonest vendor. The vendor usually agrees to send an additional invoice so a check may be cut for a bogus account from which the dishonest purchasing agent withdraws the money. Purchase orders are still issued, but there may be more than one for a vendor. Look for vendor account addresses that match employees' home addresses. Look for unauthorized orders and forged authorizations. Purchase orders should be in proper sequence and inclusive. Even in a computerized system, there should be a way to verify that every purchase order number has been used for a valid vendor account.

Invoices prove to be another source of evidence when investigating invoicing fraud. The invoicing clerk sends invoices to a vendor for more than was actually ordered. Checks for payment are still processed in the same way. This works especially well if there is a lack of separation of

responsibilities between the person approving invoices and the person receiving checks and posting them to accounts, which might be the case in a small company. Look for checks payable to employees. Bogus vendors send checks from the company that are then intercepted by the associate.

Evidence concerning the POS system includes cash refund slips, void receipts, unauthorized discounting, no-sales, and bank deposit slips. When examining these types of documents look for signatures of customers that match those of associates, associates misusing the authorization codes, and failure to follow the company policies that you have established. Voids and refunds should always be tied to an original sales transaction, and many companies have the policy that it be attached to the void or refund for reference.

Witnesses should be interviewed to gather the facts of what they observed and what they know. Witnesses' statements should be written out to ensure all of the facts are documented. When interviewing witnesses it is important to stress confidentiality with them by assuring them that their statements will be kept confidential, and they should be told that there is an expectation that they keep their discussions with the interviewer confidential. Make sure you have considered all possible victims, perpetrators, and witnesses to the crime you are investigating, and prioritize them for your preferred order when you begin your interviews. Sometimes, a matrix of all employees with proximity to the crime can help determine common denominators and even pinpoint the prime suspect. However, if you do not have a prime suspect, use the matrix to determine those who are furthest away from the actual commission of the crime to start your interviews. Interview those who have the most involvement or knowledge about what happened toward the end, and save the main suspect or suspects for last. The reason for this is that each interview will reveal additional facts about the crime or theft. If you do not have strong enough evidence to indicate a suspect, you may pick up additional facts and indicators to strengthen your convictions about an individual you feel is responsible. You may also learn enough to change your mind, based on new evidence, that the responsible party is someone already interviewed as a witness or the person reporting the crime.

RISK CONSIDERATIONS

Once you have learned of the crime, have gathered physical evidence, and have taken witness statements, it becomes increasingly important to

involve others in your business like human resources or associate relations, operations management, and the corporate legal department. Do this before commencing with interviews of those suspected of involvement in the crime. Associate relations should be in the loop on all investigations. Some companies make the notification after the entire investigation has been completed. It is a matter of preference, but I have learned that investigation dispositions go a lot smoother when the associate relations partners expect the call or are actually involved in the investigation. They provide precedents previously set by the company on case disposition decisions. They can also provide past performance history about the associate you are investigating. Some companies do not feel they get the support from associate relations and make the termination decision without the input of this department. I believe that having this partner is necessary to ensure that no mistakes are made in the termination or counseling action. If allegations arise on the part of the person being investigated, it is extremely helpful to have the support of associate relations.

The legal department should always be involved to approve investigative techniques that have case law decisions applied to them. For instance, if you are planning to use closed-circuit (CCTV) for surveillance, it is smart to get legal advice. CCTV can be used in public places where associates do not have a reasonable expectation of privacy but should not be used in restrooms, dressing rooms, and locker rooms. In some states, audio recording (e.g., CCTV) is highly regulated, and both parties must consent or else that evidence is inadmissible in court and/or plain illegal. In other states, only one party must consent to recording conversations. Your attorney is the best person to help keep your investigators out of trouble; check with them on such investigative techniques as controlled buys, secret shoppers, and any investigation that overlaps ongoing legal proceedings in which an associate is involved with the company. Attorneys can also provide attorney–client privilege protection on the work product of the investigation. In most cases, the legal department must be informed of the next steps before you take them.

Operations management must be involved every step of the way in the investigation of their associates. Without the partnership of the manager or associates being investigated, it will be very hard to have access to evidence that is in their immediate work area and to them for interviews. Operations can give insights into other pending problems with the individual, which can be included in the investigation. The operational manager will help arrange the interview time and place and will help cover the store if necessary. Once the investigation has been completed, the final

disposition must involve the operational manager, who will have the final say on termination of the dishonest associate with input from the investigator and associate relations.

Creating an investigative file becomes necessary as documents and witness statements start to accumulate. This may be at the beginning of the investigation or later as needed. Some practical steps can be taken to help keep a large case file organized, and to make evaluation of the evidence effective include the following:

1. Verify and document each piece of evidence on a table of contents sheet that will appear at the beginning of the file. This is more important on larger files.
2. Carefully maintain the chain of evidence so it is in the investigator's possession at all times.
3. Operate under the assumption that every investigation will end up in a court of law, even if you will not be prosecuting.
4. Remember that any notes written about the case included during the interview are part of the case file and will be read in court. Never express opinions of a suspect or make off-color comments that you would not want repeated in front of a crowd.
5. Include the company's approved investigative case report that documents all the facts about the investigation and the narrative that describes the investigation and disposition.
6. Include all statements of witnesses and the confession of the suspect.
7. Include any promissory note or court documents pertaining to the case.

Establishing intent is going to be necessary to be able to prove a case in the event you decide to prosecute, so it is advisable to start thinking about that early on in the investigation. Associates' intent to steal from a retail business is usually proven through confession, because a good one will be written out by the associates themselves. Even if a statement is not taken, intent can be proven by their actions. Once they remove merchandise or cash from the store, intent is obvious. We cannot know what they were thinking, so we either have to get them to write it or prove it by their actions. So in determining if we should prosecute suspects, we consider if the accumulation of evidence and the statements supporting the case lead a reasonable person to believe they intended to act as they did. Did they knowingly break a law? What possible defenses or denials will they give? These are all things to consider when preparing to interview main suspects.

CONDUCTING INTERVIEWS WITH SUSPECTS

Assuming that suspects have been identified after reviewing the collected evidence and after considering all witnesses statements, the next step is to interview all potential suspects. Planning the interview is just as important as conducting the interview to obtain the desired result: a confession from the suspect. Decide where the interview will take place, preferably an uncluttered office or private room with a desk and three chairs. A door is nice for privacy but not always necessary. If there is a door, it should be left unlocked, and the suspect should be told that they are not locked in during the beginning of the interview. If the interview will be conducted in a small, single-coverage store, work with the store manager to set up coverage so the associate can be away for at least an hour and a half or longer. Some retailers make it mandatory that a witness sit in on the interview; others do not require it. A female witness is necessary if a male is interviewing a female. A male witness is necessary if a female is interviewing a male.

Next, run through the interview in your mind, and jot down some questions. What rationalizations will you use to help make it easier for the suspect to confess? How will you address denials? Do you have confidence in your evidence and your ability to obtain a confession? The way the interview is conducted will have a direct impact on whether a confession is obtained. If you go into the interview having doubts about suspects' involvement, it will show up in your voice and your physical behavior as an interviewer. Your interviewee will pick that up and you will not get a confession. Some retailers are very numbers oriented, and investigators are encouraged to build their caseload to show increased productivity. If investigators are numbers driven, it is an unproductive environment and does not do much for confidence. Confidence builders include the following:

- Being comfortable with the evidence gathered because it proves suspects' involvement.
- Having enough rationalizations available and jotted down in your interview file.
- Thinking ahead about the denials and jotting down how to handle them.
- Knowing everything about the crime being investigated.
- Knowing everything you can learn about your interviewee.

I received interview training from Wicklander-Zulawski, a Chicago-based company. They are the experts in techniques used for interviewing and interrogation, and their basic course is called "Interview and Interrogation Techniques." Before an interview I would always create a rough outline of the interview format I learned from them with my notes specific to the case I was about to interview for. I am not going to attempt here to do justice to teaching the reader how to interview. We will reserve that for the book written by Douglas Wicklander and David Zulawski titled *Practical Aspect of Interview and Interrogation* (1993) or one of their workshops that take two full days. For the purposes of the present book, I spent some time talking with Mr. Zulawski about some current topics that practitioners often ask about and that I thought might be interesting.

Q: A large part of our book deals with the psychology of the culture of integrity, and that was presented in the first three chapters. How do you view integrity as related to associate dishonesty?

A: The culture of integrity begins with management's dealings with the public and its associates. Management should address the idea of integrity from the start of an employee's career with the organization. Managers should present a distinct message that employees are not permitted to steal and the company believes in integrity. A lot of times it is implied by the business, but it is important for management and loss prevention to explicitly say it and set expectations for employee behavior. Dishonest employees assess the risk of detection versus the possible reward if they steal. If the reward outweighs the risk, a theft occurs. There are at least three parts to a loss prevention program: awareness, audit, and investigation. All of these help reduce the level of internal theft at a company.

Q: When an investigator is conducting an interview and the subject will not confess despite having good evidence and picking up signs that the subject is being less than truthful, what advice do you have?

A: If an investigator is having consistent problems obtaining an admission with a solid investigation and evidence, he or she is probably doing something wrong. Examining the strategy being used to open the conversation and the overall structure of the interview is the best way to identify the problem. The strategy and structure employed has a lot to do with the interviewer's success or

failure. Once the investigator has progressed to a point in the interview where the suspect is making repeated denials the chance of salvaging it fades. In our experience problems and denials in an interview are generally caused by something that the interviewer did or said to the suspect. Another cause of a difficult interview is subjects who have had an opportunity to prepare themselves for the interview and to create a strategy of denial to protect themselves. Some suspects are difficult to deal with for a variety of reasons. An interviewer should have anticipated a more difficult interview because of their personality or their previous experience being questioned. People tend to react to conflict in a similar fashion each time they are in a similar situation. As a result, the interviewer can profile these individuals' likely responses based on what they have done previously in dealings with managers and other associates. The interviewer can anticipate that employees who have acted aggressively previously will likely do so again since this is a preferred strategy. Another example of a difficult interview might occur in a union environment where employees are encouraged to ask for union representation when they are interviewed. Having a union representative in the room often disrupts the interview process and makes it more difficult to obtain an admission. The investigator operating in this type of environment is generally well advised to develop enough information to terminate the employee without an admission since obtaining one may be very difficult. Each of these instances can usually be planned for, and the investigative process should focus on developing evidence that can be used independently of an admission to terminate the individual's employment. Associate relations can give advice on what information is necessary to terminate the associate. If we are unable to obtain an admission, associate relations will have already decided what must be established to terminate the dishonest associate.

Q: What are your thoughts on using negative-based statements that can document lies and discrepancies as opposed to the facts?

A: There is little value in taking a statement from a suspect if it simply denies involvement in the crime—for example, "I didn't steal the deposit." However, if the denial is accompanied by the individual's alibi or an in-depth account of events, it may be very valuable. Such a statement can be analyzed using statement analysis

techniques to look at the structure of the alibi and possible omissions that may lead to further questioning. In addition, by documenting details the investigator has locked the subject into a story that may be subject to investigation. By disproving the lies and identifying significant omissions in the subject's statement the interviewer can destroy the credibility of the individual's testimony. When there is evidence of dishonesty or a violation of policy, we may use a participatory accusation. In a participatory accusation the interviewer allows the subject to talk about his or her alibi, understanding of a policy, or the sequence of events in an incident. The investigator holds back the evidence allowing the subject to lie, thus increasing the power of any evidence discovered during the investigation. If a suspect stole a deposit, for example, the person might have added to the story that he does not have the combination to the safe and was not present in the store on the day the money went missing. Contrary to these assertions the investigation has revealed that the manager gave the suspect the combination and there is a videotape of the individual in the store on the day the deposit was taken. Using this type of an accusation the interviewer has trapped the suspect and established that he has clearly lied. For the participatory accusation to work the interviewer should lock down all the plausible excuses the suspect might have for the evidence. For example, if a store manager is seen putting merchandise into his car, what plausible explanations could he have for doing so? Transferring product, giving a donation, or perhaps returning merchandise could all be possible scenarios the manager might use to explain away the seemingly damning observation. However, once he has discussed how product is transferred, donations given, and returns made—none of which include putting it in his car—he can no longer use them to explain away the observation.

Q: How important is it to operate under the assumption that every investigation will end up in a court of law, even if you will not be prosecuting?

A: Always prepare investigations as though you are going to prosecute or be sued for your actions. Do not do or say things you would not want to come out in a courtroom full of people. Lawyers are going to prepare an argument to defend their client, and your statement, case notes, and investigation will be examined and

204

criticized for any shortcomings. They will look at what you did and more importantly what you did not do.

Q: When I attended the WZ Interviewing and Interrogations Techniques workshop, I learned about building a matrix, or Employee Data Sheet, for cash theft or cases where many people had access to the lost cash funds. Are these tools still recommended?

A: Exception reporting has gone a long way toward replacing the data sheet in targeting dishonest associates. The data sheet captures biographical information and characteristics about employees that help rank the associates from high to low risk of stealing. By looking for characteristics associated with people who steal and then organizing these items in a data sheet, we are able to assess the likelihood of theft activity by the employee. Those employees falling into the high-risk category are more likely to steal than those in the low-risk categories. The data sheet can also be useful when trying to narrow down a field of suspects or determining where to focus an investigation. This is a tool that can often help narrow the investigative targets and the cost of an investigation.

Q: Lately there has been litigation alleging forced confessions. What is your advice toward avoiding that risk?

A: First and foremost is a careful investigation followed by a substantiated confession detailing the individual's participation in dishonest activities. Attorneys tend to take cases with a good storyline where they believe they can win because of the weakness of the case. The attorney creates a plausible argument that puts the interviewer and company in bad light. Most companies bring a witness to the interview so they may testify as to what went on and what was said. The company now has the interviewer and witness to testify what happened plus a written or recorded statement from the employee admitting dishonesty. Many police departments have mandates requiring all interrogations to be videotaped so there is no dispute over what happened or was said. Some retailers have taken up this practice and require recording of all interviews. Finally, a statement from the suspect containing substantiation supporting the investigative findings goes a long way to defend the company. The voluntary statement is the crown jewel at the end of the case, which can create significant problems for the opposing counsel.

Q: What is your most valuable advice to investigators or loss prevention managers starting out in their career of investigating and interviewing?

A: Every new investigator should develop the essential skills for the job. These skills provide the foundation for future development and increased responsibilities. Investigators should be looking for something that sets them apart from coworkers. One essential skill is learning to interview and close cases. As a starting point, attend a Wicklander-Zulawski & Associates Interview and Interrogation Techniques seminar to learn the fundamentals of the interview process. After that, use what was taught in class exactly as it was taught. Most people do not have enough experience to decide whether what they are going to try will have a positive or negative effect on the subject. The WZ technique has developed over years of trial and error by experienced interviewers, so there is no need to recreate the wheel. Next, look to profession certification, such as becoming a certified forensic interviewer (CFI) or certified fraud examiner (CFE), to establish your credentials. Certification is a credential that goes above and beyond work experience and will set investigators apart from others in the industry. Remember, the skills taught in an interviewing class are really communication techniques relating to persuasion that will serve well in an interview or the boardroom. There are so many senior executives who credit the interviewing skills they developed as one of the most important aspects in their rise to success.

Before an interview it is smart to review suspected associates' personnel files to record their correct name and address, date of birth, date of hire, and position in the interview notes. This file can be a wealth of information about individuals' educational level and prior life experiences from their employment application. This could be a help in the interview because you will be able to relate to interviewees' educational level and understand their likes and past to try to develop a rapport with them.

The following paragraphs provide an introduction to the possible interview stages; investigators are encouraged to explore details surrounding interviews in classes for more in-depth understanding. Start the interview with some friendly questions to establish rapport and establish your own credibility. This introduction should be used to explain who you are and your role with the company. Talk about what an investigation is and why one is necessary. Spend between 15 and 25 minutes on this

introduction, and bring up common themes that help associates feel more relaxed and recognize that they have something in common with you.

Ask some nonaccusatory, fact-finding questions such as to verify the address of the associate. Ask if they understand the policy relating to the violation or theft you are interviewing about. Watch their physical reactions and verbal responses to understand how they respond to questions that you would expect them to answer truthfully. This is important because it helps to establish a baseline to compare against when soft accusations are made. For example, we would expect suspects to answer questions about their length of employment or current title honestly without feeling threatened or put on the spot. They should be able to talk about their address and previous education without feeling any stress, unless your investigation deals with lying on a résumé or application for employment. If that is the case, select other introductory questions.

As the interview progresses and rapport has been established, you should move into some rationalization with subjects to help them rationalize that it is in their best interests to tell the truth. An example of rationalization might look like this: "Well, Jeremy, I've been speaking to company employees for many years, and I have always been able to help them feel better about the situation once we have gotten all of the facts out on the table and the company can understand why you made the decisions you did about that deposit." If interviewing over the phone, it could go like this: "Jeremy, I have been speaking to associates like you for many years; do you think that if this were a very serious issue that I would be speaking to you over the phone? I would be meeting with you in person instead, right?"

If you feel like the interview is progressing well and the subject has been very cooperative, if you have been keenly aware of the suspect's behavior and have been looking for submission in posture like lowering of the eyes, lowering of the head between the hands, and sitting back in the chair in a more relaxed manner, you might make a soft accusation using an assumptive question like, "Well, Jeremy, you are a good-natured individual, and it is very hard for me to believe that you planned this; wasn't it a spur of the moment decision?" At this point Jeremy's response will determine the next statement. Jeremy can respond that he did not plan to take the money and that it was spur of the moment. This is his initial confession. On the other hand, Jeremy can respond with a denial. If denial is what Jeremy chooses, do not even let him get the denial out entirely, interrupting him to start him back on the path of rationalization. It is necessary to continue the rationalization themes until you hit upon one he identifies with. This process is perhaps the hardest part of the

interview process because you must be able to find themes to talk about and keep control of the conversation until a confession is made.

If Jeremy does make a small confession, you must keenly pick up on that and begin to develop it. Another assumptive question might be appropriate: "Jeremy, what is the most you have ever taken in one day while working at XYZ? $500 a day?" Jeremy might say, "Absolutely not. I never took more than $100 in a day." Here is the second admission that helps support the first softer confession. It is important to avoid questions that can be easily answered or that can be construed as leading the associate. Allow Jeremy to tell of his involvement on his own insomuch as he is able to develop the picture. Ask open-ended questions about other incidents that took place, when, for how much, and who else was involved.

Once you are able to get all your questions answered, it is time to begin a written statement explaining to interviewees that committing their statement to writing will help protect them by ensuring that the truth is documented in their own words and that the truth does not change. In support of the investigation the statement of confession has a number of important uses, primarily to describe the crime in associates' own words for criminal and civil hearings. Statements can impress upon a jury that the confession was made voluntarily. Some company legal departments prefer an informed consent document because it sets the tone of what is to come. Informed consent forms record the name and address of the associates about to be interviewed along with their position and location of their job. It lets associates know they are being asked to cooperate in a company investigation. It states that they are not being detained against their will and they can leave the room. It also states that if they choose not to cooperate, they will be subject to possible employment action, including termination for failure to comply with company policy, which requires them to cooperate with investigations. This idea of informed consent may appear to be an obstacle in getting cooperation. I have used it in all face-to-face interviews but not in phone interviews. I have never experienced one interviewee who read the consent and left the room. I have experienced a few who would not sign it, and that is okay because I just continued with the interview. On the positive side, informed consent makes it much harder for suspected associates to make a claim that they were detained against their will for little or no reason. In the event that associates sign the document and then determine later to leave the interview unfinished, you have strong grounds to act on their uncooperative behavior. While that will not solve the crime, it might help eliminate a bad apple from the store.

The confession can be written or recorded, depending on the company's policy. Written statements should be taken on lined paper like a legal pad or in a statement format approved by your company's legal department. Statements have an introduction, a body, and a closing. In the introduction interviewees will identify themselves with their name, address, place of employment, location of their work unit, and date and time of the statement. They will state that they understand they are making a statement of their own free will without any threats or promises. The statement must be written out by interviewees in their own handwriting, and any mistakes they make should be changed and initialed by them to acknowledge the change. In the body of the statement you may give some prompting to ensure that necessary identifying information is captured, especially if the statement is being taken on a lined legal pad without the formatting. If a format is used, you will want to be sure that the information is filled in thoroughly, as many statements reviewed are lacking in the area of thoroughness.

The body of the statement will be where interviewees write out their confession including all the details of the theft. This part of the statement must not be dictated by you. Leading questions should be used only if interviewees evade the facts of their involvement. The best way to start is to explain to interviewees that this is their chance to tell the truth about their involvement and help decision makers know that they are sincere about making amends with the company. Most people will want to make things better. There are those who will not see it that way, so you must be aware of what is being written. Occasional breaks in writing can be taken to review what was written. It is preferred that you learn to read upside down, which comes with practice. A good explanation of what is expected will get interviewees started and will get most of the facts documented. Questions may be asked to have the interviewee document what is needed. An example would be, "Jeremy, why did you remove the $100 from the deposit?" Jeremy might reply that he needed to make a car payment and did not have the cash. This helps to prove the intent and that there was a use for the stolen $100. Besides the who, what, where, how, why, and how much that must be captured in the statement, it is necessary to obtain a statement of knowledge that the action was theft. You might have to ask the question directly. Another approach would be to ask interviewees how they feel about the action now in light of their confession. The intent is to get them to apologize and to show their remorse because they knew it was wrong.

The conclusion of the statement will be an acknowledgment of the interviewee that they are making a statement of their own free will. The most important thing that must be said is they affirm that the statement they made is true. They might also mention how they were treated during the interview process. This statement should be signed by the interviewee, you, and a witness. It is also a good idea to include the times the interview began and ended in the conclusion, and the interviewee should write these times. If a promissory note is to be taken, it should be at the conclusion of the interview. A promissory note is a civil document used as an agreement with associates that they will pay back what they have stolen. Promissory notes should not be used when associates will be prosecuted. Most police departments will not even entertain taking your case if a promissory note is signed because it turns your issue with the associate into a civil issue. The interview is concluded by thanking associates for their cooperation in the investigation.

Thus far, I have not said a lot about how to treat a suspected associate. At all times during the investigation and during the interview, courtesy and a businesslike demeanor are necessary. Never threaten suspects with physical harm or criminal prosecution to extract a confession. Always keep in mind that they are just that—suspects—and your job is not to find guilt. That is the responsibility of the courts. Our job as investigators and interviewers is to find the truth. As a company investigator, our responsibility is to remain objective throughout the investigation and its outcome. We should refrain from forming an opinion that suspected associates are guilty. We may make a statement that we have obtained overwhelming evidence pointing to the associates' involvement. Then leave it to the courts to determine guilt or innocence. I have avoided using *interrogation* to describe the interview process because of the harsh stereotype associated with it through the media and television shows. Treating interviewed associates with dignity is essential to maintaining the reputation of a retail loss prevention department.

Once the investigation is concluded, you should discuss the results with the human resources manager and immediate supervisor of the suspected associates and make a recommendation for termination of employment. If no confession is obtained, then all details and merits of the case will need to be reviewed to determine what action should be taken with interviewees. Prosecution of the confessed can be initiated by calling the police to the locations to take a report and take them into custody while they are still present, or charges may be filed at the court if the decision is not made to prosecute immediately. Prosecution should be pursued in

cases of criminal activity where there is a theft of cash, fraud, or theft of merchandise. Of course, law enforcement should be called in on work-place violence or violations of laws. When a policy violation is being investigated, it is likely there is no evidence of a law being broken. For instance, in the investigation of unauthorized discounts, there may be a violation of your company's policies. That may be a violation of policy but not against the law. The business legal department can help determine how to proceed.

Most state laws allow retailers to make a civil demand of shoplifters and in many cases of dishonest associates who commit refund fraud or steal merchandise. A civil demand is one for the payment of a set fee, such as $100, in addition to the recovery of what was stolen. Some states may allow double the damages. The best way to navigate the civil demand laws is to work with a company such as Civil Demand Associates that specializes in those types of collections. If your company is intent on col-lection of civil demands in house, consulting the legal department is the best avenue. Be aware that in the majority of states a civil demand should not be pursued if criminal prosecution has been initiated.

PHONE INTERVIEWING

Phone interviewing is a viable tool when investigators are weighing the cost of a trip to meet with a suspect in person in light of the alleged loss. Some retail businesses use a centralized investigative unit in which ana-lysts use exception software to mine the data for potential cases, and, after pulling together all of the evidence from POS reports and exception reports and sending the local field manager into the store to pull docu-mentation, they turn the investigative file over to the investigator to con-duct the interview and complete the case. Some benefits of conducting phone interviews, besides the potential expense savings, involve mak-ing it easier to prove that suspects were never forced to cooperate with the investigation because they were on the phone and could have simply hung up the phone to end the interview. Another benefit is that today's younger generations are intimately connected to cell phones. They shop using their phone to get opinions and make decisions and to communi-cate with friends using their phones. They are very comfortable talking on the phone to the point that it is a preferred communication mode. While interviewers cannot see associates' physical behavior on the other end of the phone, with practice interviewers are able to pick up cues from their

vocal tones. With a few minor adjustments, managers can set up the interview and get the location ready. They do not have to witness the entire interview but come in at the conclusion of the interview, place the phone on speaker, and listen to the interviewee verbally repeat the admission. They would then stay in the room and assist with taking the statement from their associate.

Use of a loss prevention case management system will help with investigative case report review where approved cases can be closed out by supervisors. A good case management system can help organize the reporting of case statistics and conduct analysis on the number, locations, types, and amounts of the cases the loss prevention department is handling. There are a number of case management systems available today. Some are Internet based, and the data are stored in the case management software companies' databases. It is always accessible, but you have to be connected to the Internet to complete case reports and view reports. If your company's Internet connections are robust and rarely drop off, then this may be a viable and less expensive option. One example of this type of case management system is Wazagua (http://home.wazagua.com). If your business likes to own software that achieves and provides both an online and off-line reporting tool, explore Loss Prevention Management Software (LPMS; http://Lpguys.com), which will reside on your company's server. These are just two examples of a number of case management systems available to the practitioner.

This is the short story of internal investigative practices of a loss prevention department. Whole books have been devoted to the topic of interview and interrogations and criminal investigations. This is an overview of investigative practices with some emphasis on risks to the business if investigations are not handled correctly. Investigations must go through a review process by the leadership of the loss prevention department to assure quality control of the reports, evidence files, and statements. Developing good partnerships with your legal, human resources, and operational professionals will ensure good decisions are made all through the investigative process. Being meticulous through the investigation and concise in reporting will help to ensure good court ready investigations with minimal risk.

12

Selecting the Best for Your Loss Prevention Department

SELECTING ASSOCIATES FOR SUCCESS

Finding the right fit for a loss prevention position can be a challenge. After you begin the process, you will quickly learn that not everyone fits the mold. Most will fall into the Papa Bear (too hard) or Mama Bear (too soft) chair, and few will fit in the Baby Bear (just right) chair. The "just right" individual will exhibit many characteristics that were a combination of many other individuals who were interviewed with regards to a person's ability and skill. The recruiter for the position must be able to differentiate between a motivated business professional and an "old-school ex-cop." Experience in the business will be a definite plus when it comes to the selection process. Over the years you have been able to see what works in the business and what does not when it comes to personality. The trickiest part of recruiting for loss prevention is finding the right combination of analytical skills and an affable upbeat personality. If you settle for someone who possesses only one and not the other, you will most likely have problems down the line. The job posting must be very specific on whom you will consider for employment. Countless employees in retail organizations want to be in loss prevention because, as they will put it, it seems like a cool job and they are attracted only for the thrill of the chase. If you

are requiring a college degree, make sure that you specify the type of degree you are looking for, which will weed out people you do not want.

Many colleges and universities offer associate's and bachelor's degrees in criminal justice, police sciences, and corrections, which provide a substantial background for the law enforcement aspects of loss prevention or asset protection. However, these majors are weak in preparing students for loss management/security management, business administration, or accounting, all things a retail management position might require. Do not forget that retailers are looking for business managers who specialize in the loss prevention or asset protection fields. Being well rounded is very important here.

JOB DESCRIPTIONS

The following job description was taken from a Gap Inc. posting through http://LPJobs.com. The posting is for a district loss prevention manager (DLPM):

> The district loss prevention manager is responsible for applying loss prevention expertise and devising a loss prevention strategy within assigned districts encompassing 10–30 stores. The DLPM will take a proactive approach to resolving losses within assigned stores through training and awareness, creating and delivering loss prevention training to heads of stores, merchandise managers, and district managers. The position will be responsible for all loss prevention investigations, operations, training, and budget for multiple stores in assigned districts and will recruit, hire, train, develop, and supervise 10–20 loss prevention personnel. The DLPM will also manage vendors, physical security, and contract guards and work closely with all levels of management to ensure that all aspects of Loss Prevention are in compliance with company standards.

RESPONSIBILITIES

- Responsible for working with general managers and district managers to identify inventory shortage issues and recommend resolutions
- Deliver loss prevention training to head of store and other key field positions
- Responsible for ensuring execution of and compliance to target store and shortage reduction programs
- Assess store and district needs and employ appropriate deployment of loss prevention resources (CCTV, EAS, public view, and manpower)
- Develop district-specific action plans for reducing shortage
- Conduct investigations and interviews in response to inventory shortage, cash loss, and breach of company policies and procedures

214

- Proactively monitor controls to identify employee theft
- Assist with internal investigations as directed by supervisor
- Coordinate the recruiting, hiring, and training of loss prevention personnel
- Ensure completion of loss prevention training program for loss prevention personnel
- Identify top talent for next-level career opportunities through succession planning
- Develop and administer individual development objectives, quarterly check-ins, and annual reviews for 10–20 loss prevention personnel
- Manage monthly travel and expense budgets
- Manage loss prevention staffing budgets in assigned districts
- Conduct store visits to ensure compliance to company safety, policy, and procedure standards. Provide direction and training to ensure that potential issues are identified and corrected.
- Assist in the creation of action plans to achieve operational compliance
- Work closely with management to communicate and teach operational standards
- Offer recommendations and solutions in crisis situations such as workplace violence, protests, and demonstrations
- Communicate all safety-related policies using all available communication vehicles
- Supervisor of 10–20 loss prevention personnel in assigned districts
- Communicate daily activities to regional loss prevention manager and district managers
- Interface with field and corporate business partners (i.e., human resources, legal, operations, and employee relations)

Minimum Requirements

- Excellent written and verbal communication skills
- Excellent delegation and follow-up skills
- Loss prevention investigation and interview experience required
- Excellent time management and prioritization
- Basic knowledge of computer applications including Microsoft Excel, Word, and PowerPoint
- High-school diploma or equivalent, college degree preferred
- Wicklander & Zulawski or Reid interviewing and interrogation certification preferred
- 3–5 years of retail loss prevention management experience
- Ability to travel to stores within assigned area and maneuver around sales floors, stock room, and offices
- District loss prevention manager must be able to work for periods of time at a desk on a computer
- LPC/LPQ (Loss Prevention Certified/Loss Prevention Qualified) preferred

As this job description demonstrates, it is not absolutely necessary to have a college degree to work in loss prevention. In contrast, many jobs associated with a specialization usually require a degree just to get an interview, and many organizations will not negotiate on this prerequisite

and will eliminate résumés that do not meet certain education require-
ments. So why don't all postings for loss prevention positions require
the same? The answer is partly due to the fact that the industry still does
not have enough degreed candidates to make it a requirement. There are
few organizations that require a degree, and they struggle to find enough
qualified candidates to fill their positions.

The résumé is an important part of the review process because it will
be the first clue to whether a person qualifies for the position. A loss pre-
vention résumé is not much different from others, but depending on the
position, you will be looking for specific information (Figure 12.1).

EMPLOYEE SELECTION

As part of this chapter, I solicited the help of Gene Smith, president of the
Loss Prevention Foundation, a not-for-profit organization charged with
the responsibility of administering the retail loss prevention industry's
certification and membership programs. Prior to joining LPF, Smith was
the president of Downing & Downing, North America's largest executive
search and consulting firm specializing in providing human resource
solutions for retail loss prevention, safety, and audit. During his 15-plus
years with the firm, he was involved in conducting assessment interviews
and career counseling with thousands of industry associates. Smith was
also involved in conducting many industry organizational reviews dur-
ing his tenure. Previous to that, Smith spent 12 years in the retail loss
prevention industry. Smith was involved with selecting the right loss
prevention candidate for years during his position as president of a lead-
ing loss prevention recruiting and consulting firm. He knows what top
loss prevention executives are looking for and what they reject, and he
identified the key areas of consideration when searching for candidates,
beginning with the selection process. Employers must know what their
needs are, specifically. Simply knowing you need to add head count in
your department is not good enough. Every department within an orga-
nization needs specifics, and loss prevention is not any different. Identify
whether you need the following:

- Investigators
- Communicators
- Analyzers
- A person with a specific profile

Figure 12.1 An example of a résumé submitted for a loss-prevention position.

- Cultural fit
- A person who offsets your own weaknesses
- A person who complements your strengths

You can define whom you need through an organizational assessment. Once you have determined the type of person you need, it is time to move on to identifying how you will attract that person. Simply posting a job description might not be enough to get the ideal candidate. Your goal should always be to hire the best available candidate, not just a good candidate. You will want to use all the resources available to find the best person. Your main objective will be to conduct a thorough search because you owe it to yourself and the organization. Settling on the first person who looks good is the wrong approach. Your initial focus should be on identifying "A" players, both as candidates and as sources for referrals. Once you identify an "A" player then they will recommend "A" players to you. Reputation in the industry is also important to attract the good prospects. "A" players want to be affiliated with other "A" players who are reputable, not with people or organizations who have a poor reputation. Smith identified five areas that need to be tapped for proper recruiting to occur:

1. Networking
2. Employee referrals
3. Job boards
4. Internal recruiters
5. External recruiters

NETWORKING

Loss prevention professionals know other people in loss prevention who may be willing to fill your position. This is a good way to get candidates because you will most likely not be referred to someone who is not up to par. People making the recommendation to you do not want to be looked at negatively for sending less than quality candidates over to you; therefore, their own reputation is on the line. Because they have a stake in it, they will send you only people they know are good. The issue with only networking during the recruiting process is that the people with whom you are networking are limited in accessing talent. They will know only what surrounds them and nothing else. It is a good way to start, but it cannot be the only way.

EMPLOYEE REFERRALS

As with recommendations from networking individuals, employees put their reputation on the line,—even more so than networking people because they will deal with you and your complaints daily if the person is not any good. The employee referral may come from within your own department or outside of your department. This is a trusted way to get quality candidates because the stakes are high. Employees who refer someone else know they deal with the aftermath if the person they referred costs the organization unnecessary money or time. Unlike the networking referral, employees who refer will also have to answer to the organization when the cat is out of the bag that they sent in a lemon. This is also a good start, but the downfall with employee referrals, again, is that they do not have access to that many people, and if they are outside of the loss prevention department they might not know the specifics of who is needed.

JOB BULLETIN BOARDS — E-RECRUITING

Most organizations today use e-recruiting. This is definitely one of the most widely used ways to recruit candidates for any business. There are even Web sites allocated to specifically posting loss prevention jobs, such as lpjobs.com. E-recruiting will reach the most people with the littlest effort. Your diamond is hiding among the hundred others you will probably never consider, but it will be work to uncover the diamond. Because e-recruiting reaches so many people, the response to job postings will be enormous. Even if your posting is very specific, such as a minimum of 5 years' multistore experience, many will test their luck to see if you might not notice they have only 5 months' experience as a single-store loss prevention person. Now it will be your job to weed through all the people you do not want to select the ones you will consider interviewing. Unlike networking and employee referrals, no one else has a stake in the process; therefore, you are relying on only your own skills to identify candidates.

INTERNAL RECRUITERS

A good rule of thumb is to start with the e-recruiting and let the organization's internal recruiters narrow the scope. These groups of individuals find candidates every day for all departments, and they know what

they are doing. However, it is important to spend some time with them to make sure they know the specific expectations of loss prevention candidates. They are trained to look for large gaps in employment, short stays at other employers, and other key determinants that tell you how this person behaved in the past. Unfortunately, this is often where their expertise stops. Because we are a group of unique individuals whose careers focus on persuasion and influence, prospective candidates can snow unsuspecting internal recruiters. I remember this happening when I was recruiting for a regional loss prevention position. The pool had been narrowed down to about five final candidates. At this point, only the internal recruiters—no one in loss prevention—had spoken to any of the candidates. We also had a recap from the recruiter on his thoughts regarding each and every person. The final five were all qualified and could do the job according to the recruiter, and it was easy to tell which of the five he favored more. I spoke to one of the "favorites" during a phone interview. This is one individual who snowed the recruiter in some way. The individual was responsible for two flagship stores, extremely high volume, in a metropolitan area. This person spoke all the loss prevention jargon and knew what organizations were looking for. However, because the position entailed loss prevention responsibility for nearly 250 locations, I was more concerned about time management and prioritization skills than anything else. I knew that the ideal candidate would need to know how to properly prioritize his or her time and indirectly influence a large group of people to produce the desired results. I also knew that a person who is responsible for two locations, regardless of volume, may not have the experience necessary to manage such a high number of locations. This is where I focused the interview. I asked the candidate his approach to managing loss prevention for 250 locations and having positive results for the locations. This is the paraphrased answer I got:

> I plan to get up real early and work really long days so I can get to all of them.

That took care of the entire interview for me. This person knew how to effectively manage two locations because he went from one store to another and had direct contact daily with both. This person had no idea how to manage a vast number of locations without having daily involvement in any. The recruiter missed this for some reason. If you are using an internal recruiter, make sure the person is specifically trained on recruiting for loss prevention and understands the business of loss prevention.

EXTERNAL RECRUITER

There is no startup time with external recruiters because they know the industry. They can easily sift through the minutiae and see where the cream rises to the top. They can also identify passive candidates and connect the dots where others falter. Where they are most handy is in getting to the A players who are not currently looking for a job but who will listen to an opportunity. These are the people who are not surfing the job boards and are not known by your specific networking affiliate but who could be the best candidate. External recruiters are probably the easiest and quickest way to find the best pool of candidates, but as with the others the catch with this one is cost. The other four ways are relatively inexpensive, but external recruiters will definitely cost you. There are two different types of arrangements, contingent and retainer:

- Contingent arrangements: You do not pay the search firm anything unless you hire the person. The amount is based on a percentage of the salary. The current industry average is 20% of the first year's salary. Within the contingent confines, there are also two more specific arrangements, which are exclusive and nonexclusive.
 - Exclusive: You give your search to only one search firm and no others.
 - Nonexclusive: You give your search to multiple firms for competition.
- Retainer agreements: The search firm manages the entire search to include all candidates from all resources. You will usually pay 50% up front and 50% when it is completed. With the retainer agreement, the search firm wants to be guaranteed for its time because there is more work involved but also provides you with a guarantee as well. The current industry standard is that if the person does not work out within the first 90 days, the search firm will find a new replacement for free.

One point that Smith emphasized in this section is that you are not hiring just to hire. You are making a financial investment in someone. This is a total financial investment, including salary, bonus, car, training, benefits, and cost of ineffectiveness of transitioning into the new position during the learning curve. The financial obligation is about triple the salary.

Smith went on to discuss selecting the right candidate. The recruiting techniques will generate résumé flow, and that is what you need. The next step is to properly develop a screening process. It must be determined

who will weed through the résumés. It should not be just a human resources (HR) clerk. It should be a higher-level loss prevention person who has hired successfully before, partnering with a HR person who also has hired for LP before. There are not perfect candidates. You want someone who meets as many requirements as possible. The analogy Smith used is that it is like going fishing in a pond. At the end of the day, you have pulled out the best and can throw back the ones that are not good enough. The screening process objective is to narrow the search to three or four candidates. One point noteworthy for this part is that you do not want to let the speed of filling a position impact who you will hire. Many organizations, including loss prevention departments, fall victim to the speedy hire. This is most recognized during times when the projection for solid sales begins to decrease. If a department feels like a hiring freeze is approaching, the first person qualified will be grabbed so the position is not lost. The best approach is not to have a timeline. Only hire the best when you are convinced you have found the best available.

Part of the screening process is to do assessments such as the following:

- Psychological
- Personality
- Cultural
- Aptitude

Performing these types of assessments will help select the best. This will also eliminate the people who do not pass and cannot move further in the process. Next, you will need to conduct some initial employment reference checks. Employment reference checks can be one of the most effective ways of judging someone's long-term success. You will also want to do some initial interviews. Make sure you have already established the interview process and that the panel of interviewers knows exactly what you are looking for. Ensure that all interviewers on the panel know they are there to judge personality and cultural fit, not technical competencies. When it comes to technical skills, people are more reluctant to lie about that. For instance, if you ask someone how to derive specific equations in Excel and they give some ridiculous answer, you know they are not familiar with Excel in the way you need them to be. People are reluctant to lie about technical skills that are required because they will be called onto the carpet quickly about it. A candidate is less likely to lie about having computer skills required for a potential job because the individual knows he or she will not be able to perform the job once it starts. On the other hand, candidates often lie about getting along with people and about

their personal behavior. When candidates are asked if they are a "people person," many will say yes because this topic is subject to interpretation and technical skills are not. They could interpret being a people person as their ability to verbally communicate in an appropriate manner, and your interpretation of a people person may be that someone who gets along with others is an extrovert. Personality will often come out during a face-to-face interview. A wise person once told me that to truly understand candidates, take them to a restaurant for their interview. I was curious about picking a restaurant as the venue, and the person described the following scenario:

When you take people to a restaurant you can see how they truly behave if something is not right. Therefore, you want to make sure something is a little wrong with their meal. Maybe it is too cold or dry—something just needs to be wrong. Now you sit back and watch what they do. If they do nothing and just accept what is wrong, you know they do not like conflict and let things slide. If they are upset and approach the server in a rude manner, you know they have problems with self-control. If they complain about it but do nothing else, you know they are ineffective in addressing problems. What you want to happen is that they recognize something is incorrect and let you know there is something wrong. When the server comes back, in a very professional manner, they describe the problem: "Excuse me, I ordered a salad without blue cheese and this one has blue cheese." You also want them to provide the server with the solution: "Can you please take this one back and bring one out that does not have blue cheese?" Now you know that they will attack a problem head on, inform you about it, and have the solution ready to go. I cannot say from personal experience if this works or not for getting the best candidate, but theoretically it seems like it might.

Another great screening tool is to tour a few stores to see how they greet the store associates and if they help find service for customers. See if they see the same control deficiences that you see. Ask them what they normally would do on a store visit.

The interview process is the most ineffective way to hire someone if you judge someone only on the way they interviewed, according to Smith. When looking to hire someone, you must look at all the components. It is much better to know who that person worked for in the past and what the employer thought about the person. One question to ask yourself is if you are hiring for show or hiring for go. That means that some candidates will absolutely floor you with their professional appearance and demeanor, but that does not mean they will perform well if hired. The most important factor cannot be that one person interviewed better than the other person. Part of the process is knowing the programs they have worked in and people they have worked for. If you need someone to be in charge of

a specific area, such as supply chain, ensure that the person has worked in some kind of supply chain capacity in the past. Do not base your entire opinion of the person on the interview; rather, use it as one component of making the choice.

For the interview process, questions and answers are often used. To some degree they work, but that is not how effective interviews are conducted. Think back to past or present times of interviewing employees for dishonesty. There is a script, but you know what happens if all you do is read it in a question or answer format. The admission is much more difficult to get or may never come. The most effective interviewers use a conversational approach to reach the admission, and the same should be true for interviewing employment candidates. You want to get to know the person so he or she can open up to you. Smith believes that the interview process is like unwrapping a gift. Your challenge is to properly unwrap the gift piece by piece so you can get to what you want on the inside. The key is to ask a few questions and get the person to talk so you can listen. At the end of the interview, you must do additional reference checks. You also want to do face-to-face interviews as opposed to only phone interviews.

As for the additional reference checks, you do not want to eliminate someone based on one bad reference. There are many people who will give unfavorable references for anyone who left the organization. You do not want to access a person's background more than you do the person. One item you are trying to assess is where the interviewees are in their life. Those who are involved in personal issues are more likely to have performance issues at work. It's not to say that every person is the same and handles stress in the same manner, but personal problems often complicate any new endeavor. You will most likely find out about the personal issues if you conduct the interview properly. Even if this person's skill set far exceeds the other candidates', personal issues coupled with starting a new job can be a recipe for disaster. Someone's personal situation is the most accurate indicator of how he or she will perform in the immediate future. If there is nothing weighing on the person, all focus will be on the new job. If personal issues such as divorce or a death in the family are present, the new job will have to share time with the preexisting personal issues, which cannot be shed. You cannot have a person's undivided attention even though the candidate might think he or she is able to give 100%. You need to figure out if the person is able to do the job and is willing to do the job.

Hiring a person for loss prevention can be difficult, but with some effort the payoff can be great. Take your time and use all the resources available to uncover the best talent available. Remember, as stated a few pages back,

- don't rush your decision because you foresee a hiring freeze, lest you be stuck with someone who is unqualified or doesn't fit in,
- having a bad employee is worse than having no employee,
- don't skip out on conducting the reference checks and doing your homework about individuals.

An individual's past is a predictor of your future. If they could not make it to work on time for the last 5 years, do not think they have had a miraculous epiphany that makes them go to work on time in your organization? Use the skills you have learned as a trained interviewer on the person you want to hire and look for the red flags. Do not put all of your eggs in one basket because a person has a great-looking résumé. You want to make sure that you actually like the individual as a person and can work with the person.

Effectiveness

As with many jobs, some individuals shine while others are just getting by. To be effective as a loss prevention professional, it takes personality, knowledge, skills, and commitment. Unlike some other types of professions, those in loss prevention who are squeaking by stick out like a sore thumb because of their statistics and lack of accomplishments. Those who are shining have the numbers and accomplishments to show for it.

As I was just beginning my career in loss prevention, I was required to hire store detectives. The entire hiring process was new to me, let alone the fact that I had to make sure the new hires could catch shoplifters to keep the position. Because the store had good numbers going in, I was allowed to hire two part-time store detectives. I recruited at a local university by placing ads on the job board. After many interviews, I selected two male students who were in their senior year of college. One of them was going into elementary education, and the other had an internship with the Central Intelligence Agency (CIA) after he completed a few more classes. As much as I knew that stereotyping shoplifters did not work, I did not use that same knowledge when it came to who I hired. I thought for sure that the person going into the CIA would excel and would run circles

around the store detective planning on becoming an elementary school teacher. I could not have been more wrong.

I trained both of them the same way I was trained. I spent many hours walking the floor with them together and individually. After I turned them loose, I was amazed at what I saw. Within the first few days of being alone, the soon to be schoolteacher was competing with my numbers. Every morning when I came in and he had worked the night before, there would be incident reports on the desk. Some of the items that were taken were so small that I wondered how he was able to see the concealment. You must also remember that these were the days without cameras. The only tools we had were our eyes and our sense of wrongdoing. The nights that the CIA store detective worked, there were no incident reports on the desk in the morning. I could sense the frustration from the CIA store detective when we spoke. He was frustrated because he was not catching anyone. Because of the hours I had available, I could not overlap that much with either of them, but because the numbers were not good for one, I had to start overlapping at least 2 hours so I could see what the problem was. Together we were able to catch shoplifters, but by himself the CIA candidate did not work very well. The schoolteacher's numbers continued to climb, which made the CIA detective even more frustrated. It did not seem to matter how much time I spent with him—his numbers did not come close to the schoolteacher's numbers. This lasted about a year until they both graduated. The schoolteacher would come back and work during holidays and some of the summer, but I never heard from the CIA person again.

As I began to analyze the differences between the two, I started to understand why one did better than the other. The schoolteacher had no expectations coming in other than that he wanted to do a good job and make some money to help pay for college. He was footing the bill himself, with no help from anyone. The CIA individual came in expecting to do well because he assumed his criminal justice degree would somehow help him catch shoplifters. He was not paying anything for college; rather, his parents were paying for everything. He took the job because it was related to his field and thought it would be fun. The schoolteacher was a very humble individual who was very friendly and genuine. The CIA store detective had a fairly large ego, was social but not overly friendly, and seemed to have an agenda. I remember him discussing the schoolteacher's numbers with me and being disappointed that he was catching that many. He never saw the effort as joint and team related. He was

mostly disappointed at the fact that someone in a field such as elementary education could outdo him.

Because I was so new in the world of loss prevention and having direct reports, I did not address issues such as teamwork or the effort of catching shoplifters as collective as opposed to individual. I simply trained, retrained, and trained again in the hopes that he would come around. I also did not address the preconceived notion of who he thought he was and would be in this role. As the years went on and I continued to have direct reports in the same organization and different organizations, I thought about these two people and their behavior. I also realized where I went wrong in not addressing the behavior that helped contribute to the CIA detective being unsuccessful. I also watched others whom I worked with over the years exhibit some of the same behaviors as both the CIA detective and the schoolteacher. Loss prevention people who were more similar to the schoolteacher often were more successful than ones who were similar to the CIA detective.

PERSONALITY

People in retail loss prevention cannot reduce shrinkage alone; they must rely on those whom they work with to be involved. Because of this, personality plays a part in whether the person will be successful. Loss prevention people must be able to influence and persuade others to do what is necessary to prevent losses. They must also be able to do it well enough that the results can be sustained. If their efforts revolve around fear and intimidation, the results will not be sustained and other problems will arise. For someone to effectively influence or persuade others to do something, that person must be respected and trusted. To gain respect and trust from others there must be some sort of relationship between the people.

The loss prevention people who are effective in reducing shrinkage take the time to build relationships, earn trust, and give respect to those whom they work with. They do not expect that people will respect and trust them because of their position; rather, they know that it will come over time and with effort. They know that they need not act as a know-it-all to boost their ego but project their level of competence through the training they conduct to make others loss prevention conscious. They understand that the goal is to get the people to a level of commitment with loss prevention initiatives, not to make them

compliant to what they are told to do. They understand that they are one small part of the bigger equation and that their collective contributions help better the organization. They will share their knowledge and information with anyone who is willing to listen and not hoard valuable information for the fear that someone might be able to move ahead of them with it. They conduct themselves with the utmost professional behavior, which is reflected through their communication, appearance, and persona. They believe that all employees bring value to the organization and have something to contribute. They train others in a manner that makes things right, not in a way that points out everything that is wrong. They celebrate what is right and good and find clever ways to correct the wrongs. They live their life as they do their work; there are no variations from doing the right thing all the time. They work hard because that is what they were hired to do, and they do not allow their personal agenda to drive their behavior. The loss prevention people who are effective are those who you want to sit in a room with to have a discussion, not those whom you cannot wait to leave the room.

KNOWLEDGE

Unfortunately, loss prevention is not a profession you can wing. You have to have knowledge to successfully do the job. Because many of us start out catching shoplifters, we gain the knowledge regarding human behavior rather quickly, which will be used throughout our careers for detecting dishonesty. We learn early on that anyone is capable of anything. Those who do not work in the profession will often dismiss suspicions based on who the person is, whereas we know that it makes no difference who it is because anyone can do it. We learn that people's personal lives make a difference in their work decisions and that those decisions can negatively impact the organization. Those who are effective are always trying to gain new knowledge, understanding that it is a never-ending process.

Aside from human behavior, knowledge on organizational systems and policies also helps aid in the success. Those who are successful take the time to learn the systems such as the point-of-sale (POS) system. They understand that to quickly detect dishonesty they must know what is wrong and what is right. They will know the systems as well as the employees who run the registers.

They will also keep themselves abreast of any new information that has come out. For instance, if there is a change to the employee purchase of merchandise policy, such as a limitation or reduction in percentage, they will know that the policy changed. To keep this information organized, a binder of valuable information should be kept. The binder should have copies of documents that pertain to loss prevention as well as changes to policies that were issued. The binder is good to have when employees say they were not aware of that; then, the document can be pulled out and shown that it was indeed sent to the store.

The knowledge of effective loss prevention persons does not end within their own organization. They are also aware of issues affecting loss prevention outside of their own organization. They keep themselves apprised of any new legislation affecting their line of work and communicate the information to the appropriate people.

SKILLS

Within the profession of loss prevention, certain skills need to be mastered. Two of those skills are auditing and investigations. From store level to the director level, auditing and investigating will be the biggest portion of the job requirement. The goal of auditing is to uncover any fraudulent activity or correct training issues. To properly audit, one must understand all the questions on the audit and know how to get to the information. For beginners, it best to have a paper copy of the audit and how to get to all the information written underneath all the questions. If a question pertains to a specific policy, the effective loss prevention people will have a copy of the policy to refer to. One important part to auditing is the recap that is sent out to the necessary parties. Most executives will not go through an audit question by question; rather, they are looking for the high-level overview of what was found during the audit. Being able to properly write the audit recap is critical in being effective. Doing the audit is half the job; the other half is to effectively report the findings so others can take action. Those who try to rush the audit recap process will often come across as incompetent because others will recognize they did not take the time to review the entire audit. The effective individual will also take the time to explain the audit findings to the person who is responsible to fix it. If it is the store manager, they will be given a verbal recap of the audit and a printed version prior to the departure of the auditor. The effective person

will also help find solutions to issues that came up during the audit, not only present the opportunities. It must be certain that the person in charge fully understands what is required to correct the deficiencies.

The other skill to master is investigating. From finding the needle in the haystack to getting the person to admit to wrongdoing, investigations are a part of everyday life in loss prevention. It is not uncommon for loss prevention people to have better interview skills than law enforcement. The effective loss prevention person will take the time to develop their case. They will research any and all avenues where misappropriation could have taken place. They will be able to decipher a training issue from a dishonesty issue before they ever talk to the employee. They will be able to review documents during an investigation and know exactly what does not make sense even though the manager provides a logical explanation. They will discuss the person or persons involved, including their application and work behavior with their direct supervisor. They will be able to predict the lies that will be told and already have a rebuttal waiting before the investigative interview begins. During the interview they will project a level of confidence unlike anything the employee has seen before because they have left no stone unturned. The denials from the interviewee will be met with strict resistance, and the only conversation that will continue is the admission of guilt.

Effective persons will be able to extract all dishonesty that has happened at their organization through conversation with employees and management, not only the dishonesty detected through investigative techniques. They will be able to get employees to provide a statement that implicates them in wrongdoing and either provide a promissory note or hand off an airtight package to law enforcement for prosecution.

Being an effective communicator is also part of the role of effective loss prevention personnel. They are often asked to conduct training sessions or present on a topic related to loss prevention. How they relay the message is as important as the message itself. They have to display conviction and passion for the topic in addition to showing their knowledge of the subject matter. Effective persons will leave the audience wanting to know more and excited about loss prevention.

Effective loss prevention people are well-rounded individuals who possess the necessary skills to do the job. They continue to sharpen their skills through individualized training and take responsibility for developing their own skills further.

COMMITMENT

People who work on a factory assembly line do the same thing every day. Their requirement is to attach one piece to another and to ensure it makes it to where it is supposed to go. Their commitment, or lack thereof, may be noticed during the workday. Loss prevention people are doing something different every day. Each day holds a new and daunting task to tackle to safeguard the assets of the organization. When loss prevention people "check out," it is easy to notice. The effective person's commitment to the job will be evident. Each case is evaluated carefully to ensure key learning points are extracted not only to rectify the immediate issues but also to prevent future incidents from occurring. Loss prevention people who are fully committed are never really off the clock. They think about their work every day, and most people around them will know more about the profession of loss prevention than any other topic. Effective people are proud to work in the field of loss prevention and will do what it takes to get the job done. Effective people will not have a scope that is narrow; their scope will be wide enough to influence all risks and threats that affect the organization they work for. Their level of commitment does not end at their day-to-day functions but continues in understanding the big picture of the organizational challenges. Effective persons will be involved with more than just their own job and will extend themselves further to learn all they can about loss prevention.

REVIEW THE APPLICATION AND
ASK THE RIGHT QUESTIONS

Searching for the right person who has the personality, knowledge, skills, and commitment for loss prevention is very complex and demanding. Use the physical details of the application for employment to identify questions that should be asked during candidates' interview. Review the application that candidates fill out against the résumé. Believe it or not, I have seen applications that do not match the résumé information, even when candidates had access to the résumé while filling out the application. You might catch contradictions in educational information, the type of degree, or years attending a school. You might catch contradictions in the years that the candidate worked at previous employers. Look at every line and see if it makes sense.

Some very common-sense lines on the application for employment that should be filled out will really help you understand that level of commitment. Is the candidate willing to travel? Relocate? Does the candidate want full-time employment? All these questions are very important but often get glossed over and may result in a big surprise after hiring a regional manager who does not want to travel or expects 10% travel instead of the position requirement of 75% travel. Most applications have questions on eligibility to work in the United States. Most applications also ask the question, "Have you ever been convicted of a crime other than a minor traffic offense?" These are questions that might be left unanswered, and that is more a problem than answering yes. The truth about employment eligibility and background records can be evaluated; omissions could mean that the candidate has something to hide and should be verbally addressed in an interview before employment.

Look at the work experience section of the application to evaluate the dates employed. Are there gaps in employment history? Those may be a sign of unemployment or a sign of institutionalization. Explore any gaps in the interview as well as omissions of information about the employers or reasons for leaving the last employer during the interview. Is there enough information about the educational institutions to actually verify the level attained? Perhaps the most important lines on the applications are the signature lines after the statement of accuracy and the drug-free workplace statement. Leaving these lines unsigned and undated could be a subconscious message that applicants are not comfortable with what they would fill in on the application. By all means, ask them to sign those lines when they are attending the interview and see how they react to that request. Another thing that makes me reconsider candidates is that errors and omissions on the applications speak to their level of detail and persistence. These are just a few things that I look for; I am sure there are more that I have missed.

Once you get to the interview, there are lawful inquiries and unlawful inquiries that the interviewer must be aware of. Lawful inquiries that may be asked of a candidate include the following:

- Asking whether the applicant has ever worked for this organization under a different name
- Asking whether the applicant can meet the specified work schedules
- Inquiries made to establish that the applicant meets the minimum age requirement for the position

- Asking whether the applicant can perform the essential functions of the job as they have been described
- Requesting a photo after hire for verification on the I-9 form
- Inquiry into actual convictions that relate to fitness to perform a particular job
- Asking for the applicant's current and previous addresses
- Questions about type of education and training or experience in military service as it relates to the job
- Conducting a credit background check for a candidate if that is relevant to the type of job function

Unlawful inquiries that may not be asked of a candidate include the following:

- Inquiring about the candidate's name in a way that would indicate the applicant's ancestry or national origin
- Questions about marital status, pregnancy, number and age of children, or needs for child care
- Inquiries requiring the applicant to produce proof of age in the form of a birth certificate, or asking any questions that identify applicants over the age of 40
- Any question that directly or indirectly results in limitation of job opportunities in any way, including general inquiries such as, "Do you have any disabilities?" which would tend to divulge handicaps or health concerns not reasonably related to fitness to perform the job
- Requesting photographs or inquiring about an applicants' height or weight
- Inquiring about arrest records to use to determine qualification for a position
- Specific inquiries into foreign addresses that would indicate national origin, including any inquiry about the birthplace of the applicant or his or her parents
- Asking the type of discharge or service in a foreign country
- Inquiries regarding the candidate's credit rating (Although a credit background check may be lawful, credit ratings are not reported in such checks)
- Any questions concerning sex, race, eye, hair, and skin color
- Any inquiry to indicate or identify religious denomination

This is a fairly comprehensive list of what questions are allowable. During the interview a large part of the line of questioning should be directed at the skill level of the candidate on critical thinking and problem solving, teamwork, motivation, and leadership skills. If the questions do not sound right or seem risky, it is best to check with your associate relations department or recruiter for advice.

GETTING TO THE NEXT LEVEL

Because retail loss prevention is so specific, the competition for high-ranking positions is fierce. The competition is high not only within the industry but also in the organization. Also, because of the nature of the people who are in loss prevention, striving to be better than the next person is never-ending. Again, with limited high-level positions, only so many people can move to the top. To get where you want to be, there are many things to consider. For some expertise in this area, I again solicited the knowledge of Gene Smith. Smith has made it to a level that many loss prevention people aspire to be, but it did not come easy. Smith has had contact with almost every high-ranked loss prevention executive in the nation and knows what it takes to move up in the industry. He provided a five-step process for loss prevention people to follow if they want to move up in the industry:

1. Goal setting
2. Self-discovery
3. Find a mentor
4. Implement career plan
5. Readjustment

Goal Setting

Once you decide that loss prevention is your career, develop a career plan of how far you think you can go. The career plan that defines your goals needs to be done in a formal planning process, not a cliché. You will want to get job descriptions for the jobs you want to aspire to. The descriptions will give you a better understanding of whether you possess the basic skills required for the job. If you are lacking in some areas, the career plan should encompass gaining the knowledge you need for the position. The

career plan should also be broken down into reasonable amounts of time. Most career plans will have several years of achievements that need to be met. An example of a career plan is as follows:

INDIVIDUAL DEVELOPMENT PLAN			
Employee Name	**Position Title**	**Organizational Element**	**Supervisor's Name**
Jane Doe	RLPM	District Office XXX	John Smith
Section I - CAREER GOALS			
Short-Term Goals (1–2 Years)		*Long-Term Goals (2–5 years)*	
1. To contribute in the field of loss prevention		1. Enhance leadership skills	
		2. Find new and innovative ways to improve the department	
Section II - INDIVIDUAL DEVELOPMENT PLAN (Completed by Supervisor and Employee)			
Development objectives needed to reach goal		*Developmental Assignments, etc., including target completion dates.*	*Other Activities, Departments, others Involved*
Goal #1: To contribute in the field of Loss Prevention outside of my organization			
1. Conduct presentations on internal theft.		Dec-10	
2. Partner with people in the field of LP in other companies.		Ongoing	
3. Get on a distribution list for LP communication.		Sep-10	
Section II - INDIVIDUAL DEVELOPMENT PLAN *(continued)* (Completed by Supervisor and Employee)			
Development Objectives needed to reach goal		*Developmental Assignments, etc., including target completion dates.*	*Other Activities, Departments, others Involved*
Goal #2: Enhance leadership skills to further develop the position of regional loss prevention manager.			

235

1. Partner with the training and development department on current development initiatives.	Ongoing	Training and development department
2. Assist peers in creating an individual development plan.	Oct-10	Peers
3. Become a mentor for a district loss prevention manager.	Apr-10	DLPM
Goal #3: Find new and innovative ways to improve the department, convey the prevention message, and focus on organized retail crime.		
1. Assist in the development of a loss prevention recognition program for associates.	Dec-10	Awareness Committee
2. Create a shoplifting prevention program.	Mar-10	
3. Create awareness tools for shoplifting program.	Jun-10	
4. Create and implement a new loss prevention manual.	Dec-10	Training and Development

Section III - Formal Training and Accomplishment Schedule				
Remarks	Formal Training (e.g., interagency, out-of-agency, private sector, correspondence)	Projected Cost	Target Completion Date	Actual Completed Date
Employee's signature		Date:		
Supervisor's signature		Date:		

Note: This IDP is subject to change depending on availability of funds, courses, and candidate's requirements.

This plan is inclusive and focuses on a very specific goal, which is to get promoted. Some people in the field of loss prevention are very content with their current position and just want to do the best they can with their existing role. If that is the case, the career development plan should focus on enhancing the current role and becoming the best. During the next phase, self-discovery, you will know if your career development plan is a realistic snapshot of what you can achieve or if it is a wishlist of items.

Self-Discovery

Looking deep down into one's psyche can be a revelation like no other. Many of us want certain things in life, but they are not always achievable. College athletes may have the drive and desire to play professional sports, but their ability may not allow them to. A person with advanced degrees in business may want to become a chief executive officer for an organization, but the person's leadership skills may never allow that. It is no different with the profession of loss prevention. For many, catching shoplifters is the beginning stage of developing an ability to grow with the profession of loss prevention. Some of us probably excelled in shoplifter apprehending, but that does not mean we are all cut out to become directors of loss prevention in the future. Your career may not blossom in the manner you anticipated for various reasons, even some that are out of your own control. It is no secret that being able to relocate in the field of loss prevention allows you to advance quicker than others who are not.

If you are in metropolitan areas such as New York, Chicago, and Los Angeles, relocating may not be necessary. There are many higher-level loss prevention positions available in large metropolitan areas where corporate offices of retail businesses thrive. However, if you are in Omaha, Fargo, or Chattanooga, things might be different. It is not uncommon to have field people based in different parts of the country, but corporate positions, including director and vice president, usually require relocation to the corporate office

At present, the work–life balance is very important in corporate life. If family and friends are very important to a candidate for advancement, making a choice that is prudent for family and friends will be necessary. Weigh all the alternatives to transferring around for promotions, and involve family and friends to the extent that their opinions are valuable to the decision-making process.

Loss prevention professionals must understand if their skill set and personality will allow them to soar past all their competition. A good rule of thumb is to get a job description of where you want to go. Many organizations today are looking for college degrees as a requirement for regional loss prevention manager positions and above. If you do not have a college degree, consider working for the degree at one of the community colleges with flexible hours and computer classes. Consider tuition reimbursement with negotiating employment packages to make it definitely achievable. Consider networking, and ask experts in the field of loss prevention what they did to be successful to get where they are. After they describe their

journey to you, think of ways to adopt some of their methods for success into your own development plan.

During the self-discovery process, one should assess their own strengths and weaknesses in order to determine which position is most suitable and to develop long term career goals accurately. A full understanding of where you are in your own skill sets, knowledge of the business, and overall standing in the community of loss prevention is paramount in moving ahead. Although this may be self-discovery, a clear understanding of what others think of you is important as well.

Find a Mentor

Every organization has a mentoring process. Finding the best mentors and being careful of the motives of the individual offering to mentor you are important. If the person you are considering to ask to be your mentor is anything less than admirable and of high integrity, keep up the search until you find the right person. Because loss prevention is so competitive, leaders understand they can stand out in a crowd if they have developed a peer or subordinate to be ready to advance. Mentoring another is an accepted way for companies to polish and develop their managers with potential.

Selection Process

It may be easier to identify a mentor in your own organization because they are more accessible, but going outside of the organization can be advantageous. If selecting someone in your organization, make sure the person knows the culture and the organizational structure. Other assets to look for in the person you select for a mentor are the person's business acumen. Is the individual able to navigate the office politics and still come across as approachable and open to discussion? It is not a bad thing to find a leader who is nurturing. Mentors should not be expected to develop you into an excellent specimen of a promotable superstar. They will not be doing all the work; you will. They are there to listen well and act as a sounding board to your thoughts about the business and your development plans. They may give advice, but experiences prove those who listen best and let the mentee make some mistakes and take some risks are best and most appreciated.

When selecting your mentor, it could be someone you like as a person and have some type of chemistry with. You will need to feel that this person has a vested interest in your success and is not just going through

the motions. This person will also need to ensure that he or she has the time to mentor you. One thing to remember is that great mentors love to be copied. They do not hoard their knowledge in fear that someone will surpass them. You are also looking for someone who loves to educate, teaches why things are done (the thought process behind the action), and uses logic to solve problems. This person will discuss possible solutions but will not give you the solution. By discussing the possible solutions and not giving away the answer, this person teaches you how to effectively solve problems.

Just keep in mind the ideal person may not be in loss prevention. If you want to further develop your leadership skills, selecting a mentor outside of loss prevention but still in retail may be the way to go.

Implementing Your Career Plan

You have to invest in your career plan with sweat equity. You will want to volunteer to go the extra mile and take on some special projects. One alternative is to read business books and leadership books, even if you do not put that on your career development plan. The derived benefit will be understanding the bigger business picture. Many loss prevention people believe that just because they have the highest statistics in the department they should be promoted. This is in practice—usually not what happens.

Smith believes it is not important to be the best shoplifter apprehender; it is more important to be able to hire and lead the best shoplifter apprehender. He went on to say that some of the best coaches in professional sports were average players. It takes a lot more than technical skills to get ahead. It takes the ability to understand what is required for the job and the ability to communicate and persuade others. What many newly promoted leaders find out once they achieve the dream of an executive-level position in the field of loss prevention is that technical skills are ironically enough required less and less. The loss prevention executives functioning in each organization are executives overseeing a specific department. They are not much different from the executives leading marketing, training and development, or operations. Their main function is to ensure the success of the department through the work of their subordinates. That being said, their ability to lead others surpasses their need for specific technical skills.

You always want to have an updated résumé available. You never know what phone call you will receive from a recruiter or old friend, when you will need to send one out right away. Your career development plan may

outline all of the things necessary for you to get where you want to go, but your current organization may not be able to accommodate the plan. If your career development plan is done effectively, it may lead you out of your current organization and into the arms of another organization that can embrace your end result quicker. Smith also believes that what separates "A" players from "B" players is that "A" players take ownership for their own personal development. They find out what is needed and go for it. They invest in their own career with time and money. If part of your career development plan calls for seminars on leadership and the company will not pay for it, the "A" players will pay for it themselves because they understand that it is necessary.

Readjustment

As we discussed earlier, just because people want something does not mean they will get it. The last phase of moving ahead is the readjustment process. After you have completed the other four phases, you will need to readjust your goals to face reality.

You will readjust goals based upon the following:

- Results of self-discovery process
- Feedback from mentors
- Ability to effectively implement career plan

It is good to go through the readjustment process once every 3 years. Goals will also adjust due to the following:

- Personal reasons, within self
- Family
- Changes in organization

People who set out to become loss prevention executives when they were single may have to adjust their goals if they get married and start a family. At one time they were able to move around or make sacrifices to advance with no strings attached. Some husbands and wives will have to give their significant other a chance to advance if they have been supported along the way. This is especially true if both spouses have promising careers. I have been in this predicament personally, and I know that you absolutely cannot allow yourself to overshadow your spouse and put your spouse in a place where he or she just goes along to get along. I have a saying that I live by: I am not willing to jeopardize my spouse's career to further my own. Countless marriages have been lost to career choices

with one of the people involved with the relationship. The reason for the demise is usually that one person did not consult the other and just did what suited them. Careers in loss prevention are no different. Individuals must weigh all aspects before they can have a clear understanding of how far they can go. Once all factors have been considered, you can have an updated version based on the compromises you had to make.

MANAGING LOSS PREVENTION PROFESSIONALS

Is managing loss prevention professionals any different from managing other employees? The answer is absolutely yes. Most of us are in this field because we want to help people and uphold the rules and regulations of the organizations, we want to fight for what is right and fair, and we want to know that our efforts are recognized through the reduction of losses and the removal of dishonest employees. Employees who work in a different capacity within the same organization as loss prevention people probably think about the aforementioned items but are not employed there because of it. Therefore, when it comes to persons supervising a loss prevention professional, their ethics, morals, values, and integrity must be uncompromising. If the supervisor is willing to bend the rules just a little bit, it will immediately be noticed, and a strike will go against that person. Unlike the common employee, most loss prevention people will not retaliate against their supervisor with theft-related activity, but there are exceptions to that as well. Most will simply withhold effort or just leave the organization entirely, neither of which is good for the individual or the organization.

Many of us owe a lot to people in the field of loss prevention for whom we have worked in the past or present. Some have taught us how to catch shoplifters, and others were there when we completed our first internal investigative interview. Even bad supervisors can teach something, which is how not to be like them. Personally, I owe a great deal to loss prevention people for whom I have worked and for whom I am currently working. Each of the companies for whom I have worked and the individuals to whom I have reported have taught me something about loss prevention or business that has contributed to my success in this industry.

MILLIE'S STORY

For me, it all started with a loss prevention professional named Ron Holiday. Ron hired me as a store detective in 1994. He placed an ad on my college job board, and I replied. I

used the part-time job as a co-op to earn credits for graduation. Ron figured out rather quickly that I am pretty competitive, so he used that knowledge to lead me. He would leave out his incident reports for all the shoplifters he caught before I arrived to work for me to see. This motivated me to want to "outdo" Ron and catch more than him. It was a successful night if I had more incident reports on the desk than he did. He would also tell me what a great job I was doing and how quickly I caught on to identifying and catching shoplifters. Our store became one of the top producers in external theft cases in the region, and we were competing with inner-city stores. I remember being so excited coming to work each day to see how many shoplifters I could catch and outdo my boss. Within the same year that Ron hired me, he also left the organization to take a higher position. He recommended me for his position, which I received shortly after his depar-ture. I used the leadership knowledge that Ron showed me to hire and train my own store detectives. I too left incident reports out and had them competing against one another. I never lost contact with him and have always consulted him on career decisions that came up throughout the years. Ron is the person who started me in this business and showed me how to get people to want to work for you. He was never negative, and even when I needed correcting he did it in the most diplomatic way. I always wonder if it had been someone with poor leadership skills instead of Ron, if I would have stayed in loss preven-tion. I guess I will never know the answer to that.

I stayed with Kmart about 4 years and then accepted a position with OfficeMax. The position I took was that of corporate loss prevention supervisor—a position unlike anything I have ever done. I would no longer be involved with catching shoplifters, nor would I see the inside of a store very often. The interview process to get the position at OfficeMax was nothing less than grueling. I was surprised when they called and offered me the position. I later found out that not many store-level loss prevention people transition directly into a corporate role without multistore experience. The person who hired me at OfficeMax was Will Powell. Will was a well-rounded business professional. He knew not only loss prevention but also the intricate workings of the business world. I caught on rather quickly to the technical aspects of the corporate world, but I was missing one big necessary component: polish. *Polish* is a term many management people use to describe those who have business acumen and communications skills and understand the nuances of office politics. I had the biggest problem getting the corporate office employees to do what was necessary, like use their badge and not tailgate into the building. Will watched my interactions with others and pulled me aside one day. This day changed the course of my corporate personality forever. He told me not to be "that bull in a china shop" and that corporate employees were not like "the store people." He went on to say that the corpo-rate people would tell you that you are the biggest idiot in the form of the friendliest e-mail. I was used to a small confined group that I had a lot of control over and did not understand how to get thousands on my page. Over the course of time, Will put the polishing touches on that were necessary.

After Will left the organization, I began reporting to Don Burkett. Don is a guy that you can rely upon for the facts; he is very meticulous and intense. He is probably the best systems person I have ever met in my career. Don also did not tolerate poor quality work. One of my responsibilities was to write and rewrite policies. I remember turning in some

of those policies, having them marked up in red ink, and returned to me at my cube. This was Don's way of telling me to do it right the first time. After a few times of that, I repeatedly proofread my work before I turned it in. Don also taught me that you have to find the information you need, because someone is not always there to help. There were different projects I was working on but had little knowledge about. Instead of going to Don, I learned to problem-solve myself to get the answers I needed. This was a valuable lesson that had worked wonders over the years for my life and career.

I stayed with OfficeMax about 3 years and then accepted a position at my current organization. I started off as regional loss prevention manager; I did not come with much field experience but with a wealth of corporate experience. My learning to play nice with others during the OfficeMax years helped me become very successful in building good relationships with my field partners into the future. As with corporate employees, field managers are indirectly influenced by loss prevention, and the relationship is one of the most important components in making you successful in your position. I was able to get to know my new supervisor well over the years and really understand what he stood for.

Bob is one of the most upstanding human beings I have ever met. He attributes a portion of his uncompromising integrity to his father-in-law who taught him a valuable life lesson. Bob's father-in-law cashed out at a bowling alley and went to his car. Upon entering the car, he noticed that the attendant had given him one dime too many. He was afraid that the attendant would be short and get in trouble so he walked back to the bowling alley, in the pouring rain, to return the dime. Bob witnessed this event and it set the tone of how he would look at life and honesty. Bob's lesson was that no matter how small, doing the right thing is always right. This is how Bob leads his people today. Bob is the kind of person you can sit down and chit-chat with and talk about all the things you do not like. He will never pretend to go along with something that is wrong because others expect it to be done. He does not necessarily agree with you, but he does give you the chance to state your case. And when he does not agree, he tells you how he would do it and you can decide for yourself if that is the route you want to take. The autonomy he gives his people allows them to achieve their very best. No one is afraid to take risks in his group, and he always supports initiatives. People are never shot down or discouraged, no matter how silly it may seem. Bob's lesson to me is that loss prevention people must live their life like they live their career. It is not good practice to pretend to have uncompromising integrity whiile at work but, when you are in a setting that isn't work related, your ethics are non-existent. They will be halted at the thumb of their supervisor. Encouraging loss prevention people to take risks without the fear of failure will allow them to strive for greatness.

I have been very fortunate in my career all along the way. Each and every person who has supervised me has instilled one thing or another. Each is unique in his or her own way and had a strength I needed to develop. Each invested the time to develop me to exceed the role and further my career. I know not everyone will be this fortunate, but I am sure there are supervisors out there like Ron, Will, Don, and Bob. Take time to learn them and extract the good parts. No supervisor will have every leadership skill, technical knowledge, or personality to suit everyone, but all may have one or two traits that prove to be beneficial for you.

CONCLUSIONS

This chapter has given you many fine processes and tips on hiring the very best loss prevention associate. You got the word from an expert in the business of people, at one time creating relationships and now strengthening those relationships by improving the quality of life for practitioners in the industry through his leadership of the Loss Prevention Foundation. It is very obvious that training and expectations have momentous effects on the newest and brightest talent coming into our industry. You may have heard that people do not quit jobs; they quit people—namely, their managers, because they were treated poorly, lied to, left to perform without proper training, and perceived that their leaders had poor integrity. Go back to Chapter 2 in this book and recall the culture of integrity, substituting us who are now the employee. It is all relative.

CONCLUSION

This book covered many different aspects of the retail loss prevention profession. Both the novice and professional practitioner will be able to gain some insight into the world of retail loss prevention and maybe even embark on a few functional areas they were not aware of. Retail loss prevention is a highly specialized field that many do not even realize exists. As shoppers go through the mall or department stores, most are not thinking about what is happening behind the scenes. As shoppers are putting their merchandise in the cart and wondering how they are going to explain what they just spent to their significant other, loss prevention practitioners are thinking about how to keep costs low for them by eliminating internal and external theft. Not all professions will allow people to change the way they think about society, but retail loss prevention is one that does. It is very hard to leave your work at work when every time you go to buy groceries, clothes, shoes, or anything else you think about your work. For the authors, it has been about 10 years or more since we caught a shoplifter, but we are still very aware that they may be around as we shop. One suspicious move or look from a fellow shopper still gets the adrenaline running and the flight-or-fight response activated. We also find ourselves watching employees when we are in the customer mode as they ring through transactions at the register or have conversations with people who come to visit them. The knowledge you gain as a loss prevention practitioner never allows you to discount your feeling about something being wrong. Your senses will forever be heightened, and your need to make things right never goes away.

A person who truly embraces the profession will become a business leader unlike any other. Many people believe that because we deal only with "loss prevention issues" we are not qualified to do anything else. They could not be more wrong. We, unlike most departments within an organization, deal with every aspect of the business. From a sales perspective, we will be the ones who understand why a particular store is or is not generating the expected revenue. We will be the ones who dig down deep enough to understand the underlying causes of performance, when others will simply repeat the same objective or terminate the individual. Our ability to understand human behavior is developed over time and will help to mold us for significant leadership positions. Loss prevention

people learn to truly understand the "whys" behind every action and reaction to rectify the causes of the problems. We do not sit back and deal with the symptoms of the problem; rather, we determine the root cause because we know that is where the issue starts. One of the recurring themes in this book was relationships because it is one of the most important functions of your jobs. Most loss prevention practitioners are not directly responsible for stores or the people who supervise those stores. Because of this, our ability to influence and persuade others to do what is necessary relies on our ability to build meaningful relationships. If we can build trusting relationships, we can move people in the organization in the direction we want to go. Another theme discussed was expectations. If employees understand the direction they are going and they are told the truth about everything, they are less likely to become a loss prevention problem.

The strategy of setting integrity expectations immediately and conveying the message of intolerance for counterproductive behavior is a must. I cannot emphasize enough how important this tactic is for field managers, and they will reap the rewards of such a method. All are crystal clear about what is expected and what is not. This method will allow employees to operate under an umbrella that promotes an atmosphere of trust, respect, and compliance for the rules and regulations of the organization. In turn, the results and efforts will be genuine and achieved with commitment, not just out of compliance.

As you can tell from all your reading, loss prevention starts from the inside out. If we take the time to delve deep into shrinkage and employee dishonesty, we will uncover the issues. Putting out fire after fire will not resolve your problems entirely. Putting out fires without dealing with the main cause of the problems will only prolong the issues. The book provided examples of building an audit process, how to investigate in retail loss prevention, and how to build a department and discussed the current epidemic of organized retail crime. If you are reading this book, you are likely in this field, are interested in the field, are in retailing, or are a criminal wanting to understand how to avoid us. It is the authors' hope that you take the areas that you need to learn about and read carefully. One resounding theme throughout this book is how strongly the culture of the company affects the success of your loss prevention program.

One additional point we would like to leave you with is this: if an organization is built on an ethical infrastructure that promotes integrity, loss prevention issues will be lessened. It is our job to help build that infrastructure, influenced deeply by company culture, and to guide employees on how to remain honest and do the right thing. Most employees do

not become employed with the intention of stealing or defrauding their employer. Something happens along the way to change their motives. If we are watching closely, the change can be caught in time, and a bad decision can be stopped. It is all about the passion for doing what is right, even when no one is looking.

BIBLIOGRAPHY

Agnew, R. (1992). Foundation for a general strain theory of crime and delinquency. *Criminology*, 30(1): 47–87.

Association of Certified Fraud Examiners. (2010). 2010 Report to the Nations on Occupational Fraud and Abuse. http://butest.acfe.com/rttn/rttn-2010.pdf (accessed October 29, 2010)

Baer, J. (2002). Is family cohesion a risk or protective factor during adolescent development? *Journal of Marriage and Family*, 64: 668–675.

Bolin, A., and Heatherly, L. (2001). Predictors of employee deviance: The relationship between bad attitudes and bad behavior. *Journal of Business and Psychology*, 15: 405–418.

Braithwaite, J. (2000). Shame and criminal justice. *Canadian Journal of Criminology*, 42(3): 281–298.

Colbert, A. E., Mount, M. K., Harter, J. K., Witt, L. A., and Barrick, M. R. (2004). Interactive effects of personality and perceptions of the work situation on workplace deviance. *Journal of Applied Psychology*, 89: 599–609

Cornell University. (2006). Workplace Diversity. http://www.ilr.cornell.edu/library/research/subjectguides/workplacediversity.html (accessed on October 29, 2010)

Federal Bureau of Investigation (FBI). (2007). FBI partners with retailers to fight organized retail theft: press release. http://www.fbi.gov/pressrel/press-rel07/database040507.htm (accessed October 29, 2010)

Field, J. (2008). Job satisfaction model for retention. http://talentedapps.wordpress.com/2008/04/11/job-satisfaction-model-for-retention/ (accessed October 29, 2010)

Giddens, A., Duneier, M., and Appelbaum, R. (2005). *Introduction to Sociology*, 5th ed. New York: W.W. Norton & Company.

Glasgow Erickson, K., Crosnoe, R., and Dornbusch, S. (2000). A social process model of adolescent deviance: Combining social controls and differential association perspectives. *Journal of Youth and Adolescence*, 29(4): 395–425.

Harter, J., Barrick, M., Colbert, A., Mount, M., and Witt, L.A. (2004). Interactive effects of personality and perceptions of the work situation on workplace deviance. *Journal of Applied Psychology*, 89: 595–609.

Higgins, G. and Ricketts, M. (2004). Motivation or opportunity: Which serves as the best mediator in self-control theory? *Western Criminology Review*, 5(2): 77–96.

Hollinger, R. (2003). Why do employees steal? Part 1: Motivations for Dishonesty. *Loss Prevention Magazine*, October: 13–14.

Hollinger, R.C. and Clark, J.P. (1982). Formal and informal social controls of employee deviance. *Sociological Quarterly*, 23: 333–343.

Hollinger, Richard C., and Adams, A. (2008). 2008 National Retail Security Survey Final Report. Gainesville, FL: Department of Criminology, Law and Society, University of Florida.

Huxley, R. (2000). Moral development of children: Knowing right from wrong. http://www.selfhelpmagazine.com/article/child_morals (accessed October 29, 2010)

Johnson, L. and Phillips, B. (2003). *Absolute Honesty: Building a Corporate Culture That Values Straight Talk and Rewards Integrity.* New York: AMACOM.

Langton, L.E. (2004). Can general strain theory explain white-collar crime? A preliminary investigation. http://etd.fcla.edu/UF/UFE0004785/langton_l.pdf (accessed October 29, 2010)

Lerner, R., Noh, E., and Wilson C. (1998). The parenting of adolescents and adolescents as parents: A developmental contextual perspective. http://parenthood.library.wisc.edu/Lerner/Lerner.html (accessed October 29, 2010)

Mikulay, S., Neuman, G., and Finkelstein, L. (2001). Counterproductive workplace behaviors. *Genetic, Social, and General Psychology Monographs*, 127: 279–300.

National Retail Federation (NRF). (2009). 2009 Organized retail crime survey. http://www.nrf.com/modules.php?name=Documents&op=showlivedoc&sp_id=3137 (accessed October 29, 2010)

Paul, R., Niehoff, B., and Turnley, W. (2000). Empowerment, expectations, and the psychological contract-managing the dilemmas and gaining the advantages. *Journal of Socio-Economics,* 29(5): 471–485.

Robinson, M. (1999). The theoretical development of CPTED: 25 years of response to C. Ray Jeffery. *Advances in Criminological Theory,* 8: 427–462.

Safeway-Walgreens (2004). *Organized retail crime video: Interview of a professional booster.* Cook County Sheriff's Police, IL.

Santrock, J. (2005). *Adolescence.* 11th ed. New York: McGraw-Hill.

Scott, S. (2004). *Fierce Conversations: Achieving Success in Work and in Life, One Conversation at a Time.* New York: The Berkley Publishing Group.

Stamper, C. and Masterson, S. (2002). Insider or outsider? How employee perceptions of insider status affect their work behavior. *Journal of Organizational Behavior,* 23(8): 875–894.

Thorsborne, M. (2003). Integrity. *The Seven Heavenly Virtues of Leadership.* http://www.aim.com.au/publications/bkchapters/seven_ch3.html (accessed October 29, 2010)

Vazsonyi, A., Hibbert, J., and Snider, J. (2003). Exotic enterprise no more? Adolescent reports of family and parenting process from youth in four countries. *Journal of Research on Adolescence,* 13(2): 129–160.

Wells, J. T. (2001). Why employees commit fraud: It's either greed or need. *Journal of Accountancy,* 191(2): 89–92.

Wold, Barbara. (2010). Taking stock: Seven relationship-building business strategies. http://www.retailinasia.com/article/2010/07/taking-stock-seven-relationship-building-business-strategies?page=1 (accessed October 29, 2010)

INDEX

Printed in the United States
by Baker & Taylor Publisher Services